AIA Detroit

The American Institute of Architects

Guide to Detroit Architecture

AIA

EXIT 51B
375
Civic Center
75
Toledo
1 MILE
EXIT 52
Mack Ave
1/2 MILE
Warren Ave

Detroit

The American Institute of Architects Guide to Detroit Architecture

Eric J. Hill, FAIA
John Gallagher

WAYNE STATE UNIVERSITY PRESS DETROIT

Library of Congress Cataloging-in-Publication Data
Hill, Eric J.
AIA Detroit : the American Institute of Architects guide to Detroit architecture / Eric Hill and John Gallagher.
p. cm.
Includes bibliographical references and index.
ISBN 0-8143-3120-3 ((paper) : alk. paper)
1. Architecture–Michigan–Detroit–Guidebooks. 2. Detroit (Mich.)–Buildings, structures, etc.–Guidebooks. 3. Detroit (Mich.)–Guidebooks. I. Gallagher, John. II. American Institute of Architects. Detroit Chapter. III. Title.
NA735.D4 D4 2003
720'.9774'34–dc21
2002012742

∞ The paper used in this publication meets the minimum requirements of the American National Standard for Information Sciences—Permanence of Paper for Printed Library Materials, ANSI Z39.48-1984.

Title page: St. Josaphat Church in foreground with Renaissance Center in background. Photograph by Balthazar Korab.

A special project by

Michigan Architectural Foundation

The American Institute of Architects

For my wife, Cynthia,
and children Bradley, James,
and Emily
— Eric Hill

For my wife, Sheu-Jane
— John Gallagher

In Memory of Gordon Bugbee, AIA
Professor of Architecture,
Lawrence Technological University

Contents

About the AIA Guide

PURPOSE

This new *AIA Guide to Detroit Architecture* builds on the old. Prior editions surveyed the best of the best over the vast metropolitan region. We've taken a different approach, including both a broader view of Detroit itself and a handful of unique places outside the city's limits. Our immediate purposes are to introduce citizens and tourists alike to a rich architectural heritage and to serve as a starting point for the more serious student of the art.

ORIGINS

The first Guide was written for the 1971 national convention of the American Institute of Architects (AIA) in Detroit, and the 1980 update appended a summary of notables built since. This edition started with the same premise as the second: add what's been built over the last twenty years, put a new cover on it, and you're done. No problem. But, like a building program without a budget, the project grew. The original guide was "largely drawn from" *The Buildings of Detroit: A History* by W. Hawkins Ferry (with the author's blessing and counsel). We're not certain, but additions to the 1980 update appear to have been excerpted largely from company brochures. We decided with this edition to begin anew, and, in our exuberance to revisit buildings, we broke the rule of the gift horse. We looked.

PROCESS

We looked far and wide, engaging both the professional and the academic communities in the process. We invited all 1,100 members of AIA's Detroit Chapter to nominate candidate buildings and environments for potential inclusion. We harvested historic registers and nearly six decades of design award programs sponsored by the AIA. We invited senior historians from the area's three architecture schools to weigh in. We visited candidate buildings and built a photographic archive of existing conditions.

With research in hand we convened an advisory committee to help define the project's scope. The previous guide had surveyed

"Detroit architecture" from Warren to Pontiac to Ann Arbor. We considered trimming the territory to the City proper, but concluded that such limits might result in a distortion of a different kind. We considered the overnight tourist from Nairobi, the weekend visitor from Traverse City, and the exchange student from Seoul. Ultimately, we reformulated the guide to include those special environments outside the city limits that illuminate the essence within, and combine to define greater Detroit's unique place in the world of architecture.

The numbers regarding this process are informative. By reducing the guide's geographic reach, we retained about half of its original entries. We then added more than two times as many "new" entries, for a total of about 370. Of these, (only) about fifty were built since 1980. In all, this essentially "new" guide is less about updating the recent past and more about rediscovering our distant past. We found there's more to like in Detroit architecture.

INCLUSION

Good design, however elusive and subjective, was the primary criterion for inclusion here. While significantly expanded, this new survey is far from encyclopedic. About two-thirds of the buildings are listed on local, state, and/or national registers of historic buildings or districts. A fifth have received design awards from the AIA. Of the remaining buildings built before 1950, most are eligible for historic designation. If this sounds elitist, that's because such is the nature of architecture as fine art, and of guides to it.

To a list dominated by buildings, we've added a handful of bridges, monuments, fountains, parks, and cemeteries that exhibit design qualities worth noting. We've included neighborhoods and specialty districts for their remarkable coherence or sense of place. Some selections epitomize a style, and others represent one of the few remaining examples of a style in our area. Some were selected over comparable others due to their more convenient location on the tour map. A few entries were included for their civic importance, functional role, and/or sheer size.

Did personal tastes play a role in what is included here? No doubt. We inevitably omitted one of your favorite buildings or overlooked some attribute or flaw in those we did include. While we are grateful for the opportunity and regret our misdemeanors, our primary motivation has been to tell a good story about good design, and thereby to play some small role in preserving it.

ORGANIZATION

This guide is organized from the top down: from larger to smaller geographies to neighborhoods and precincts to individual buildings. The points of a compass originating at the Downtown core organize the broad scope of this guide. Our essential Detroit comprises nine geographies presented in the following order: Downtown, Midtown, North, West, and East (all within the city), plus Grosse Pointe Lakeshore, Cranbrook, GM Technical Center, and Ford's Dearborn.

Each of the five geographies within the city is subdivided into identifiable precincts or neighborhoods. The Downtown area is organized more or less in line with the geometry of the People Mover system, its stations, and its counterclockwise path. Most other Detroit journeys will require a car—at least to transport you to and from, if not around. This is Detroit, after all.

Maps are provided for each of the geographical areas and each of the precincts or neighborhoods within.

SOURCES

Our sources are many and varied. We visited all potential entries to gain a firsthand understanding of their merits and contexts. For the more recent buildings we invited the architects to describe their work, and a few did so. For the more historic entries we consulted a number of writings, which are included in the bibliography. We refer the more serious student of the art to three particular sources for additional information and viewpoints: Ferry's *The Buildings of Detroit*, Eckert's *Buildings of Michigan*, and the surveys compiled by the State Historic Preservation Office (SHPO). Ferry's work is the most comprehensive in scope, and Eckert's is the more recent. For all buildings and districts listed in the state register, SHPO provides additional information online at www.sos.state.mi.us/history/preserve/michsite/index.html.

INFORMATION

Each nonresidential entry begins with its current name, followed by the original name, if applicable, in parentheses. Residential entries are presented under the names of the original owners. Undoubtedly we have erred in some original attributions and missed some name changes, especially if recently implemented. The dating protocol endeavors to identify original dates of construction completion, with initial dates provided first and dates of renovation or significant additions following, as may be applicable. Similarly, original architects are named first, followed by later hands, if different. Architects are identified by their record name at the time of the building's design. While we certainly value the contributions of engineers and builders, we generally do not name them.

If an architectural style is identifiable, we offer a considered opinion. Many buildings were designed under the influence of diverse precedents, and thus exhibit a hybrid of stylistic references.

We have tried to avoid technical jargon, but some terms are irreplaceable. We refer the reader to any number of specialty dictionaries and glossaries, a few of which are included in the bibliography.

Symbols in the left margin of entries provide interesting factoids and references in shorthand fashion, including: historic registry at the national, state, and/or local levels; AIA design award at the national, state, and/or local levels; whether or not a building is endangered; and whether a building's interior spaces are open to the public.

PHOTOGRAPHY

Most of the photography included in this new edition is of recent origin. Some outdated photographs are used to more completely illustrate the original conditions of the building and/or its context—the Ford plant on Piquette is an example. A select few photographs were not updated if an earlier image is itself a remarkable work of art.

SAFETY, SECURITY AND ACCESS

Architectural appreciation—gawking and clicking cameras at buildings—often attracts attention. We ask that you take care in your journey.

Not all public buildings are readily accessible to an admiring tourist. Churches are usually open during times of service. The houses included here are generally private, except as noted, and we ask that you respect that privacy.

DISCLAIMER

The opinions expressed here in no way represent the views of any sponsoring organization. While a guide's content is inevitably dated before its ink is dry, its value as a time capsule, defects and all, can only increase with time.

EMERSON

He was right in his belief that two of the most powerful human emotions are memory and hope.

Key to Symbols

P — **Public** — Open to the general public

SP — **Semi-public** — Only specific areas accessible

PR — **Private** — Not open to the public

$ — **Admission** — May require an admission fee

C — **Closed** — Closed or vacant

NSC — **Historic Building** — National, State and/or City levels

N S C — **Historic District** — National, State and/or City levels

NSC — **AIA Design Award** — National, State and/or City levels

National Historic Landmark

Endangered Building

N — National Register: District, Multiple Buildings

N — National Register: Building

The National Register of Historic Places was established in 1966. Historic resources are nominated for listing by the State Historic Preservation Officer in each state or territory, and also by federal agencies, which have that responsibility for historic resources in their ownership. There are three forms of National Register listing: Individual, District, and Multiple Property. Individually listed resources meet the National Register criteria on their own. Districts are areas in which the assembled resources meet the National Register criteria; individual properties may or may not be individually eligible. Multiple property listing provides a framework for listing of a number of significant properties linked by a common property type or historic context; the individual resources need not be located together, but must all relate to a single significance or common history which makes it desirable to list them as a group. In a multiple property listing, all the resources listed must be individually eligible for the National Register.

S — State Register: District, Multiple Buildings

S — State Register: Building

The State Register of Historic Sites, established in 1955, lists individual resources and historic districts; listing brings with it eligibility for a state historic site marker. Listing is approved by the State Historical Commission on nomination by the State Historic Preservation Office; owner consent, or consent of a majority of owners, is required for listing.

C — Detroit Designation: Multiple Buildings

C — Detroit Designation: Building

The City of Detroit's program for the designation of historic districts was established in 1969; all designations are referred to as historic districts whether containing one structure, many, or none. Designation is accomplished through the passage of an ordinance by the Detroit City Council after a study conducted by the Historic Designation Advisory Board; the criteria are essentially the same as for the National Register. Requests for historic designation may be submitted to the City Council by any party "with an interest."

Acknowledgments

DONORS

Principal Benefactors

Graham Foundation for Advanced Studies in the Fine Arts
Albert Kahn Associates
SmithGroup

Patrons

American Institute of Architects—Detroit Chapter
Associated General Contractors of Michigan
Herman Miller
Michigan Architectural Foundation
Balthazar Korab

Sponsors

American Institute of Architects—Michigan
Professional Concepts Insurance
The Taubman Foundation
Detroit Free Press

Contributors

HarleyEllis
Progressive AE
Rossetti Architects
TMP Associates, Inc.

Supporters

French Associates
Gensler
Project Planning and Management, Inc.

Friends

DiClemente Siegel
Robert and Rae Dumke
Archive Design Studio
Edward and Lynne Francis
J. Michael Kirk, AIA
Phillip and Diane Lundwall
Morrison-Knudson Corporation
J. Howard Nudell Architects, Inc.
Silveri Architects
Stevens Architects
Swanson Meads Architects, LLC
John Tagle Associates, Inc.

SELECTION COMMITTEE

Gordon Bugbee, AIA—Lawrence Technological University
Anthony Martinico—University of Detroit Mercy
Anatole Senkevitch—University of Michigan
Steve Vogel, FAIA—University of Detroit Mercy
John Gallagher—Detroit Free Press
Eric J. Hill, FAIA—Albert Kahn Associates and
University of Michigan

PHOTOGRAPHY

We are indeed fortunate that Balthazar Korab has served as the principal photographer for this publication. He created more than two hundred new images, and contributed more than one hundred additional photographs from his extraordinary archives. We are indebted to his commitment to the project and his unparalleled service to the architectural community. SHPO, the Michigan State Historic Preservation Office, contributed several images, and we thank Laura Ashlee and Frank Quinn for their efforts. Thanks to Cranbrook Archives for Saarinen contributions. We are also grateful to Albert Kahn staff Fred Handley and Christian Sandel, who photo-documented many existing site conditions throughout the city.

GRAPHIC DESIGN AND MAPS

Savitski Design created a compelling graphic design that advances the genre to a new level. Many thanks also to Taft Cleveland, Stephen White, and Ricardo Pappini of Albert Kahn Associates for their splendid mapmaking in support of the design.

SPECIAL THANKS

The Michigan Architectural Foundation Board of Trustees; AIA Detroit: Rae Dumke, Hon. AIA, and Lynn Francis; Keranen Associates: Gary Quesada; Detroit Historic Designation Advisory Board: Bill Worden and Deborah Goldstein; Cranbrook Archives: Mark Coir; Albert Kahn Associates: Stephen Q. Whitney, Serena Haque, and Alice Baker; University of Detroit Mercy: Professor Anthony Martinico, Tony King, Jason McNatt, Tadd Heidgerken, Scott Swanson, Eduardo de'Sa, Justin Bialek, Crystal Nanney, Nicholas Juhasz; Lawrence Technological University: Professor Gordon Bugbee, Sam Moschelli, Michelle Goldstein, David Reed; University of Michigan: Professor Brian Carter, Professor Anatole Senkevitch, Kara Kressbach, Ray Lennard, Christian A. Hedrick; Wayne State University Press: Arthur Evans, Kathryn Wildfong, Alice Nigoghosian; Rebecca Binno; Lisa DiChiera; Diane Jones; Jean Dodenhoff; Charles Licari; Mary Hebert; Nancy Dziedzic.

Introduction

Detroit began on the riverbank. Native Americans long had recognized the value of the narrow straits as a river crossing and trading site. Indeed, many early roads, now grown to multilane status, followed Indian trails. Cadillac, that savvy and ambitious Frenchman, knew a strategic spot when he saw it. So did the British, who came later, and the Americans who followed them, including a judge with a restless intellect named Woodward. Today, three hundred years after Cadillac's landing, we celebrate what the city has become. The world knows Detroit for its industrial might and Motown sound. But, in truth, Detroit has been many things during its three centuries.

In the first hundred years forts and pioneer cabins nurtured the fur industry. For decades after Cadillac, Detroit was merely a colonial outpost in a vast wilderness. "Ribbon farms," long and narrow homesteads platted in the French manner, swept up from the river and penetrated inland forests. Windmills, while rare on the more recent American landscape, were then among the most common sights on the skyline, with four arms decked in sailcloth to catch the wind. Built to mill grain, these towers were a sign that farming was as important as fur trading to early Detroiters. Today about all that remains of the eighteenth century is the grid of river-to-inland streets that follow the lines of early farms and still bear the names of their colonial proprietors, including Beaubien, Riopelle, and Chene.

Fire destroyed the remnants of colonial France in Detroit in 1805. Within weeks Judge Augustus Woodward arrived from Washington, D.C., where he had learned firsthand of L'Enfant's plan for our nation's capital. He soon convinced authorities to let him map out a great city. But Woodward's plan was even more elaborately baroque than L'Enfant's, with a repetitive pattern of major and minor radials and circles, or circuses, at key junctions. In fact, it proved far too intricate to ever be carried out in the face of opposition from property owners. Just imagine having your neat rectangular piece of pasture reconfigured into a slice of pie. Still, Woodward's plan established the idea of wide boulevards radiating from a central place near the river; and it created the semicircular street grid that has defined our Downtown to the present day. As we survey today the dynamic urban results, we are thankful indeed for visionaries, however eccentric—see cover.

Thus, the stockaded encampment gave way to a serene little village sitting on a supremely ambitious plan. Temple-front porticoes soon populated the streets, and church steeples competed with ship masts to define the skyline. It wasn't until 1827 that the final riverbank fort was demolished. By then, the nature of the metropolis to come had already been set. Aided by territorial governor Lewis Cass's newly widened avenues radiating from the center, the growing town burst its boundaries and spread out, if not sprawled, to the north, east, and west. Detroiters, it seems, have always built first and only afterward looked back to see what they have created. That impetuous process continues today.

The architects of nineteenth-century Detroit took their cues from styles imported from Europe by way of the East Coast. The neoclassical lines of Georgian, Federal, and especially the Greek Revival upscaled the look and feel of the city. Porticoes and colonnades were common. Then, at mid-century, architects introduced the more melancholy Gothic Revival primarily in church architecture, such as the Jordan brothers' Fort Street Presbyterian Church and Gordon Lloyd's Christ Church on East Jefferson. A profusion of mansard-roofed design soon followed with an ease born of the city's French heritage. Elaborate Second Empire mansions and townhouses, mini-chateaus and Parisian hotels, and civic buildings blossomed in the city's core and extended up Woodward Avenue, which replaced East Jefferson as the elite place to reside. Combined with the city's later embrace of Beaux-Arts Classicism, it's not surprising that Detroit was once referred to as "the Paris of the Midwest." Sadly and not a little ironically, it was our French architectural legacy that was nearly decimated in the century that followed.

The second hundred years brought the first Industrial Revolution, which changed the face of the city, especially at the banks of the Detroit River. At the beginning of the nineteenth century, the river served many purposes. But by mid-century it was reduced to a transportation way, and what the maritime industry hadn't claimed, the railroad had all but consumed by century's end. It wasn't until the middle of our third century that we reclaimed a share of the riverfront for civic purposes, and into the fourth century that we show signs of valuing the river as our greatest natural resource.

Frontier Detroit

Poised to lead a second industrial revolution at the beginning of the twentieth century, Detroit emerged as a leader in the world of architecture. What Henry Ford and his architect, Albert Kahn, created here was a new functionalist architecture, in which building design more nearly matched its intended use. Chicago architects had already proclaimed that form follows function, but it took Detroiters to carry that principle to its full expression. The area's early industrial landmarks had a profound impact on European modernists like Mies van der Rohe and Le Corbusier.

While automobile production changed the design of factories and soon the architecture of other uses, the proliferating product itself soon changed the design of cities. And, here again, Detroit fleetingly showed the way to the modern metropolis.

In 1900 the compact city barely extended beyond what is now Wayne State University on the north or Belle Isle on the east. But with the automobile the floodgates opened. Immigrants seeking factory jobs poured into Detroit and built a city of neighborhoods. And as the city rapidly grew, the lines between commercial, residential, and industrial uses were blurred. By 1930 the city had pushed its borders out to Eight Mile Road. Detroit saw the advent of worker housing—mile after mile of inexpensive bungalows and other simple dwellings clustered around the growing number of factories. The industrial plant began to replace the church steeple as the organizing icon of the neighborhood. Following New York's example, city planners crafted zoning ordinances to impose order on this chaos. Zoning solved part of the problem. More recently the abstract dicing of the city into single-use districts has become viewed as the crux of the problem itself.

Indian Village

Similarly, residential developers devised architectural codes that carefully defined what a neighborhood would be. Indian Village, Boston-Edison, and other fine subdivisions first built and then kept their character through careful regulation of lot size and restrictions on materials and architectural styles. These solid residential districts would remain important anchors decades later when Detroit struggled to keep its economic footing. After nearly a century we are relearning the power of such architectural codes to ensure the design quality and sustainability of our communities.

In many respects, including architectural, the period from 1920 to 1930 was Detroit's Decade. The 1920s saw a sunburst of skyscraper design in the Downtown core with such city-defining towers as the Buhl, the Penobscot, and the Guardian buildings. The Book brothers' development of Washington Boulevard merged the design of New York's Fifth Avenue with that of a Parisian boulevard. The New Center core emerged as the first "edge city," with a magnificent ensemble of office buildings including the General Motors and Fisher buildings. In the face of rapidly encroaching commercial and industrial development, city leaders preserved space for a Cultural Center in the Woodward corridor, and the City Beautiful movement was imported to invoke standards of taste appropriate for a world-class city. To the north an enterprising newspaper publisher began to build an educational community dream called Cranbrook. And to the east the Age of Affluence saw the transformation of the Grosse Pointes from resort to suburb as dozens of elegant mansions defined the sweep of Lake Shore Drive.

All this heady prosperity came with a price, as the auto enabled a social mobility that was nearly Detroit's undoing. In this context, all too many landmark buildings lasted no more than a generation or so. A few of the more exceptional pieces were thankfully and literally moved about as if vehicular themselves. "Detroit on wheels" took on an architectural meaning. Most notably, or notoriously, the widening of Woodward Avenue in the 1930s, just as the wheels fell off the economy, was a particularly callous idea designed to solve the elusive problem of traffic congestion. Many of Woodward's beautiful churches were defaced or unceremoniously shoved back. To add insult to injury, within a decade traffic engineers were planning freeways that would eviscerate whole neighborhoods, including the cultural heart of the African American community. The automobile had become king.

New Center's development symbolically presaged the later mass exodus from the city's center to its edges, then on to outer rings of suburbs and edge cities. After World War II, auto companies sited their new plants far from the city, both to escape the effects of militant unionism and to find the land needed for now-sprawling industrial complexes, optimally designed on one level. As an unfortunate byproduct, older factories fell into disuse. And just when factory jobs were moving out, the mass transit means to reach them began disappearing as well. A new socioeconomic model based on mobility replaced a system long centered on place. The challenges facing workers recently moved up from diverse regions of the South grew to dire proportions. Intercultural and interracial tensions heightened. The melting pot came to a boil, and Detroit's long decline had begun.

A city that loses half its population in forty years, as Detroit did, cannot reasonably sustain urban vitality nor stem architectural decline. On a base level, many of the city's finer houses, office buildings, and hotels were stripped of woodwork, light fixtures, and other treasures for their salvage value. Great buildings like the Michigan Central Depot were left to vandals and graffiti artists. Background buildings and architectural gems alike have been allowed to deteriorate or vanish under the forces of the elements. All too often the resulting brownfield sites sit vacant,

Brush Park

Civic Center

resurface as parking lots, or redevelop in suburban forms shaped by the auto and built of materials designed to last as long as the mortgage. Accordingly, the devolution of the Detroit landscape in the final decades of the twentieth century was unremittingly bleak. If we've learned anything of late, it's that architectural form follows far more than function. Since the beginning of time, buildings and cities have been shaped by a combination of forces, including social, economic, political, religious, technological, and environmental.

Today all that remains of the French colonial heritage are a few street names and a handful of parishes descended from their originals. Of the city's stately Greek Revival period, a limited selection of houses remain. Of the elegant Second Empire and sturdy Romanesque mansions that once lined Woodward and Jefferson avenues, a mere handful still stands. The imposing City Hall that graced Campus Martius was razed in 1961. Few of the dozens of sumptuous houses built along Lake Shore Drive in the early 1900s outlived their first owners. The historic Chene House, one of the city's few remaining Federal-era houses and a link with our French past, was leveled a decade ago to make way for a pancake house. Irreplaceable nineteenth-century churches are falling into disrepair. World-renowned factories where the auto industry was born sit as ruins. Broad avenues once framed by buildings and teeming with traffic today resemble bleak urban prairies, and a chill wind blows. While a New Orleans or a Boston routinely adapts its two-hundred-year-old buildings to modern uses, Detroit continues to discard its past at a shocking pace.

But there are signs of hope, too. Construction cranes dot the skyline once again. Big-ticket projects like Comerica Park, GM's Renaissance Center renovation, and Compuware's move to Campus Martius all deserve headlines. A revitalized theater is attracting world-class opera. Three casinos are adding a little glitter. Loft apartments and condominium conversions are reusing century-old buildings and bringing middle-class residents back to the city. Restaurants and nightclubs are filling in street-level floors and spilling onto sidewalks. Selective neighborhoods are revitalizing, and a few subdivisions are even in the making. Property values are rising. Detroit may yet again emerge from its long decline. The past shows that Detroit can surprise us with its resil-ience and capacity for rebirth.

Thus, we survey our built environment today with mixed feelings. This book aims not only to serve as a handy guide to the city's architectural delights; it also sounds an alarm. Some of the four hundred or so entries included here are endangered. Enlightened plans and progressive codes, however well conceived and intentioned, cannot make a great city. Nor is money alone the answer. If architecture is a conversation across the generations, Detroit is a city in danger of losing irreplaceable voices of its past. Detroit is filled with built treasure, but, like an architectural Rodney Dangerfield, it gets too little respect. On the other hand, a heightened public awareness of good architecture and good city building, encompassing the preservation of the old and the design of the new, is a promising place to start.

Best of all, the spirit of architectural enthusiasm that led to this guidebook remains strong. How that spirit translates into a livable city, or, as Aristotle said, a city whose purpose is to promote the good life for all citizens, is one of the most pressing questions facing the architectural profession today. We believe some of the answers are embedded in our built surroundings. We invite you to join us as we celebrate three hundred years of Detroit by design.

Downtown skyline

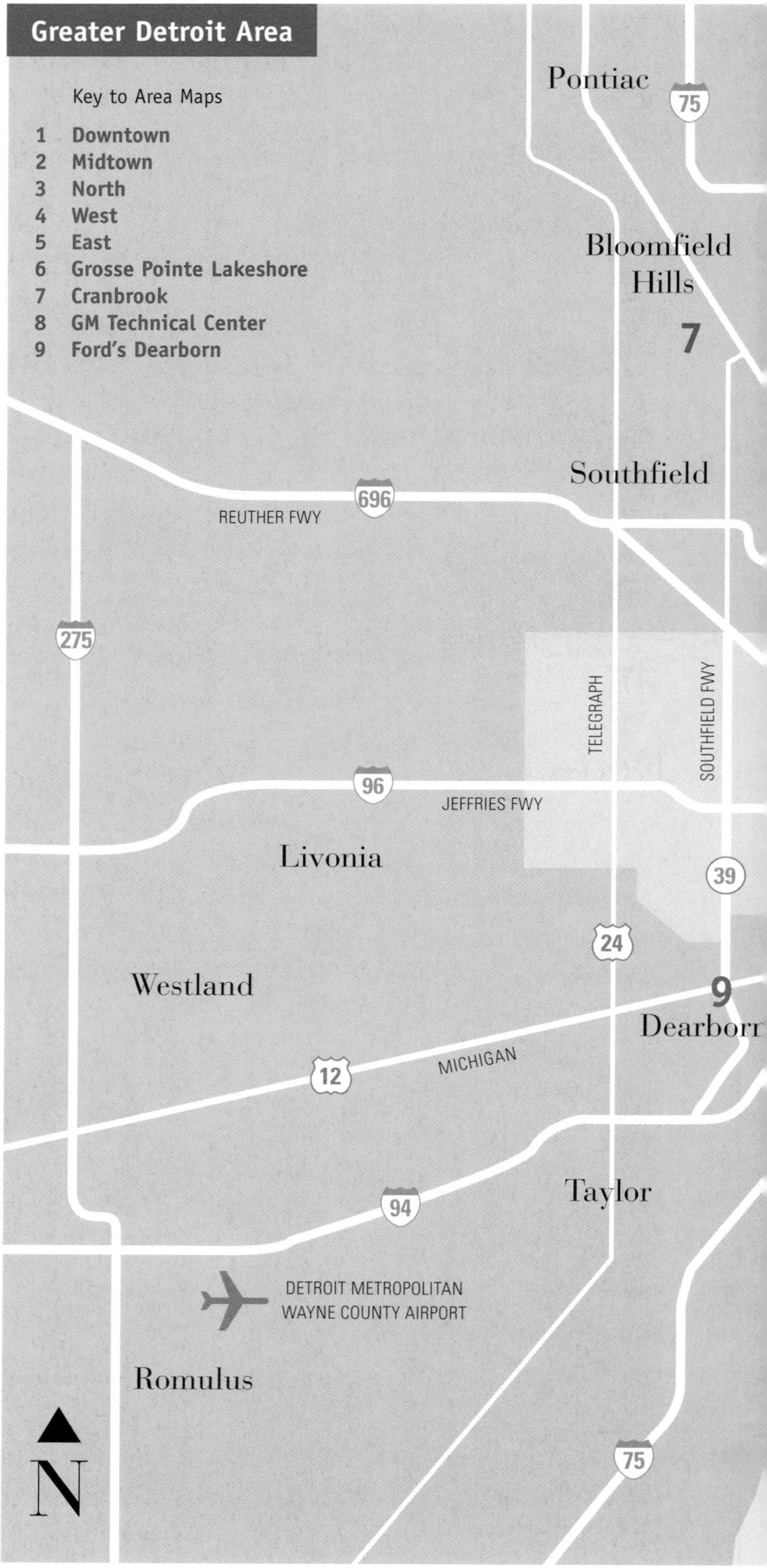
Greater Detroit Area
Key to Area Maps
1 Downtown
2 Midtown
3 North
4 West
5 East
6 Grosse Pointe Lakeshore
7 Cranbrook
8 GM Technical Center
9 Ford's Dearborn
Pontiac
75
Bloomfield Hills
7
Southfield
696
REUTHER FWY
275
TELEGRAPH
SOUTHFIELD FWY
96
JEFFRIES FWY
Livonia
39
24
Westland
9
Dearborn
12
MICHIGAN
Taylor
94
DETROIT METROPOLITAN
WAYNE COUNTY AIRPORT
Romulus
75
N

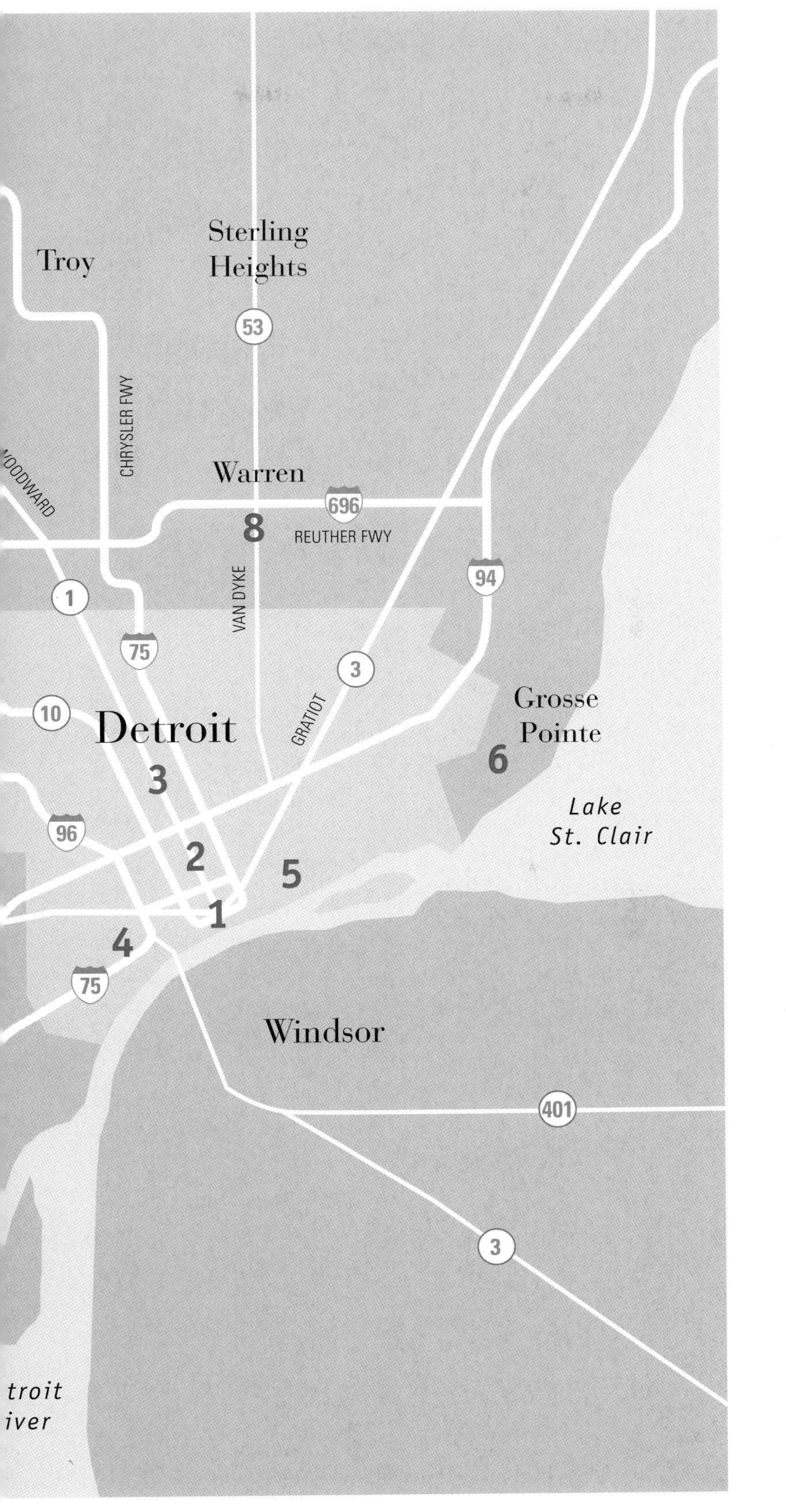
Troy
Sterling Heights
53
CHRYSLER FWY
WOODWARD
Warren
696
8
REUTHER FWY
VAN DYKE
94
1
75
3
10
Detroit
GRATIOT
Grosse Pointe
6
3
Lake St. Clair
96
2
5
1
4
75
Windsor
401
3
troit
iver

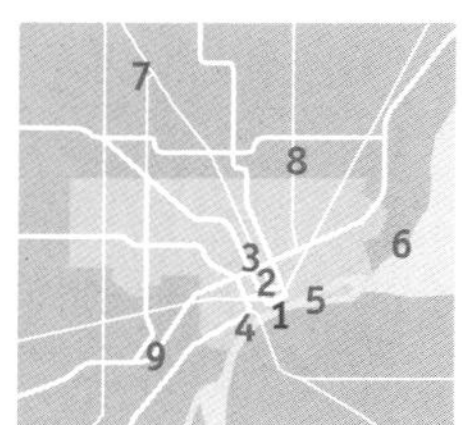

1 **Downtown**
2 Midtown
3 North
4 West
5 East
6 Grosse Pointe Lakeshore
7 Cranbrook
8 GM Technical Center
9 Ford's Dearborn

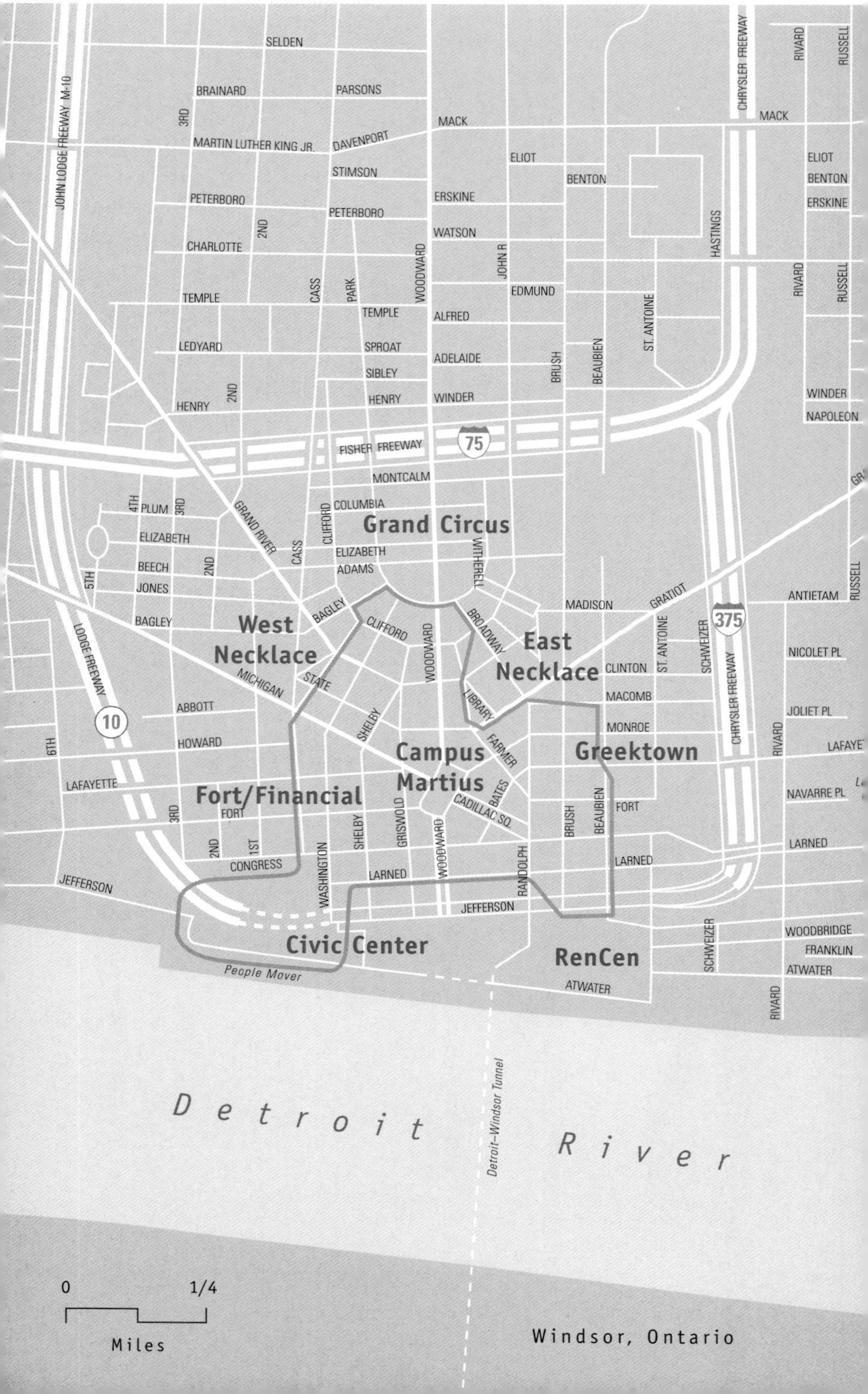

Grand Circus
West Necklace
East Necklace
Campus Martius
Greektown
Fort/Financial
Civic Center
RenCen
People Mover
Detroit–Windsor Tunnel
Detroit River
Windsor, Ontario

0 1/4
Miles

Downtown

Downtown

One mile square, roughly. Traversed on foot in half an hour, or glimpsed by a commuting motorist in about forty seconds. Acre for acre and pound for pound, the constellation of architecture and urban space within this tiny piece of real estate is among the richest and most diverse on earth. Overlaid on now invisible traces of Pleistocene terrain, ancient campfires, and eighteenth-century forts is an urban geometry that seemingly expands from Campus Martius with big-bang force. For the ground-bound pedestrian the experience of Downtown's maze-like "necklace" can be downright disorienting. Accordingly, we encourage the reader to refer to the maps.

Our Downtown journey follows the counterclockwise path of the elevated People Mover, beginning with the Civic Center and spiraling, more or less, to the Campus Martius core. The reader may elect to ride at any time, and an introductory round trip on the PM offers a worthwhile overview.

Civic Center

A good place to start, the Civic Center area is both historic and hopeful. Hart Plaza provides a centering place of orientation, but hardly represents a "center," a sense of place, or what the Greeks called *genius loci*. Why is that? Perhaps it's the formlessness of the expanse. Unlike, say, Piazza San Marco in Venice, Detroit's main public space lacks scale, coherence, and connection, especially to the River.

The area's history is as deep and layered as any in the city. First, this is our place of origin. Native Americans surely settled at this strategic strait between the lakes. Cadillac landed here, we think. Over time came layers of hut, cabin, business, industry, infrastructure, and asphalt.

In 1890 Mayor Pingree proposed a civic center at the foot of Woodward, but the idea and area languished through three decades of disagreement. In 1924 the American Institute of Architects sponsored a young professor from the University

of Michigan, Eliel Saarinen, to compose a center with a war memorial. Depression and World War II postponed development until Saarinen and Saarinen—Eliel and his son Eero—returned in 1947 with a new Civic Center model (pictured, above). The veterans' hall was built in 1950. The city-county government building and the auditorium followed suit, but not exactly according to the plan, in 1955.

Perhaps the greatest departure from the Saarinens' vision was the nature of the proposed public space itself, which they envisioned as a predominantly green sweep of lawn and naturalistic tree clusters gently terracing to the river. What was built was a largely hard-surfaced piece of environmental art with landscape garnish. The model was undoubtedly compelling. Speaking of models, the superhuman enlargement of Joe Louis's fist at the intersection of Woodward and Jefferson is hard to miss and admired by many.

On many levels, the Civic Center is something of an enigma. Only a trace of its layered history remains. Only a hint of its awesome river vantage is apparent from the Jefferson sidewalk. On a practical note, the pedestrian traverses Jefferson under advisement; as your guides, we implore you to observe that West Jefferson is a freeway on/off ramp. The clenched fist may say it all.

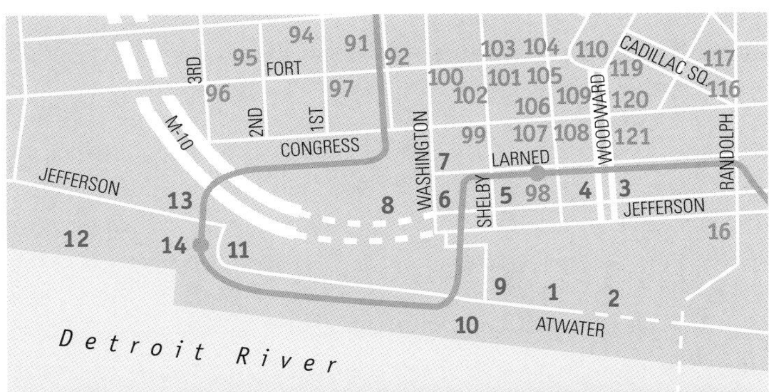

CIVIC CENTER AREA

1 PHILIP A. HART PLAZA
2 HENRY AND EDSEL FORD AUDITORIUM
3 COLEMAN A. YOUNG MUNICIPAL CENTER
4 ONE WOODWARD
5 150 WEST JEFFERSON
6 PONTCHARTRAIN HOTEL
7 DETROIT FIRE DEPT. HEADQUARTERS
8 COBO HALL AND CONVENTION CENTER
9 FORD/UAW BUILDING
10 CIVIC CENTER RIVERFRONT PROMENADE
11 JOE LOUIS SPORTS ARENA
12 RIVERFRONT TOWERS
13 PEOPLE MOVER
14 JOE LOUIS ARENA STATION

1 PHILIP A. HART PLAZA; HORACE E. DODGE AND SON MEMORIAL FOUNTAIN

Jefferson and Woodward Aves.
Smith, Hinchman, and Grylls, with Isamu Noguchi, 1979

At the center of Downtown's waterfront, Hart Plaza was designed to serve many purposes, including the city's ethnic festivals, Independence Day, and less predictable Stanley Cup celebrations. Noguchi's fountain, the focal point of the plaza, is impressive when wet, and even more when lighted and wet at night. Absent special events, the vast hardscape can be awesomely empty.

2 HENRY AND EDSEL FORD AUDITORIUM

Jefferson and Woodward Aves. (Civic Center)
O'Dell, Hewlett, and Luckenbach, 1955

Saarinen's 1924 plan for the Civic Center placed an auditorium on the east facing west and framing a central civic space. The dream became reality in 1955, although the building fronts Jefferson and regrettably turns its back to the river. In line with reigning principles of the day, the design was kept simple inside and out. Its visual impact depends on its elementary massing, its subtle interplay of material and texture, and color contrast. The dark granite contains blue flecks that are more readily appreciated up close. Even the most casual observer will know the building's intended uses, and that's one of the big ideas of modern functionalism. Time has proven that this long vacant and now endangered classic is not easily adapted to serve uses other than its original purpose.

3 COLEMAN A. YOUNG MUNICIPAL CENTER (CITY-COUNTY BUILDING)

Jefferson and Woodward Aves.
Harley, Ellington, and Day, 1955

Designed at the zenith of the International style, Detroit's City-County Building won praise in its day for its clean lines and modern efficiencies. The composition, especially the west tower, draws inspiration from the United Nations Building, which in turn is indebted in many ways to the Swiss master architect Le Corbusier. Today, though, we lament the lack of street-level amenities. The building also is too far removed from Hart Plaza to create any meaningful sense of "Civic Center" edge. *The Spirit of Detroit* statue is the work of world-renowned sculptor Marshall Fredericks.

1

2

3

4 ONE WOODWARD (MICHIGAN CONSOLIDATED GAS COMPANY)

1 Woodward Ave.
Minoru Yamasaki, and Smith, Hinchman, and Grylls, 1963

Minoru Yamasaki embellished the formula of Mies van der Rohe by wrapping a graceful vertical grillwork around this thirty-two-story office tower. He heightened the effect of shimmering lightness with a reflecting pool and thirty-foot-high glass-enclosed lobby. Those three-story sheets of glass were the tallest ever installed at the time. Each of the two-story precast concrete panels is joined at the center to form hexagonal window openings. The bronze ballerina in the pool is by Giacomo Manzu. After MichCon moved its corporate offices, the building underwent a few name changes and is today known simply by its address: One Woodward.

5 150 WEST JEFFERSON

150 West Jefferson Ave.
Heller and Leake, and BEI Associates, 1989

America's postmodern skyscraper boom of the 1980s arrived in Detroit fairly late. Built by Denver developer John Madden, 150 West Jefferson was the first office tower to rise in Downtown since Renaissance Center. With bowed front, green-framed windows, and flag-topped summit, it added a dash of after-modern style to the skyline. But the building's siting is less assured. While the tower "faces" Jefferson, most visitors enter through a nondescript doorway off Larned, and from there take an elevator to a warren-like lobby on the second level, all of which is rather awkward.

6 PONTCHARTRAIN HOTEL

Washington Blvd. and Jefferson Ave.
King and Lewis, 1965

Downtown's first major hotel built since the 1920s, "The Pontch" was faceted so that each room has an angular bay allowing views both of the river and the city. Cadillac's Fort Pontchartrain du Detroit was built more or less on this site in 1701.

7 DETROIT FIRE DEPARTMENT HEADQUARTERS

Larned at Washington Blvd.
Hans Gehrke, 1929

This powerfully massive and richly detailed work reassures the public it serves and protects. Gehrke built a practice designing functionally pragmatic yet symbolically adorned fire stations all over the city.

4

5

6

7

8

COBO HALL AND CONVENTION CENTER

1 Washington Blvd.
Giffels and Rossetti, 1960; addition by Sims-Varner, 1989

By 1900 warehouses and light industry covered this prime waterfront site. When higher civic priorities prevailed a half century later, only the likes of an under-used railhead district could provide enough Downtown land area for a new convention center. The downside is that boxy, blank-walled assembly halls are as indifferent to a river view as a freight train.

Louis Rossetti, the elder, designed the gleaming convention center and arena with a sophisticated modern hand. Sims-Varner later added the monumental loggia that moves people up, down, and through a long interior city block. The sheer extent of this space is nearly incomprehensible, as the custom-patterned carpet seems to warp with the curvature of the earth. The superhuman scale extends to the exterior, where cascading cubic forms dramatically define the building's entries. The northeast corner (pictured) is the definitive architectural statement, although the rest of the unrelieved Congress Street elevation is ominously speechless.

And if you liked the film *Metropolis*, you'll love Cobo's backside. In what just may be the quintessential Detroit cityscape, sweeping freeways, spiraling auto ramps, and flying people tubes reach a feverish pitch (8b). To some the interwoven assemblage resembles the aftermath of a tornado. Topping it all, the People Mover threads through Cobo like a strip of celluloid, offering seemingly unintended glimpses of the convention floor below through a serially interrupting maze of structure, pipe, and suspended ceiling grid. All this movement around and through the big top can be shockingly new to the unsuspecting tourist. Indeed, it was circus entrepreneur James A. Bailey who once said, "The public likes to be humbugged." Bailey was born near this site in 1847.

9

FORD/UAW BUILDING (VETERANS MEMORIAL BUILDING)

151 West Jefferson Ave.
Harley, Ellington, and Day, 1951; renovation by Smith, Hinchman, and Grylls, 1996

This blocky, ten-story structure was the first piece realized in Detroit's long-planned Civic Center. The white marble façade facing Downtown bears a twenty-eight-foot eagle relief sculpture by Marshall Fredericks in memory of veterans who died in war. Smith, Hinchman, and Grylls's recent renovation of the building for the United Auto Workers and Ford Motor Company's joint training facility was acclaimed by AIA Michigan.

8 a

8 b

9

10

CIVIC CENTER RIVERFRONT PROMENADE

P

Riverfront from Hart Plaza to Joe Louis Arena
Albert Kahn Associates, and Sasaki Associates, 2001

This linear park provides public connection to and along the waterfront as it dresses up Downtown's front door—to the River and to Canada. The design includes figurative quotations from Detroit's maritime and industrial heritage. The serpentine seat wall resembles a giant rope uncoiled along the metaphorical boardwalk. The coiled rope source at the west end was designed for a future civic sculpture of monumental proportions. The nearby mini-park is laid out to recall the geometry of Detroit's eighteenth-century ribbon farms. A powerful new figurative sculpture by artist Ed Dwight is dedicated to the Underground Railroad at the stairs from Hart Plaza (10b).

11

JOE LOUIS SPORTS ARENA

P$

651 West Jefferson Ave.
Smith, Hinchman, and Grylls, 1980

"The Joe" is home to the Detroit Red Wings, one of the original and great hockey teams in North America. Because the arena is now somewhat obsolete in its lack of lower-level luxury suites, some have suggested turning it into a new city aquarium.

10 a

10 b

11

12 PR

RIVERFRONT TOWERS

300 Riverfront Park Dr.
The Gruzen Partnership, 1984; second phase by
The Martin Company, 1988

Architects for the first two towers toward the west seemed a bit preoccupied with massing forms and surfaces. Later designers of the third installment took better advantage of the breathtaking views.

13 P$

PEOPLE MOVER

Downtown
Parsons Brinkerhoff, 1987

The People Mover elicits a range of emotions. First, the decision to hoist this engineering stunt on an unsuspecting public realm was surely not aesthetically driven. It's hard to find words to describe this viaduct's impact on the Downtown architectural scene. In one stroke it dehumanized the street as it defaced many fine buildings. On the other hand, the People Mover stations comprise an interesting array of solutions, from free-standing objects to appendages integrated into host buildings. As a whole the system provides convenient access to the city's resources, including all-important parking. And forgetting the financial and architectural costs, it does provide a unique overview of the cityscape, allowing the voyeur-traveler to check out who's working (and who's not) on the second floor of Downtown Detroit. Finally, and best of all, the artwork commissioned for the People Mover stations is uniformly splendid. Accordingly, we highlight these works here.

14 P$

JOE LOUIS ARENA STATION

Like a traffic cone inexplicably standing amidst a swirl of movement, this Trekkie vertical transport unit fits right into its multimodal setting. Artist Kamrowski's "Voyage" surrealistically interprets all this motion and energy in two murals of Venetian glass mosaic. Next stop, Millender Center.

12

13

14

RenCen

This district includes many diverse buildings, and nonbuildings, competing for our attention. The whole seems less than the sum of its parts. Here, the juxtapositions of scale, style, dimension, and modality seem other-worldly at best. Car is king, however poignant and pragmatic, as two freeways merge to decelerate on the Jefferson landing strip.

15 SP

MILLENDER CENTER AND STATION

555 Brush St.
1985

What's most interesting about the Millender Center complex is how it was designed and built. As a relatively rare achievement of the Model Cities Operation Breakthrough initiative, this mixed-use building was built in large pieces out of state and shipped to Detroit. Kitchen and bath units were assembled on site like a giant kit of parts.

The need to accommodate the People Mover elicited the most appealing phrase in an otherwise banal modern statement. Millender Center station includes a colorful Pewabic tile mural by artist Alvin Loving. Exit here for a walking tour of the RenCen District and return to Renaissance Center station, which is just across the street.

16 NS SP

OLD MARINERS' CHURCH (MARINERS' CHURCH)

170 East Jefferson Ave. at Randolph
Calvin N. Otis, 1849; relocated 1955

The oldest stone church surviving in Detroit, Old Mariners' was erected to solace seaman visiting the busy port of Detroit. It stood originally at the base of Woodward Avenue in the heart of the dock and warehouse district. As one of Detroit's many examples of "architecture on wheels," the church was moved in 1955 to make way for the new Civic Center.

Architecturally and historically, the building we see today is not what Detroiters of 1849 saw. The original structure was a two-story, thoroughly urban building that resembled a nineteenth-century British Methodist chapel. The church proper was on the second floor while the ground floor was sublet to defray expenses—in this case, a post office was the tenant. While the south and east elevations are mostly original, the north and west sides are mostly fictional. As a result of the move the grade was lifted on the Hart Plaza and Jefferson Avenue sides, wooden

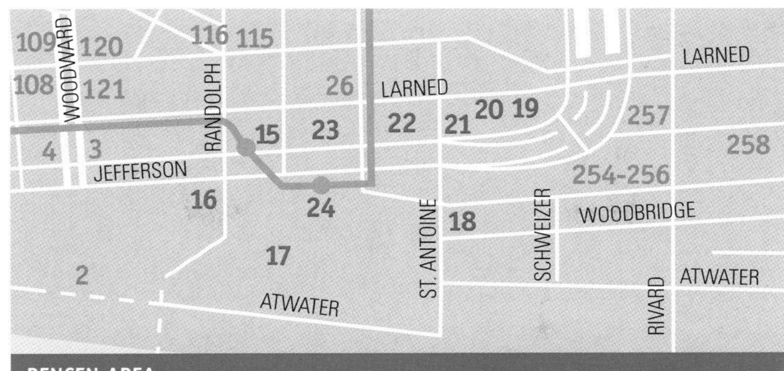

RENCEN AREA

15	MILLENDER CENTER AND STATION
16	OLD MARINERS' CHURCH
17	RENAISSANCE CENTER
18	THE DETROIT RACQUET CLUB
19	DOWLING HALL
20	UNIVERSITY OF DETROIT MERCY–SCHOOL OF LAW LIBRARY
21	SAINTS PETER AND PAUL CHURCH
22	BEAUBIEN HOUSE
23	JEFFERSON AVE. PARKING STRUCTURE
24	RENAISSANCE STATION

15

16 a

pinnacles and battlements disappeared, windows and buttresses were added to the north elevation, and a romantic tower was added to the west. From southeast to northwest, a city house morphs into a country house, reminiscent of a rural English parish church.

Today, having added "Old" to its name, Mariners' stands hemmed in by the Detroit-Windsor Tunnel on one side and busy Jefferson Avenue on the other, yet it has survived to become a treasured symbol of the past.

17 RENAISSANCE CENTER

East Jefferson Ave.
SP John Portman and Associates, 1977; renovations by Skidmore, Owings, and Merrill, 2000–

Although it's been given a bad—and probably unfair—rap by local architectural cognoscenti, there is no denying that this blockbuster is a city-defining landmark. At the very least, Henry Ford II's development decision committed money and prestige to Detroit's revitalization in the face of a mass Downtown exodus. And, two decades later, this gift that keeps giving was purchased by General Motors to serve as its world headquarters, and to further energize the city's renewal.

Now, to the architecture. To be sure, Portman seems to have designed RenCen more in the abstract than as an outgrowth of place. The sculptural composition of four thirty-nine-story octagonal towers and one seventy-three-story gleaming cylinder, rising like giant fingers from its massive plinth, is terribly compelling. The experience within, however, is mixed. Here, the Brutalist juxtaposition of forms, surfaces, and dark and light is exciting indeed, but practically speaking the visitor can become desperately disoriented. There's a lesson about scale and symmetry here.

General Motors' courage and SOM's design editing promise to clarify, adjust, and expand the original design's potential. The interior circulation ring already reduces anxiety and adds to the spatial thrill. Removing those off-putting concrete berms on Jefferson will surely improve the streetscape and RenCen's connection to the city. And the Winter Garden, which sweeps out to a planned riverfront plaza and promenade, brings focus and renewal to the whole.

The idea of a self-contained citadel is a timeless solution to city building and rebuilding. Inevitably, as its environs have been rejuvenated, RenCen's fortress-like isolation appeared all the more gratuitous. Its resilience in turning inside out is testimony to the strength, not weakness, of the original design idea.

16 b

17

18  PR

THE DETROIT RACQUET CLUB

626 Woodbridge
Albert Kahn, 1902

This functionally straightforward building has quietly gone about the business of having fun for a hundred years. Its unusual use, date, and architect are of interest here. Like its reputed prototype in London, the building was originally designed for both racquets and curling, a combination whose logic escapes us. Indeed, curling was dropped, and the "curling barn" was removed from the building's back, by 1920. To what extent the design is indebted to its source is not known, although the handsome entry feature conveys a proper English Arts and Crafts attention to material and detail. Much of the interior finishes and furnishings have been preserved. The steel roof structure over the Racquets court, with its integral skylights and operable vents, prefigures Kahn's pioneering factory design several years later. Yet from the street there's hardly a clue that a game involving a projectile whizzing through space at 185 miles per hour is played here. Architect Robert Venturi would prize this little jewel as an early "decorated shed."

19 SP

DOWLING HALL, UNIVERSITY OF DETROIT MERCY (DETROIT COLLEGE)

651 East Jefferson Ave.
Gordon W. Lloyd, 1890

This urbane sidewalk-hugging block was built originally for Detroit College and is used now by the University of Detroit Mercy School of Law. An English immigrant, Gordon Lloyd was the dean of the city's architects at the end of the nineteenth century. The rugged façade shows Lloyd working in the popular Romanesque style of the day. Some suggest that Lloyd was more proficient in the Gothic mode. The interior, while updated, still includes evidence of Lloyd's original intent.

18

19 a

19 b

20 SC SP

UNIVERSITY OF DETROIT MERCY SCHOOL OF LAW LIBRARY

Larned, behind Dowling Hall
Smith, Hinchman, and Grylls, 1977

This modern addition to Dowling Hall creates a minimalist counterpoint to the older building. The glass-and-brick structure includes a three-story skylit student lounge and intimate courtyard.

21 NS SP

SAINTS PETER AND PAUL CHURCH

629 East Jefferson Ave.
Francis Letourno, 1848; alterations, 1860s and 1911

The oldest church building in Detroit was under construction from 1844. Francis Letourno (or Latourneau) was an enterprising builder who also built lighthouses on the Great Lakes and even steamboats. For this Roman Catholic church he turned to classical precedents instead of the more prevalent Gothic Revival of the day. The subdued exterior, recalling the work of English Regency architect John Soane, features Ionic pilasters and a heavy frieze designed to conceal the sloping roof.

The interiors are splendid, albeit almost entirely later than the building's construction. The sanctuary ceiling (21b) was originally a half-round barrel vault, which produced disastrous acoustic effects. A flatter vault replaced the original in the 1860s, while the full barrel vaults at the side aisles are believed to be original. The entry rotunda (21c) and side vestibules were added in a 1911 remodeling designed to make the church seem more elegant. The organ case is the only original interior element surviving. Through it all, this sophisticated building remains a monumental landmark of church architecture in Michigan.

Also significant is St. Catherine's Chapel, built in 1918 on the rear of the main church in an architecturally sympathetic style. Created both as a daily chapel for parish school children and for smaller wedding parties, the chapel remained in use until the 1970s. It was later converted to parish administration, the use it serves today.

Just to the east of the main church is a former Jesuit residence that now belongs to the University of Detroit Mercy School of Law.

20

21 a

21 b

21 c

22 NS SP

BEAUBIEN HOUSE (CHARLES TROMBLY HOUSE)

553 East Jefferson Ave.
Unknown architect, 1851; restoration by AIA, 1981

This stately townhouse is one of Detroit's oldest surviving houses. At one time, about a dozen similar residences stood nearby until they were demolished in the 1950s, when land was tragically cleared for parking lots. The modest seven-room structure was lovingly renovated by the Michigan chapter of the American Institute of Architects in 1981. Since then, it has served as headquarters for AIA Detroit, AIA Michigan, and the Michigan Architectural Foundation.

23 SC SP$

JEFFERSON AVENUE PARKING STRUCTURE

Jefferson Ave. and Brush St.
Neumann | Smith and Associates, 1996

This award-winning design advances parking structure design one small step for mankind. Respectful of its neighbors, the building celebrates human movement and scale over that of the automobile—a bold, if nearly heretical, move in Detroit.

24 P$

RENAISSANCE STATION

Artist George Woodman interpreted RenCen's forms in brilliantly colorful patterns of hexagonal ceramic tiles. Local sculptor Marshall Fredericks created the "Siberian Ram," cast in bronze and set against a very green Pewabic tile backdrop. Next stop, Bricktown.

22

23

24

Greektown

What we call Greektown began as a pioneer farm, became a German ethnic enclave in the mid-nineteenth century, and later evolved into a Greek commercial district. It consists largely of two- and three-story commercial structures anchored by St. Mary's Catholic Church complex to the east. Today the first floors of most buildings house restaurants, and those storefronts have been modified over time as owners customized them to suit their trade. In the 1980s the collection of older warehouses on the south side of Monroe was refit as the Trapper's Alley market-place. Street-level signs, some good and some expedient, collectively contribute to the corridor's appeal. In the late 1990s the construction of the Greektown Casino on the rear of Trapper's Alley facing Lafayette added a major (some say overwhelming) new presence.

Greektown (along with the neighboring strip of brick buildings on Beaubien known today as Bricktown) illustrates shifting attitudes in urban planning over the past half-century. Fifty years ago, urban planners happily would have swept aside this collection of mostly nondescript Victorian buildings to make way for something like the modern Blue Cross-Blue Shield campus nearby. Today we've learned to treasure its variety and scale, as we celebrate Greektown as one of the city's premier tourist attractions.

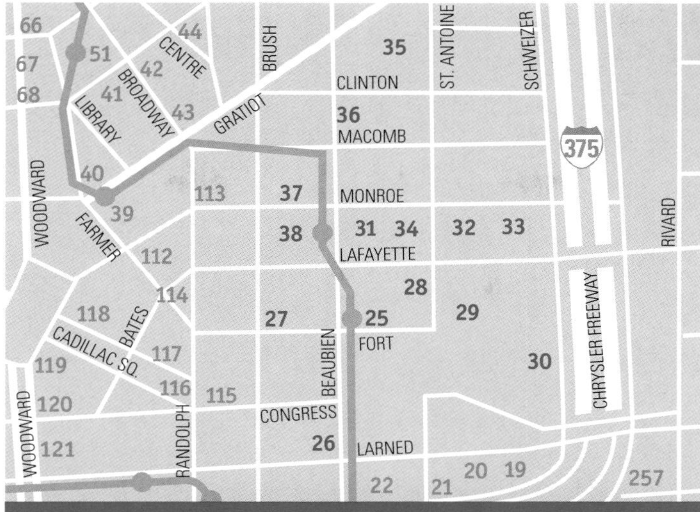

GREEKTOWN AREA

25	BRICKTOWN STATION	31	TRAPPER'S ALLEY
26	ALEXANDER CHAPOTON HOUSE	32	SAINT MARY CATHOLIC CHURCH
27	GLOBE TOBACCO CO. BUILDING	33	SAINT MARY PARISH HOUSE
28	DETROIT CORNICE AND SLATE CO.	34	SAINT MARY SCHOOL
29	BLUE CROSS/BLUE SHIELD OF MICHIGAN	35	FRANK MURPHY HALL OF JUSTICE
		36	DETROIT POLICE HEADQUARTERS
30	HOLY FAMILY ROMAN CATHOLIC CHURCH	37	SECOND BAPTIST CHURCH
		38	GREEKTOWN STATION

Greektown after dark

25 BRICKTOWN STATION

PS

Artist Glen Michaels enlarged and transferred bas-relief images to porcelain panels to create the ninety-foot-long "Beaubien Passage," which suggests a fantastic cityscape.

26 ALEXANDER CHAPOTON HOUSE

NSC SP

511 Beaubien St.
Unknown architect, 1870s

The Chapotons were one of Detroit's oldest French families. A prolific builder in the mid-to-late nineteenth century (including Detroit's "Old" City Hall to his credit), Alexander Chapoton built this three-story Victorian townhouse as a rental property. At the time, this was but one of a row of similar red-brick townhouses on narrow lots. As the commercial district expanded, all but a handful were lost. Now restored and operating as an art gallery and office, it is one of the last well-preserved vestiges of nineteenth-century residential architecture Downtown. Note the heavily expressive eyebrows over the first-floor windows. Of Chapoton's numerous buildings in the area, Globe Tobacco (27) still stands nearby on Fort Street.

27 GLOBE TOBACCO COMPANY BUILDING

NC SP

407 East Fort St.
Alexander Chapoton, Builder, 1888; renovation by
Redstone Architects, 1984

The Globe Building is virtually all that remains of Detroit's once-thriving tobacco industry. Founded by leading citizens including Hiram Walker, the Globe company built this six-story red-brick building to cure Virginia and Kentucky leaf tobacco and make cigars and pipe tobacco. Redstone's 1984 renovation into office space was achieved by carving a skylighted atrium through the building's core, while revealing original timber framing and brickwork.

25

26

27

28 NSC S PR

DETROIT CORNICE AND SLATE COMPANY

733 St. Antoine
Harry J. Rill, 1897; restoration and addition by Kessler and Associates, 1999

The Detroit Cornice and Slate Company manufactured building ornamentation made from steel, which was pressed and hand hammered, then painted to look like stone. What better way to advertise its wares than to bedeck its own building? Architect Harry J. Rill merged a structural frame resembling earlier cast-iron commercial architecture with a stylishly current flourish of Beaux-Arts Classicism. The result is a unique and delightful whole.

The building housed the original business until architect Kessler's office converted it for their own use in 1974. In yet another useful life, it was converted in the 1990s to the offices of the *Metro Times*. Bill Kessler and his partner Ed Francis recently, and with exceeding sensitivity, parlayed the original company's idea into a sleek, stainless steel wrap-around expansion to give the newspaper more room. This inventive solution represents a primer on how to successfully preserve and expand historic architecture.

29 SP

BLUE CROSS/BLUE SHIELD OF MICHIGAN

Lafayette and St. Antoine
Giffels and Rossetti, 1971; additions by Neumann | Smith, 1999

The original three-building complex by Louis "Gino" Rossetti includes a twenty-two-story office tower, three-story computer center, and five-story parking deck. Praised at the time, the idea of closing Downtown blocks to build a modern suburban-style campus is now in question. Ken Neumann's Customer Service Center addition extends the modern architecture in form and scale.

30 S SP

HOLY FAMILY ROMAN CATHOLIC CHURCH

641 Walter P. Chrysler Highway
Edward A. Schilling, 1910

Created for Detroit's Italian community, this church was designed by Edward A. Schilling in a bold Beaux-Arts style that appears somewhat quirky today in the round. One can more readily imagine this assertive façade in an intimate Roman piazza. The building surely was more at ease in its pre-freeway context at Hastings and Fort. Today the cream-colored, painted brick exterior strikes a delightfully sunny note in a city better known for its somber Gothic churches. Be sure to catch this elevation in a morning sunrise. In the larger place of Detroit's religious architecture, and especially in the Catholic church context, this articulate little building exemplifies a frequent tie between stylistic expression and the ethnic heritage of the congregation it serves. See also Schilling's equally inventive Belle Isle Casino (290).

28

29

30

31 TRAPPER'S ALLEY

Monroe between Beaubien and St. Antoine
Various architects, 1853; renovation by Roger Sherman Architects Group, 1985; alterations, 2000

Originally the Traugott Schmidt and Sons Furrier and Tannery Buildings, this collection of red-brick buildings was built from the mid-nineteenth century onward for a wool, fur, and leather business. While the street boasts a variety of styles, the overall impression is Victorian Romanesque and Italianate. In the 1980s the buildings were substantially altered and united under a vast skylight to form the Trapper's Alley festival marketplace (31b). Still later, the complex was re-reused for the Greektown Casino.

32 SAINT MARY CATHOLIC CHURCH

St. Antoine at Monroe
Peter Dederichs, 1885

St. Mary's is among the city's oldest Roman Catholic parishes, founded in the 1830s to serve Detroit's German-speaking Catholics. The current church was completed in 1885. Period sources refer to the church as "Pisan Romanesque." Architectural historians have noted both German and Italian details in its design. German-born and trained Peter Dederichs, a parishioner and noted church designer of his day, skillfully blended these influences into an exuberant creation. Oddly juxtaposed now to the new Greektown Casino, St. Mary's remains one of Detroit's essential architectural treasures.

33 SAINT MARY PARISH HOUSE

646 Monroe St.
Julius Hess, 1876

This sturdy Italian Romanesque parish house is the work of Swiss-born Julius Hess, also known in Detroit for his Grand Army of the Republic Building (75) and his Trumbull Avenue Presbyterian Church (158).

34 SAINT MARY SCHOOL

St. Antoine at Monroe
Pius Daubner, 1868

Completing the exquisite three-part harmony, this simple structure served as a Catholic school for girls for almost a century. It now operates as a parish community center.

31 a

31 b

32

33

34

35

FRANK MURPHY HALL OF JUSTICE

Gratiot and Chrysler Freeway
Eberle M. Smith and Associates, 1968

This evocative slab tower tells a story about the uses within and how they are supported. The court suites, offices, and detention facilities are individually expressed, as the bold structural framing unifies the whole.

36

DETROIT POLICE HEADQUARTERS

Beaubien and Macomb
Albert Kahn, 1923

Kahn elaborated here on his earlier foray into classicism at the Detroit Athletic Club (48). Some suggest the resemblance was ironically deliberate. In any event, the Italian palazzo model lends dignity and authority to a design that incorporates thoroughly modern construction methods. Here Kahn blends Renaissance details with pier and window patterns commonly found in his commercial architecture. At this point in his long career, Kahn was doing it all—factories, university buildings, mansions, and office buildings—and each in its own terms.

37

SECOND BAPTIST CHURCH

441 Monroe St.
Various architects, 1857; alterations, 1880, mid 1910s, and 1968

Founded in 1836 by thirteen former slaves, Second Baptist is the oldest African American congregation in Michigan. The original 1857 church was a three-story painted brick building of Gothic inspiration. Major additions built in 1880, the mid-1910s, and 1968 substantially altered its massing and character. The extent to which the original architecture survives is uncertain. Above all, this church was an important haven in the Underground Railroad. The expressive modern office structure to the east was designed by Sims-Varner.

38

GREEKTOWN STATION

This most effusive and arguably best of People Mover stations captures the festive spirit of Greektown as streetscape and as place. Artist Stephen Antonakos successfully integrated art and architecture through the medium of colorful neon tubing. Next stop, Cadillac Center station.

35

36

37

38

East Necklace

The "necklace" is a relatively new term coined for the web of radiating and concentric streets centering on Grand Circus Park and comprising the portion of the Woodward Plan that was built. The area east of Woodward, north of Greektown, and south of the stadiums includes a varied mix of uses. At its heart is the pace-setting Harmonie Park. Professional, artsy, and lofty, this pocket of urban renewal was once part of a thriving fur and jewelry district. Providing opportunities to display these luxuries today are the fine theaters, restaurants, and clubs of the area. To the east, and bridging to Greektown and its new casino, is the nucleus of the city's criminal justice infrastructure.

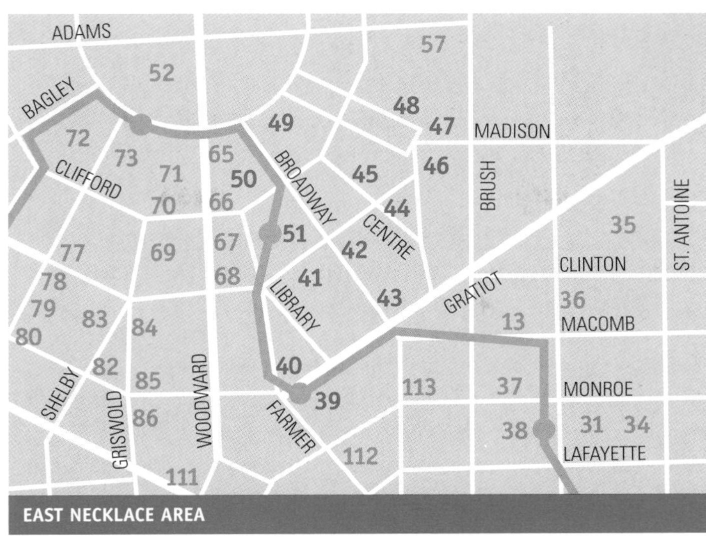

EAST NECKLACE AREA

39 CADILLAC STATION
40 DETROIT PUBLIC LIBRARY, DOWNTOWN
41 L. B. KING AND CO. BUILDING
42 MERCHANTS BUILDING
43 HARMONIE CENTRE
44 HARMONIE PARK
45 HARMONIE CLUB
46 MUSIC HALL
47 CENTURY CLUB AND GEM THEATRE
48 DETROIT ATHLETIC CLUB
49 DETROIT OPERA HOUSE
50 METROPOLITAN BUILDING
51 BROADWAY STATION

Detroit Opera House interior

39

CADILLAC STATION

P$

Pewabic tiles salvaged from the Stroh Brewery demolition were used to create a lively arcade. The murals of Detroit workers originally graced the halls of Northern High School.

40

DETROIT PUBLIC LIBRARY, DOWNTOWN BRANCH

P

Gratiot and Library St.
Smith, Hinchman, and Grylls, 1932

This building was designed to conform to an odd-shaped block created by Judge Woodward's plan. Smith, Hinchman, and Grylls designed this wonderful object-building in the Art Deco style, which originated in a 1925 exposition devoted to the *arts décoratifs*. As exemplified here, the style is classically based, but simplified. In the early 1930s, Art Deco and Art Moderne were often merged, and hence a stylistic call is hard to make with certainty. "But here," as Detroit historic designation director Bill Worden points out, "we have the real deal."

41

L. B. KING AND COMPANY BUILDING

NS PR

1274 Library St.
Rogers and MacFarlane, 1911

This early terra cotta-clad commercial building is notable for its use of the "Chicago window"—a large, horizontal pane of fixed glass flanked by smaller, operable windows on each side. The elaborate Italian Renaissance cornice was added in 1926; without it, L. B. King would be right in line with mainstream Chicago proto-modernism. Annis Furs occupied the building from 1932 to 1983, almost the last vestige of the fur industry that founded the city.

42

MERCHANTS BUILDING

N PR

206 E. Grand River Ave. at Broadway
Otto Misch Company, 1922

Terra cotta, a type of fired clay, was popular in early tall buildings because it was readily available and could be molded easily into decorative forms. In this case, we have a modern reinforced-concrete frame building clad with a thin veneer of white terra cotta, which is styled to resemble classical ornament in stone.

39

40

41

42

43 HARMONIE CENTRE (BREITMEYER-TOBIN BUILDING)

1308 Broadway

Raseman and Fischer, 1906; renovation by Schervish Vogel Merz, 1990s

This eight-story, steel-frame office structure was one of the early "tall" buildings in this part of Downtown. Because of its corner location, it has two finished façades. The style is Beaux-Arts Classicism, as expressed in a wealth of columns, cornices, and cartouches. The combination of red brick and cream terra cotta was a standard formula for the Beaux-Arts style of the time, but this seems to be Detroit's only extant example. Through the 1930s the building housed a number of prominent African American professionals, and in the 1990s it was substantially renovated by Schervish Vogel Merz as part of the Harmonie Park revival.

44 HARMONIE PARK

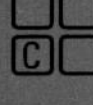

Randolph, Center, and Grand River

Various architects, 1895–1924; renovations by Schervish Vogel Merz, 1980s

Harmonie Park is a small triangular space happily left over from Judge Woodward's intersecting geometries, and a remarkable enclave of refined architecture and urbanity. The area was a haven for German immigrants, who filled this part of the city in the nineteenth century. The buildings in the district were built between 1895 and 1924. Many were designed by German-born architect Richard Raseman, notably including the Harmonie Club of 1894–1895 and the Breitmeyer-Tobin Building of 1906. In the 1980s the firm Schervish Vogel Merz began redeveloping the area, adaptively reusing this collection of historic buildings. Today, with its assorted restaurants, offices, and lofts, Harmonie Park represents what planners hope to accomplish all over Downtown—a quiet but flourishing pocket of vitality.

45 HARMONIE CLUB

267 East Grand River Ave.

Richard E. Raseman, 1895; renovation by Schervish Vogel Merz, 1990s

The Harmonie Club was built in 1895 to serve the social needs of a large German population in Detroit. The Harmonie Society was, and is, a German singing organization and staple of German social life. The four-story, buff-colored brick building incorporates a number of classical ornaments, including Corinthian columns and a balustraded balcony over the entry. The expression includes overtones of the Renaissance Revival of Munich and hints of Beaux-Arts. The round corner is wonderfully shaped to its site geometry. Harmonie Park's "Manhattan feel" is largely attributable to the sophisticated character of this landmark building.

43

44

45

46 NS P$

MUSIC HALL (WILSON THEATRE)

350 Madison Ave.
Smith, Hinchman, and Grylls (William E. Kapp), 1928;
renovation by Schervish Vogel Merz, 1991

William Kapp designed this splendid little theater for patron Mathilda Dodge Wilson. The richly yet subtly decorated exterior keeps pace with the Art Deco styling of the day, while the interior regresses to Spanish Renaissance sources. Kapp seems to have been Mrs. Wilson's most favored architect, as he created the famed Meadow Brook Hall for her in this same timeframe. The theater's name was changed to Music Hall in 1946 when the Detroit Symphony made its home there for a period. The 1991 renovation extended the building's delightful life.

47 N P$

CENTURY CLUB AND GEM THEATRE (CENTURY BUILDING AND LITTLE THEATRE)

Madison Ave. at Brush
George D. Mason, 1903, 1927; relocated, 1997

Although built twenty-five years apart, the Century Club and Gem Theatre were designed by the same man, noted architect George D. Mason. He unified the pair through the use of common materials and Renaissance-inspired motifs and detailing. The Century was commissioned by a group of civic-minded women to advance social causes and serve as a cultural center exclusively for their use. The Little Theatre (now called the Gem) was added in 1927, and a year later was leased to the Motion Picture Guild, becoming the first venue in Detroit to show foreign films. The pair was saved by Theatre District pioneer Chuck Forbes in the 1980s and moved five blocks to this site in 1997 to make way for Comerica Park. The most recent example of Detroit-on-wheels, the ensemble sits remarkably at home on Madison.

48 PR

DETROIT ATHLETIC CLUB

251 Madison Ave.
Albert Kahn, 1915

Henry B. Joy, president of the Packard Motor Car Company, established the DAC to "get the men of the automobile industry out of the saloons on Woodward Avenue." His architect, Albert Kahn, drew upon Rome's Farnese Palace and other Renaissance wonders he discovered during a tour of Italy in 1912. The result is a dignified private club that immediately became the preferred place of the auto elite. Kahn himself reportedly declined membership because the DAC did not admit other Jews at the time.

46

47

48

49 DETROIT OPERA HOUSE (THE CAPITOL THEATRE, AND MANY OTHER NAMES THEREAFTER)

NSC

P$

1526 Broadway

C. Howard Crane, 1922; restoration by The Albert Kahn Collaborative, 1998

When entrepreneurs set out to build a vaudeville theater that would show newfangled moving pictures, they erred on the side of caution. Accordingly, the Capitol Theatre was wrapped with two narrow and seemingly independent "veneers" of office building. Just in case the theater went bust, the office floors would be joined and the theater eliminated. Within a few years the emergence of talkies ensured the Capitol's success, and thus ended the first of many ensuing acts that would play out in a drama leading to the building's reincarnation as the Detroit Opera House.

C. Howard Crane, architect for the Capitol, designed many of Detroit's finest theater venues and was one of the most active theater architects in the country. The interior was rendered in a "European Opera House style," mixing elements of Renaissance, Baroque, and Rococo. The 2,700-seat hall was proportioned after European models, and its restoration has proven it to be acoustically flawless. Why each of the house's two exterior office flanks was developed in distinct but compatible styles is a mystery. The Broadway side is more formally finished in a Beaux-Arts classicist composition of white terra cotta. The Madison façade is a quieter Neo-Georgian design with red brick masonry and stone detailing. Perhaps the architect responded to each of the differing streets; if so, Crane's performance is all the more admirable.

50 METROPOLITAN BUILDING (THE JEWELER'S BUILDING)

PR

33 John R

Weston and Ellington, 1925

This highly original building, rendered in a Neo-Gothic style, was shaped to fit its polygonal site in the heart of Woodward's "Necklace." Note how successfully the building's massing both contours with John R and steps up as a visual terminus at the head of Farmer. The three lower floors housed shops catering to female customers, and the upper floors were mainly occupied by jewelry manufacturers and wholesalers. The building closed in 1977.

51 BROADWAY STATION

P$

This station's relatively neutral architectural shell is transformed through the tour-de-force tile mural designed by Jun Kaneko. The inventive pattern and robust palette were crafted, astonishingly, by hand. Charles McGee's "the Blue Nile" (see 51b at right), which is the only painting in People Mover stations, draws on African sources. Next stop, Grand Circus Park.

49

50

51 a

51 b

Grand Circus

For our purposes the Grand Circus area encompasses the park itself, a reemerging theater and entertainment district, major new sports venues, the former hotel corridor of Park Avenue, now nearly extinguished, and the northern blocks of lower Woodward. As such, it is a geographical convenience centered also on the northernmost People Mover station of that name.

52

GRAND CIRCUS PARK

Woodward Ave. at Adams
Judge Woodward, 1805; The Albert Kahn Collaborative, 1998

The elegant semicircle of Grand Circus Park is a centering piece of the baroque plan drawn by Judge Woodward after fire destroyed the city in 1805. Woodward intended for the city to be dotted by such open spaces, in turn connected by broad thoroughfares. Woodward's plan was thus a more complex version of L'Enfant's Washington, D.C., plan, with which the judge was professionally quite familiar.

In the mid-to-late nineteenth century the park was lined with elegant mansions. Gordon Lloyd's 1867 Central United Methodist Church (53) at Adams and Woodward remains from this era. Between 1890 and 1930, the park and surrounding streets were built up with high-rise commercial towers. Holding the corner at Adams and Park is the first Kresge headquarters, designed by Albert Kahn in 1914 and later renamed the Kales Building. The relative uniformity of height and massing of the surrounding buildings creates an urban place comparable to Philadelphia's famed Rittenhouse Square.

The park itself features statues of prominent citizens, including Detroit Mayor and Michigan Governor Hazen Pingree (1840–1901). The fountain to the west was named for and dedicated by Thomas Edison. The fountain statue in the east park is by Daniel Chester French, creator of the Lincoln in the Lincoln Memorial, and the preeminent American sculptor of his day. An underground parking garage was built in 1956, and the People Mover station opened in 1987. Although an exodus marked the final decades of the twentieth century, Grand Circus has benefitted from the reemergence of the Theater District and a renewed interest in urban living. The park was renovated in the late 1990s in a classical manner consistent with the spirit of the original Woodward plan.

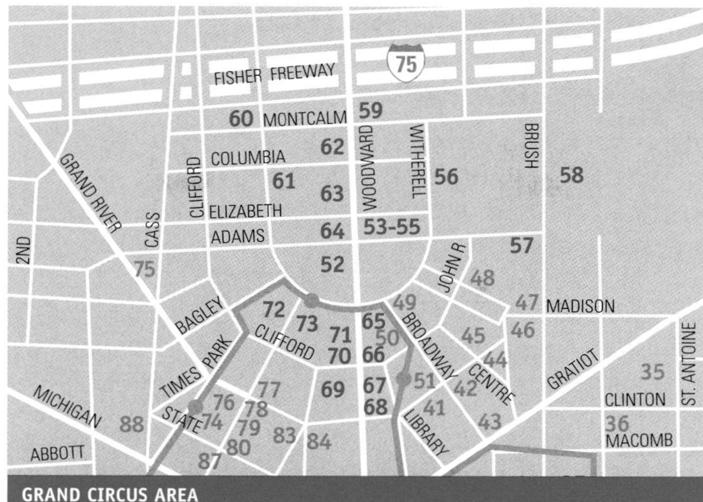

GRAND CIRCUS AREA

52	GRAND CIRCUS PARK
53	CENTRAL UNITED METHODIST CHURCH
54	CENTRAL UNITED METHODIST CHURCH PARISH HOUSE
55	WOMEN'S EXCHANGE
56	COMERICA PARK
57	ELWOOD BAR AND GRILL
58	FORD FIELD
59	SAINT JOHN'S EPISCOPAL CHURCH
60	PARK AVENUE HOUSE
61	WOMEN'S CITY CLUB BUILDING
62	FOX THEATRE
63	PALMS BUILDING AND STATE THEATRE
64	R. H. FYFE'S SHOE STORE BUILDING
65	DAVID BRODERICK BUILDING
66	WRIGHT-KAY BUILDING
67	D. J. HEALY CO. BUILDING
68	T. B. RAYL CO. BUILDING
69	WOODWARD BUILDING
70	WOODWARD ARCADE BUILDING
71	DAVID WHITNEY BUILDING
72	STATLER-HILTON HOTEL
73	GRAND CIRCUS PARK STATION

52

53 CENTRAL UNITED METHODIST CHURCH

23 East Adams at Woodward Ave.
Gordon W. Lloyd, 1867; altered and reassembled, 1936

Gordon Lloyd designed this limestone Gothic Revival church for a prominent Methodist community in the mid-nineteenth century. When Woodward Avenue was widened in 1936, a rather ingenious slicing, dicing, and reassembling operation ensued. The building was divided into five sections plus its tower. First, two sections of the sanctuary were removed, leaving the semi-octagonal central crossing, or transept, free-standing. The center section was then moved to the east to abut the chancel end. Next, the front block on Woodward was placed against the relocated transept. Finally, the tower with spire was rolled eastward and fitted into the Woodward façade. There is much fine woodcarving in the interior, dating from the time of this reconfiguration. Despite its Humpty-esque foreshortening, the church retains a remarkable presence.

54 CENTRAL UNITED METHODIST CHURCH PARISH HOUSE

23 East Adams at Woodward Ave.
Smith, Hinchman, and Grylls, 1936

A very fine and sympathetic bridge from Lloyd's more somber Victorian Gothic church at the corner to Smith, Hinchman, and Grylls's own more romantically Tudor ode to the east. This large (and expensive) building stood in the way of a more straightforward push-back of the church building in the 1930s.

55 WOMEN'S EXCHANGE

47 East Adams at Grand Circus Park
Smith, Hinchman, and Grylls, 1916

A romantically inclined client and/or designer with Smith, Hinchman, and Grylls offered a dash of medieval flavor to Grand Circus Park with this 1916 project. The Exchange was a clubhouse where women sold baked goods and arts and crafts on consignment. Beneath the façade are actually two Victorian buildings that date to the 1880s. The 1916 facelift was modeled after the Butcher's Guild of Herefordshire, England, dating to 1621. The current owners recently renewed the upper stories.

53

54

55

56 COMERICA PARK

Bounded by Witherell, Brush, Adams, and Montcalm
HOK Sports, and SmithGroup, 2000

HOK Sports hit a nostalgic homer with its return to traditional ballpark design at Camden Yards, Baltimore. Not unlike the cookie-cutter stadium blitz of the 1970s, a pattern has emerged in Cleveland, Denver, and now Detroit. As Yogi would say, "Déjà vu all over again."

"The Copa," to some, strives for the same old-time look that Oriole Park so notably achieved. But the house that pizza built (the Ilitch family owns both the Detroit Tigers and Little Caesar's Pizza) adds a more playful array of iconography, including ball-eating tigers and gravity-defying bats. Serious contemplation of where architecture ends and concessions begin is not intended. Whether it was kitsch or culture to festoon the exterior is up to each fan and critic to decide. This is the stuff of entertainment, at least.

Although the seating is nowhere nearly as intimate as in the old Tiger Stadium, the views are flawless from all over the park. And for you architecture fans, the Detroit skyline looms impressively beyond the outfield fence. Indeed, the architects have merged cityscape and ballpark as effectively here as any venue in the country. Play ball.

57 ELWOOD BAR AND GRILL

Brush and Adams
Charles Noble, 1937; relocated, 1997

The Elwood is a small but lively piece of the theater/entertainment district and is notable as one of the few "purely" Art Moderne structures in the city. Typical of its genre, the building's street façades exhibit a sleek, streamlined appearance with smooth enameled steel panels and rounded corners. Originally it stood at Elizabeth and Woodward (hence the name from "El" and "Wood"), but it was moved in 1997 to Brush and Adams to make room for the new Tigers and Lions stadiums. Despite its new location, its name appropriately remains the same.

56

57 a

57 b

58 FORD FIELD

P$

Bounded by Brush, Adams, I-375, and Montcalm
Rossetti Associates, and SmithGroup, 2002

Under construction at this writing, the new Detroit Lions den will add another major piece to an emerging entertainment district that includes the Fox and State theaters and Comerica Park. Among a handful of architects specializing in design for major league sports, Rossetti brought new ideas to an age-old building type. The architects reduced the building's impact by locating the playing field, and most of the 65,000 seats, below street level. One of the stadium's most unique features will be the incorporation of the old six-story Hudson's warehouse, which will feature 120 private suites overlooking the field. The glassy southwest corner will offer dramatic views of Downtown. All these amenities are designed to increase both fun and profit. Welcome to the modern world of major league sports and big league business.

59 SAINT JOHN'S EPISCOPAL CHURCH

NS N SP

2326 Woodward Ave. at Vernor
Jordan and Anderson, 1861

This survives as one of Detroit's earliest Victorian Gothic churches. It was known in its time as the "Patriarch of Piety Hill" for the reputed moral character of nearby residents. Architects Albert Jordan and James Anderson designed Fort Street Presbyterian Church (96) a few years earlier, but here they toned down the frenzy of Gothic detail they had employed there.

When the church and chapel were moved sixty feet eastward to accommodate the Woodward widening in 1936, the Victorian interior was drastically altered. The steel framework inserted for stabilization was left in place, covered in plaster, and transformed into nave arcades. The original space here more nearly resembled the interior of Fort Street Presbyterian.

60 PARK AVENUE HOUSE (ROYAL PALMS HOTEL)

N

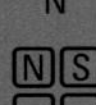

2305 Park Ave.
Louis Kamper, 1924

Park Avenue was once the heart of Detroit's hotel district, but now few hotels survive. The Park Avenue (formerly the Royal Palms Hotel) is a thirteen-story brick and masonry building with Italian Renaissance details, and one of three similar hotels Louis Kamper designed for Mr. Tuller on Park Avenue. Given the effusive antiquarianism of Louis Kamper's work in, say, the Book-Cadillac Hotel (81), this design appears restrained. The unusual, pocketed bay windows were adopted by Stratton a year later down the street. The entrance canopy is a later addition.

58 a

58 b

59

60

61 WOMEN'S CITY CLUB BUILDING

NS
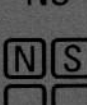

PR

2110 Park Ave.
William B. Stratton, 1924

The City Club was formed in 1919 "to promote a broad acquaintance among women." The Strattons—Club chair and Pewabic tile entrepreneur Mary Chase Perry Stratton and her equally talented husband, architect William Buck Stratton—collaborated here, or perhaps agreed to disagree. Such great pains were taken to distinguish the Club below from the residential floors above that the building appears to have been built in phases. The severely boxy mass, aproned at its midsection and seemingly headless, is at once Arts and Crafts and early Modern, depending on your vantage point. The real achievement is in the surface dressing and detail. Walls of pink and beige tapestry brick subtly change coloration from bottom to top. The receding arched entry and band of stylized Pewabic tile frame a wonderfully glassy entry.

62 FOX THEATRE

NS

SC
SP$

2111 Woodward Ave.
C. Howard Crane, 1928; restoration by William Kessler and Associates, 1988

With the Roaring Twenties hurtling along, architecture burst the bounds of traditional Renaissance forms. The movie palace proved most receptive to exotic, if not wild, experimentation. C. Howard Crane, designer of some 250 theaters around the nation, created in the Fox a picturesque blend of Burmese, Hindu, Persian, Indian, and Chinese motifs. Not a little of this flamboyance seeps to the exterior of the more restrained ten-story office building, which sports an Art Deco façade. Yet beneath these many layers is a modern multi-purpose theater. The 1988 cleaning and restoration under the watchful eye of Kessler and Associates returned the Fox to full splendor.

63 PALMS BUILDING AND STATE THEATRE

N
SP$

Woodward Ave.
C. Howard Crane, 1925

Like the Crane-designed Fox Theatre next door, the State was one of many ornate movie palaces built in the Grand Circus Park vicinity in the 1920s, and too, was encased in a larger office building.

61

62

63

64 R. H. FYFE'S SHOE STORE BUILDING

Woodward Ave. and Adams

Smith, Hinchman, and Grylls, 1919

Even in the twentieth century, long after the tall building broke from historic precedents, architects found inspiration in the Gothic vocabulary as a means of skyscraper expression. One of the best examples was Cass Gilbert's Woolworth Building in New York City, completed in 1913. Detroit's finest is Smith, Hinchman, and Grylls's soaring home for shoes. Mason's medievalist Masonic Temple (143) seems a tad heavy in comparison. But here, vertical lines sweep from sidewalk to sky, as a highly sculptural façade creates a rich interplay of light, shade, and shadow. In later years the building was converted to apartments.

65 DAVID BRODERICK BUILDING (EATON TOWER)

10 Witherell

Louis and Paul Kamper, 1928

Together with the David Whitney Building (71) across Woodward, the "two Davids" form an impressive gateway to lower Woodward from Grand Circus Park. At completion, Eaton Tower was the second tallest building in Michigan, and architect Kamper was not much more comfortable here than he was with the just-built Book Tower (76). The restrained Chicago Classical shaft is topped with a Beaux-Arts hat. Much of the original ornament has disappeared from the upper floors.

Not unusual in early high-rise design, the relatively small floor area forced the elevator core to an exterior wall. Here, the blank east wall throws the building a bit off balance. To highlight the point, the 1997 mega-mural of leaping whales, by artist Wyland, contributes to the unease. However well intentioned, such forced energy is fun to some, odd to others. The office lobby, with coffered, barrel vaulted ceiling, marble finishes, and bronze elevator doors, is special. Today, only a first-floor restaurant uses this building, although many plans have been floated to adaptively renovate it for hotel, loft apartments, and/or other uses.

64

65

66 WRIGHT-KAY BUILDING (SCHWANKOVSKY TEMPLE OF MUSIC)

1500 Woodward Ave. at John R
Gordon W. Lloyd, 1891

The prolific Gordon Lloyd designed this structure as one of the first tall buildings on Woodward Avenue. It has a cast-iron frame, making it an evolutionary step between the older masonry buildings and the steel-frame skyscrapers to come. It also was one of Detroit's first buildings designed with an electric elevator. The style leans toward the Romanesque. Originally home to the Schwankovsky music company, it housed the Wright-Kay jewelry firm for decades. In recent years it has been renovated to include a nightclub on the ground floor, with offices and residential uses above.

67 D. J. HEALY COMPANY BUILDING

1426 Woodward Ave.
Postie and Mahler, 1910

This adventuresome design mixed the progressive pragmatism of the Chicago School of architecture on the lower floors with a more eclectic top story and tiled parapet cap, now gone. We value this piece at least because there is sadly so little like it now remaining.

68 T. B. RAYL COMPANY BUILDING

Woodward and Grand River Aves.
Baxter, O'Dell, and Halpin, 1915

Strongly influenced by Louis Sullivan, this splendid corner building exhibits a sophisticated composition of form following structural function. The red terra cotta surfaces crisply distinguish supporting elements from nonsupporting surface ornament. Slender piers terminate in a visually relieving arcade. Among the finest Sullivanesque designs in Detroit.

69 WOODWARD BUILDING

Woodward Ave. at Clifford
Albert Kahn, 1915

An energetic blend of Chicago School influences, from master Louis Sullivan to his more conservative follower Daniel Burnham. Slender terra cotta piers and iron spandrels create a unique arcade at the lower tier. Classical pediment inserts appear out of context—perhaps too many ideas for one building to take.

66

67

68

69

70 WOODWARD ARCADE BUILDING (HIMELHOCH'S)

1545 Woodward Ave.
Donaldson and Meier, 1901

A fine piece of urban infill from John Donaldson in his prime. The later Woodward storefront is remarkably sympathetic to the original.

71 DAVID WHITNEY BUILDING

Woodward Ave. at Park Ave.
D. H. Burnham and Co., 1915

Originally intended for doctors and dentists, this office tower features an elaborate interior courtyard. Italian Renaissance details predominate in the exterior ornament. Unfortunately, much of the classical ornament is now gone. With this, the Ford (106), and the Dime (104) buildings, Detroit hosts one of the nation's best stocks of Burnham skyscrapers. The David Whitney building was completed by Burnham's Chicago firm after his death.

72 STATLER-HILTON HOTEL (STATLER HOTEL)

Park Ave. and Washington Blvd.
George B. Post, 1914

Designed for a prime site at the head of the Washington Boulevard spoke from Grand Circus, this eighteen-story, eight-hundred-room hotel was planned for efficient luxury. Post was a pupil of the great Beaux-Arts classicist Richard Morris Hunt and architect of choice for Ellsworth Statler. Here Post color-washed the building with a warm red masonry, highlighted with subtle stone coursing, trim, and detailing. In contrast to the more boisterous statements emanating from nineteenth-century France, the Neo-Georgian is indebted to the quieter styling of late-eighteenth-century England. The building has long sat vacant and is endangered.

73 GRAND CIRCUS PARK STATION

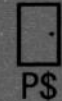

The best part of this stop is J. Seward Johnson's life-sized bronze sculpture of a commuter reading a newspaper. Note that your fellow traveler gives equal time to the *Detroit News* and *Free Press*—the "paper" includes both banners. Next stop, Times Square (Detroit version).

70

71

72

73

West Necklace

The West Necklace area is a study in urban contrasts. In many ways Capitol Square represents the overture, and Washington Boulevard the exuberant second movement.

The more intimate Capitol Square is about the past. The state's first capitol was sited facing onto this triangular park, which was renamed for the honor, however short-lived. Over time, Capitol Square gained an intimacy born of the increasingly taller wall of surrounding buildings.

Washington Boulevard is decidedly more expansive and energetic, as it reinforced Detroit's image as "the Paris of the Midwest." Washington also speaks to the city's rise and fall in the modern era, from the roaring speculation of the Book brothers to the spirited confidence of the Aloysius prelates, and on to a fearless, over-the-top intervention of 1970s urban design. Today, the area awaits a third movement of orchestrated renewal.

74 **TIMES SQUARE STATION**

Tom Phardel's Art Deco design in Pewabic glazed tile was dedicated to the late architectural historian W. Hawkins Ferry. Thus, it captures the best of Detroit in one move. Next stop, Michigan station.

75 **GRAND ARMY OF THE REPUBLIC HALL**

1942 Grand River Ave.

Julius Hess, 1900

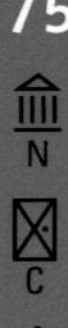

Known as the G.A.R. Building, this imposing, Richardsonian Romanesque structure takes its shape from the triangular-shaped lot it occupies. It was the largest G.A.R. meeting hall ever built in Michigan, a tribute to the veterans of the Union army in the Civil War. Here Hess applies a castle model, perfectly suited to its purpose and freestanding site. Hess died during construction, and his former partner Richard Raseman oversaw its completion. See also Hess's Trumbull Avenue Presbyterian Church (158) for a similarly inventive effort. Closed since about 1980, the building hopefully will survive the next round of urban redevelopment.

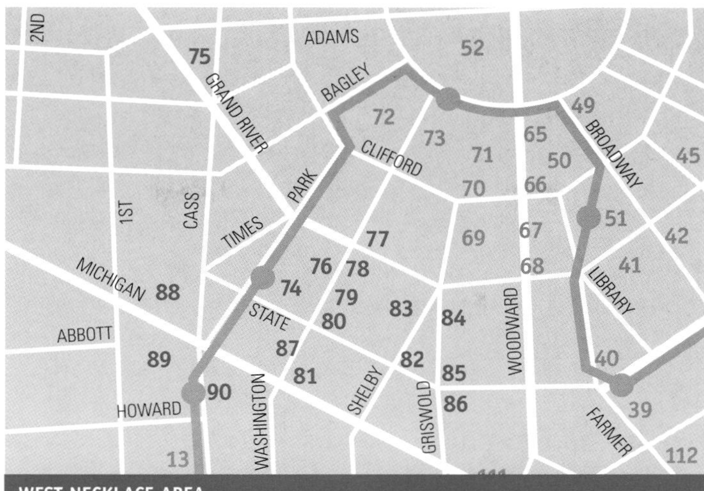

WEST NECKLACE AREA

74	TIMES SQUARE STATION	83	FARWELL BUILDING
75	GRAND ARMY OF THE REPUBLIC HALL	84	GRISWOLD BUILDING
76	BOOK BUILDING AND BOOK TOWER	85	CHAMBER OF COMMERCE BUILDING
77	PARK PLACE APARTMENTS	86	DAVID STOTT BUILDING
78	CHANCERY BUILDING	87	WASHINGTON BOULEVARD PLAZA
79	SAINT ALOYSIUS PARISH CHURCH	88	AMERITECH BUILDING
80	WASHINGTON BOULEVARD BUILDING	89	PATRICK V. MCNAMARA FEDERAL BUILDING
81	BOOK-CADILLAC HOTEL		
82	CAPITOL PARK	90	MICHIGAN AVENUE STATION

Washington Boulevard

74

75

76 BOOK BUILDING AND BOOK TOWER

1249 Washington Blvd.
Louis Kamper, 1917, and tower addition, 1926

The thirteen-story structure, built first, was a relatively straightforward modern office building, although Kamper unconvincingly loaded on a few details from antiquity, including twelve nude caryatids, or female statues, supporting the cornice.

The more ambitious thirty-six-story Book Tower followed in 1926. The artistic impression the tower leaves today is that Kamper didn't quite get the skyscraper idea. The icing almost oozes out from the multiple layers, as too much attention is paid to classical ornamentation at the expense of the building's elemental massing. He did indeed attend to the notion that as distance increases so must the scale of the ornament. Contrast this tower with the cleaner silhouette of the Penobscot Building (105), erected at about the same time.

77 PARK PLACE APARTMENTS (INDUSTRIAL BANK BUILDING)

232 West Grand River Ave.
Louis Kamper, 1928

A less self-conscious Kamper designed this twenty-two-story office building. Continuous piers and recessed windows, subtle skyline setbacks, and a unique Art Deco blend of Gothic and Beaux-Arts motifs distinguish this next volume in the Book set. The building was later renewed for residential use.

78 CHANCERY BUILDING

1234 Washington Blvd.
Donaldson and Meier, 1924

Sheathed in limestone, this eight-story chancery, including Archdiocesan offices and rectory spaces for St. Aloysius, is a charismatic original. The open upper loggia is a creative leap of faith. A versatile and clearly inspired architect, John Donaldson.

76

77

78

79

SAINT ALOYSIUS PARISH CHURCH

1230 Washington Blvd.
Donaldson and Meier, 1930

This unusual Romanesque revival church presents a memorable face to Washington and complement to the Chancery next door. The flourishes of corbeling, arcading, and carving stand out from broad planes of unadorned limestone. The rose window is all the more stunning for its context. The three-story interior is extraordinary. With this spirited Donaldson encore, St. Aloysius holds its own as a bookend to more speculative development on the Boulevard.

80

WASHINGTON BOULEVARD BUILDING

234 State St.
Louis Kamper, 1923

Perhaps more tightly budgeted, this office building for the Book brothers is at least more tightly composed. A neoclassical limestone base supports an almost modern brick shaft. In summer the operable windows animate the façade as no modern, hermetically sealed (air conditioned) building can equal.

81

BOOK-CADILLAC HOTEL

Washington Blvd. and Michigan Ave.
Louis Kamper, 1924

Coming just after the Washington Boulevard Building (80) and before the Book Tower (76), this twelve-hundred-room hotel enabled Kamper to indulge his taste for lavish splendor. The lobby and restaurant were designed in a Venetian style, and the grand ballroom evoked Florentine Renaissance. More successfully than the Book Tower, the exterior rises in a simple shaft to a cornucopia of Italian Renaissance gestures up top. Once Detroit's hotel of choice and now sadly deteriorated, the building has stood vacant and stripped of most of its interior decorative features since the 1980s.

79

80

81

82 CAPITOL PARK

Griswold between Michigan and Grand River Aves.,
including parts of State St.
Various architects, 1877–1929

This intimate park is named for Michigan's first capitol building that stood here from 1828 to 1847. The Capitol Park Historic District took shape in the late nineteenth and early twentieth centuries and comprises seventeen commercial buildings around a small triangular green space. Several famous architects, including Albert Kahn and Gordon Lloyd, contributed designs rendered in a rich array of Renaissance, Victorian, Beaux-Arts, and Art Deco styles. Many of these buildings' defining cornices were removed over the years for fear of falling ornament. (Perhaps Adolph Loos was onto something a hundred years ago in asserting, "Ornament is crime.")

83 FARWELL BUILDING

1249–1259 Griswold St.
Bonnah and Chaffee, 1915

This eight-story office building is a fine example of the Chicago commercial design formula. Structural support and nonstructural infill are clearly expressed in contrasting materials and colors. The large horizontal windows are recessed within emphasized frames. Detroit historians suggest that interior ornament was by L. C. Tiffany. Some of the original character of the building has been lost. Now in disuse, the building would appear to be endangered.

84 GRISWOLD BUILDING

1214–1230 Griswold St.
Albert Kahn, 1929

Kahn's tentative transition from Art Deco to Modern shows here in this unusual design for offices. The architect used this brick-and-stone style for a number of second-tier buildings. Around 1980, when it was added to the National Register of Historic Places, it was converted to senior citizen housing, for which it may have been better suited. As with many older buildings Downtown, the modern storefronts on the street level appear garish and out of context with the rest of the building. But the observer can still appreciate the unusual massing, the contrasting base and tower, and the early modern application of steel window sash.

82

83

84

85

CHAMBER OF COMMERCE BUILDING

1212 Griswold and State Sts.
Spier and Rohns, 1895

SP

One of the first steel-framed buildings Downtown, this thirteen-story structure is Detroit's oldest standing skyscraper. But you wouldn't know it from the massive piling of one eclectic layer on another. Architects Spier and Rohns acted as if they had just discovered Beaux-Arts Classicism. More restraint during design preparation might have resulted in a more unified appearance.

Like many of Detroit's older buildings, this one has been altered substantially, inside and out. The cornice was removed after a city safety ordinance was enacted in the late 1950s, and at some point the building's original round-arch windows were squared. Also, the light well was unfortunately glassed in, thus altering the massing nearly beyond recognition.

The Chamber building, by the way, held the tallest title for only one year, until it was eclipsed by the fourteen-story Majestic Building, down the block and since demolished.

86

DAVID STOTT BUILDING

1150 Griswold St.
Donaldson and Meier, 1929

SP

Of all the skyscrapers built in Detroit in the 1920s, few captured the ideal of Eliel Saarinen's landmark Chicago Tribune proposal as well as this. A shaft of tan-orange brick rises from a reddish granite base to the twenty-third story, where it tapers in a series of discrete setbacks. Nearly freed from historical ornamentation, the modern skyscraper was emerging as a slim, evocative silhouette. A classic contribution to the building type, and a defining exclamation point on the Detroit skyline, Stott elevates tall building design to fine art.

87

WASHINGTON BOULEVARD PLAZA

Washington Blvd. between Grand Circus and Michigan Ave.
Rossetti Associates, 1979

P

As the great retail district along Washington Boulevard deteriorated in the 1960s and 1970s, the city invited architect Gino Rossetti to redesign the streetscape to include a pedestrian plaza. The most notable feature of his plan is a bright red, steel-pipe environmental structure that stretches for blocks. It carries a continuous lightbar and meanders through the plaza, which also includes water displays and a variety of landscape features. The courageous urban design aspired to a lively street life, and while nearby senior residents enjoy its quieter features, the forces of urban abandonment have thus far prevailed.

85a

85b

86

87

88 SP

AMERITECH BUILDING (MICHIGAN BELL TELEPHONE MAIN OFFICES BUILDING)

Michigan and Cass Aves.
Smith, Hinchman, and Grylls, with Alexander Calder, 1974

This seventeen-story graft to the original tower doesn't seem to accept the host. The twenty-foot-high red stabile by Alexander Calder is at home in its minimalist setting. The original building, also designed by Smith, Hinchman, and Grylls, was completed in two phases, including an initial seven-story block built in 1912 and a twelve-story addition completed in 1927. Note the design transition from one decade to the next.

89 SP

PATRICK V. MCNAMARA FEDERAL BUILDING

Michigan at Cass Aves.
Smith, Hinchman, and Grylls, 1976

In the 1970s a number of large buildings were built Downtown that, bunker-like, did little to enhance the street life around them. This twenty-seven-story extrusion is one.

90 P$

MICHIGAN AVENUE STATION

Painter Allie McGhee infuses spontaneous expressionism into ceramic tile in this energetic mural.

88

89

90

Fort/Financial

Detroit's early forts dominated this area beginning in the eighteenth century. In the late 1820s territorial governor Lewis Cass transformed a handful of converging Native American trails into radiating thoroughfares that would define Detroit's growth through the nineteenth century—including Michigan, Grand River, and Gratiot Avenues. Similar to Baron Hausmann's transformation of Paris a generation later for Napoleon III, the broad avenues were planned primarily to facilitate troop movement between military outposts in the territory.

The magnificent Fort Street Presbyterian Church is a gothic hint at the area's nineteenth-century incarnation as a prominent place of residence. One can only imagine how this soaring landmark dominated the 1855 skyline. Since the turn of the twentieth century, the West Fort area has hosted an enterprising fourth estate. The city's two major newspapers, built within a stone's throw of each other, battled to a 1989 semi-merger here.

The reader may continue walking east on Fort, or elect to interrupt the experience with a return to the Fort/Cass station and People Mover to the Financial District station. (One of many ways in which "People Mover" has proved to be both noun and verb.)

The Financial District to the east is appropriately named for its life as the city's center for commercial banking and insurance, although modern consolidations have diluted its concentration. Nevertheless, the area as a whole comprises one of the city's highest concentrations of quality commercial architecture. Through the declining second half of the twentieth century, this Downtown pocket has remained vitally urban through thick and thin. While some of America's most prominent firms have designed significant buildings here, the district's skyline was largely shaped by Smith, Hinchman, and Grylls. Their Guardian Building stands out as world class.

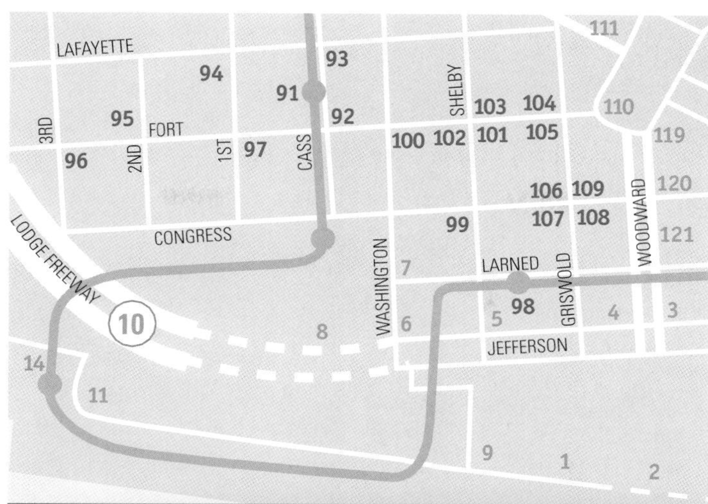

FORT/FINANCIAL AREA

91	FORT/CASS STATION	100	211 WEST FORT STREET BUILDING
92	DETROIT CLUB	101	SAVOYARD CENTER
93	*DETROIT FREE PRESS* BUILDING	102	DETROIT TRUST CO. BUILDING
94	FORT SHELBY HOTEL	103	FEDERAL RESERVE BANK ANNEX
95	*DETROIT NEWS* BUILDING	104	DIME BUILDING
96	FORT STREET PRESBYTERIAN CHURCH	105	PENOBSCOT BUILDING
97	SMITH, HINCHMAN, AND GRYLLS BUILDING	106	FORD BUILDING
98	FINANCIAL DISTRICT STATION	107	BUHL BUILDING
99	BANKERS TRUST CO. BUILDING	108	GUARDIAN BUILDING
		109	BANK ONE MICHIGAN

Financial District

91 PS$

FORT/CASS STATION

Farley Tobin's enigmatic murals complement the station's architecture. The bronze sculptures are by Sandra Jo Osip. Next stops, Cobo Convention Center and Joe Louis Arena stations, then on to Financial District station.

92 SP

DETROIT CLUB

Cass Ave. and Fort St.
Wilson Eyre, Jr., 1891

Active to this day, the Detroit Club was established to serve the social needs of the city's professional and business community. The dignified design incorporates many influences, from Second Renaissance Revival to Richardsonian Romanesque. The recessed arched entry and stair feature are unusual. The interior includes finely crafted woodwork, elegant furnishings, a broad rambling main stairway, and a huge fireplace in the main dining hall. The original woodwork was lighter in tone and less all-encompassing. Architect Wilson Eyre, Jr., of Philadelphia also designed club member Charles Lang Freer's house (189) on East Ferry Avenue. This building has been declared eligible for listing in the National Register.

93 S C

DETROIT FREE PRESS BUILDING

321 West Lafayette
Albert Kahn, 1925

This impressive piece of urban architecture holds a commanding place at the foot of Washington Boulevard. Unlike his earlier *Detroit News* building (95), Kahn's *Free Press* building used a steel frame for a more efficiently constructed thirteen-story tower for commercial tenants. The then-fashionable stepped massing of the central tower and flanking six-story wings were finished in limestone to create an appropriately monumental feel. The *Free Press* building marks the first of a series of Kahn commercial designs that includes the Maccabees Building (179) and the Albert Kahn Building (199).

94 N C

FORT SHELBY HOTEL

525 West Lafayette
Schmidt, Garden, and Martin, 1916; addition by Albert Kahn, 1927

The original ten-story building of Neo-Georgian character is the only Detroit work by the Chicago firm of Schmidt, Garden, and Martin. The 1927 Albert Kahn addition was sympathetic to a point—specifically, through the second floor. But then the twenty-one-story tower takes on a life of its own, even though the floor plans are fully integrated. This now vacant hotel is endangered.

91

92

93

94

95 *DETROIT NEWS* BUILDING

S

PR

615 West Lafayette; 1916
Albert Kahn with George Booth

Newspaper publisher George Booth was an idealist and an accomplished amateur architect. In planning a new home for the *News*, Booth wanted to refine the building's essentially industrial nature. Accordingly, he inspired his friend Albert Kahn to create a civic-minded building that would elevate the newspaper's image above the mundane. The dignified, solid massing is embellished with panels extolling the high purposes of the press. Kahn conceived the sophisticated concrete frame, and Booth directed the Arts and Crafts ornamentation, with a result that is uniquely American.

Kahn called it one of the first industrial buildings to which he was permitted to give an architectural character, and was quick to credit Booth's contributions. Having previously designed Booth's house at Cranbrook, Kahn wrote, "He draws as well as most architects, is full of ideas, and for practically every project that we have worked on for him, has submitted many workable schemes of his own." After extensive interior modifications in the late 1990s, the building became the common home of the *News* and the *Detroit Free Press*.

96 FORT STREET PRESBYTERIAN CHURCH

NS

SP

631 West Fort and Third Sts.
Octavius and Albert Jordan, 1855; renovated, 1876 and 1914

Detroit's pre-Civil War skyline was dominated by church spires, and Fort Street Presbyterian was surely among the city's finest. This church has been much admired for its lacy stonework and graceful silhouette. Some note that the architects applied a plethora of Gothic details almost like random brushwork, rather than in an entirely coherent manner. Perhaps this uneasy historicism reflects a basic building form that is not medieval at all, but derives from a later Protestant meeting house model. While fires severely damaged the church in 1876 and 1914, each time this venerable landmark was rebuilt to the original plans.

97 SMITH, HINCHMAN, AND GRYLLS BUILDING

C

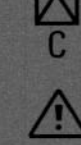

455 Fort St.
Smith, Hinchman, and Grylls, 1910, and 1970 renovation

The 1970s saw a wave of wholesale renovations of older buildings Downtown. This 1910 structure was stripped to its reinforced concrete frame and rebuilt to high modern standards and taste. The north and west walls display elegantly minimalist curtain-walls of glass attached by a grid of classy aluminum fasteners. From here the reader can continue east on Fort, or return to the Michigan station and ride to the Financial District station, past Cobo and the Joe.

95

96

97

98 FINANCIAL DISTRICT STATION

P$

A lively introduction to the core of the Financial District. As if sensing an uncomfortable fit with its architectural context, Joyce Kozloff's whimsical wall design draws from a menagerie of external sources.

99 BANKERS TRUST COMPANY BUILDING

P

Congress and Shelby
Smith, Hinchman, and Grylls (Wirt Rowland), 1925

In the 1920s it was still possible for a bank building to rise just two stories and be covered with historic ornamentation. Here designer Wirt Rowland chose an Italian Romanesque theme with massive arches. The use of terra cotta permitted Rowland to simulate a richer effect of ornate stone carving. The building later served as a stockbrokers' office and, more recently, as a fast-food restaurant. An interesting, if not pithy, progression, to be sure.

100 211 WEST FORT STREET BUILDING

S

SP

Fort St. and Washington Blvd.
Harley, Ellington, Cowin, and Stirton, 1965

The design of this office tower is notable for its restraint. Tinted floor-to-ceiling windows fit into a pre-cast concrete frame, giving the building a simple yet dignified character. Following a then current trend, the office tower was set back from the street to form a small plaza. The 1965 AIA award jury noted, "...an excellent solution to a difficult site."

101 SAVOYARD CENTER (STATE SAVINGS BANK; PEOPLE'S STATE BANK)

NSC

C

151 W. Fort St. and Shelby
McKim, Mead, and White, 1900; addition by Donaldson and Meier, 1914

Other than a mausoleum, this is the only building in Detroit designed by the legendary Stanford White and his partners. The white marble bank, one of Detroit's finest examples of Beaux-Arts Classicism, is spacious and well-lit inside thanks to the broad window arcade. A second, more ambitious White project, a proposal for a Bicentennial tower at the tip of Belle Isle (1901), never passed the dream stage.

Originally the bank occupied only half of its current site. It was doubled in size in 1914 by extending the building down to Congress, occupying the site of Calvin Otis's St. Paul's Cathedral, which in turn was relocated to East Grand Boulevard and rebuilt as the Church of the Messiah (287). Donaldson and Meier designed the addition so faithfully to the original that most people cannot detect where one stops and the other begins. Today the building serves as a computer training facility.

98

99

100

101

102 DETROIT TRUST COMPANY BUILDING

201 West Fort St. and Shelby
Albert Kahn, 1915

In designing this bank Albert Kahn drew on the lavish style of McKim, Mead, and White, as seen in the State Savings Bank (101) across the street. Corinthian columns and pilasters convey an impression of wealth and security. Yet Kahn is more conservative, here and elsewhere, as indeed he never fully succumbed to the Beaux-Arts rage.

Inside, marble walls and floors, as well as gilded coffered ceilings, continued the opulent mood from the exterior. The provision of ample natural light was an extension of Kahn's revolutionary design of the modern factory, based in no small measure on the ideal of creating more humane and productive workplace environments.

The building was enlarged in 1926 and modernized in 1966, when the Detroit Bank and Trust expanded into the new 211 W. Fort tower next door.

103 FEDERAL RESERVE BANK ANNEX

160 West Fort St.
Smith, Hinchman, and Grylls (Minoru Yamasaki), 1951

The first important building to rise Downtown in the post-World War II era was this eight-story annex to the Federal Reserve Bank of Chicago. Seattle-born Minoru Yamasaki designed this fine piece for Smith, Hinchman, and Grylls just prior to going on his own and earning fame in his own right. Rather than mimicking the existing 1927 marble bank structure, the architect clad the annex in a thin curtain-wall of alternating bands of glass and marble veneer. The building is also set back some thirty feet from the sidewalk to allow for a more generous place of arrival. This sophisticated solution ushered in a new, modern era in Downtown architecture and planning, and, given its relatively early date, is right at the leading edge of the Modern Movement in America. A well-kept secret.

104 DIME BUILDING

719 Griswold St.
D. H. Burnham and Co., 1910; renovation by Barton Malow Design, 2001

Daniel Burnham's second office tower in Detroit is shaped to allow natural light into the interior offices. The open end of the U-shape facing the street is both unusual and skillful in its handling. Classical detailing is slightly more in evidence here than in the Ford Building (106), erected just down the street a year earlier. In the Dime Building's mix of clean lines and eclectic ornament, we see the modern skyscraper struggling to be born. Recently renewed with care.

102

103

104

105 

PENOBSCOT BUILDING

645 Griswold St.
Smith, Hinchman, and Grylls (Wirt Rowland), 1928;
early stages by Dondaldson and Meier, 1905 and 1916

In the short span of a decade, Detroit's architecturally roaring twenties, the city saw an impressive array of skyscraper design, and the Penobscot remains among the best. Designer Wirt Rowland of Smith, Hinchman, and Grylls crafted a simple limestone tower on an H-plan in the Art Deco style. Rowland first extruded the building shaft thirty stories from the ground, then progressively eroded the top seventeen stories in a masterful series of sculptural setbacks. Contrast this clean, powerful massing with the overwrought classicism of the Book Tower (76), built at the same time, or the Penobscot's comparatively stodgier first and second building phases by Donaldson and Meier—completed in 1905 and 1916. Dramatic exterior lighting accentuates the tower's upper reaches at night. Contributing to skyline and streetscape alike, the Penobscot is successful from head to toe.

106 

FORD BUILDING

615 Griswold St.
D. H. Burnham and Co., 1909

This is among Detroit's oldest surviving skyscrapers, built with a steel frame instead of masonry piled thick and high. Unlike, say, the earlier Chamber of Commerce Building (85) Ford was intended to look as lean as it was built. The architect covered the exterior of the eighteen-story tower in clean sharp lines of white terra cotta so that nothing would detract from the building's aspiring height. Daniel Burnham was perhaps the most celebrated architect in the nation at the time, and Detroit would soon have three of his designs. The others are the Dime Building (104) on Griswold and the David Whitney Building (71) on Grand Circus Park.

107  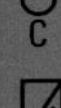

BUHL BUILDING

535 Griswold St.
Smith, Hinchman, and Grylls (Wirt Rowland), 1925

Completed in 1925, the twenty-six-story Buhl tower shows how architects were still struggling to merge the logic of tall buildings with respectable—or "safe"—historical allusions. With the Buhl, which suggests a tower extrusion of a Romanesque cruciform church, Wirt Rowland nevertheless took a significant step toward the modern. The lack of a classical cornice permitted a stronger vertical statement. And the plan, with wings projecting from a central core, brought light and air to the interiors in an era when floor plans were dominated by a maze of individual walled offices, glass doors, and transoms. A few years later and across the street with the Penobscot tower (105), Rowland would further advance his art of skyscraper design.

105

106

107

108 GUARDIAN BUILDING (UNION TRUST)

500 Griswold St.
Smith, Hinchman, and Grylls (Wirt Rowland), 1929;
renovation by SmithGroup, 2000

N S SP

Originally the Union Trust Building, this 1920s icon strikes many as beautiful, some as innovative, and others as strangely exotic. Designer Wirt Rowland of Smith, Hinchman, and Grylls blended fine brickwork with glazed tile and terra cotta to explore new combinations of color, texture, and form. Art Deco is the predominant vocabulary. Italian travertine and black marble floors, and gaily colored patterns of mosaic and Pewabic tile, recall the ebullient twenties. Window figures embody the building's recurring themes of security and fidelity. Catch a glimpse of the lively mural-covered vault on the mezzanine level. Nicknamed the "Cathedral of Finance," the Guardian was a lightning bolt of spirited inventiveness. Yet, for all the boldness of Rowland's experimentation, the Guardian remained a one-of-a-kind oddity, a relatively unexplored, and certainly unequaled, branch of the skyscraper's evolutionary tree.

The award-winning interior renovation, recently completed by the descendent firm for its own offices, stunningly continues the tradition.

109 BANK ONE MICHIGAN (NATIONAL BANK OF DETROIT)

611 Woodward Ave.
Albert Kahn Associates, 1959

C SP

After the long dry spell of the Depression years and World War II, building started up again in Detroit. The new headquarters for the National Bank of Detroit showed how much the world of architecture had changed in the interim. Gone were Gothic and Romanesque motifs. In their place, the NBD headquarters rose behind a checkered curtain-wall of glass and white marble panels—one of the first buildings designed with a staggered window pattern. The cubic mass was set back from the street to create a generous walkway. The main banking floor reinterprets the grand banking rooms of the 1920s with a sparely detailed glass curtain-wall replacing earlier massive enclosures. Following the Federal Reserve Bank Annex example (103), Modernism had clearly arrived in Downtown Detroit.

108

109

Campus Martius

A step, not a People Mover stop, away from the Financial District is Downtown's core, which is reemerging at this writing from a half century of decline. Campus Martius in many ways represents Detroit's symbolic place of origin: as an early frontier military parade ground, as a key public space in Judge Woodward's plan, as a convergence of Governor Cass's troop-moving thoroughfares, and as a galvanizing hub of the city's Tricentennial pageant.

A hundred years ago Campus Martius and Cadillac Square formed an axial set piece very much in tune with the reawakening of baroque planning in America and the City Beautiful movement. In this spirit Old City Hall was balanced by a splendid new county courthouse at the opposite end. The Second Empire city hall and Beaux-Arts courthouse spoke the same language across the intervening space and time.

The tragic demise of City Hall (built 1871, demolished 1961) was unfortunately not alone, as our center has endured more than its share of major rebuilding campaigns. The list of casualties is remarkable. The first Pontchartrain Hotel (1907) was demolished after only thirteen years. Located on the site now occupied by First National Building, the hotel was among the last designed with shared baths, and when the Statler (1914) provided a private bath with each room, the Pontchartrain was instantly rendered obsolete. Once occupying Cadillac Square itself, George Mason's handsome Central Market (1880) was demolished merely a

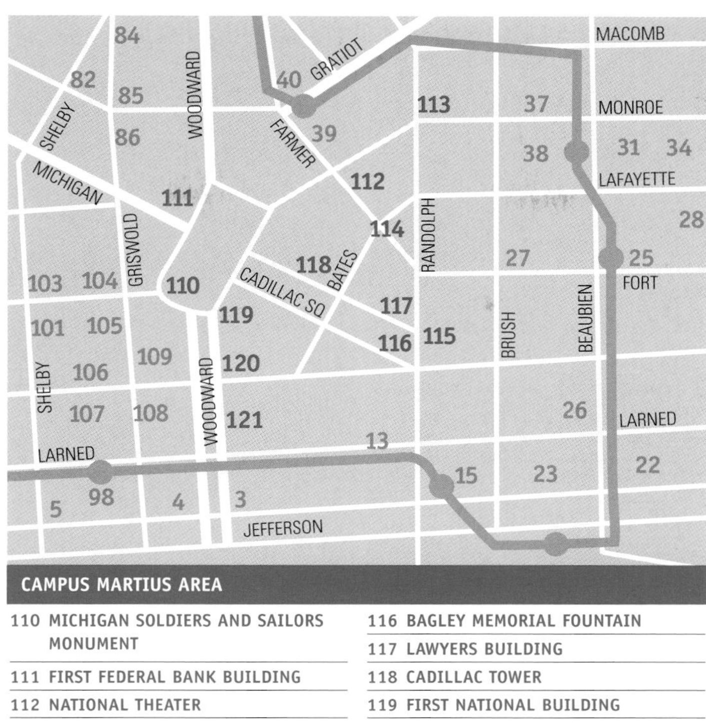

CAMPUS MARTIUS AREA

110 MICHIGAN SOLDIERS AND SAILORS MONUMENT	116 BAGLEY MEMORIAL FOUNTAIN
111 FIRST FEDERAL BANK BUILDING	117 LAWYERS BUILDING
112 NATIONAL THEATER	118 CADILLAC TOWER
113 TEMPLE OF ODD FELLOWS	119 FIRST NATIONAL BUILDING
114 WATER BOARD BUILDING	120 VINTON BUILDING
115 WAYNE COUNTY BUILDING	121 ONE DETROIT CENTER

decade after it was built, although the shed was dismantled and reassembled as the horse barn on Belle Isle. The Kern Block and Monroe blocks were demolished and left vacant for a generation. The mighty J. L. Hudson's building, the essential Downtown memory for many Detroiters, was most recently and controversially imploded.

At press time, construction is underway on a new headquarters building for Compuware Corporation. Preliminary plans show a wedge-shaped building with a monumental recessed entrance feature (pictured here). Soon to follow will be the "partial restoration" of Campus Martius Park—a full realization of the park as envisioned by Woodward, but never built, would involve removing pieces of several surrounding extant buildings. In any case, the new street pattern promises relief for what has been a hundred-year-old traffic jam.

Time will tell if it's a new and enduring day in Detroit building. While the Campus Martius vision offers promise, let's hope that this time we get it right for more than a generation or two. Disposable architecture is not the stuff great city centers are made of.

110 MICHIGAN SOLDIERS AND SAILORS MONUMENT

NSC P

Cadillac Square
Randolph Rogers, 1872

This monumental work honoring Civil War service rises in four tiers to an apex fifty-six feet above the ground. The main body of the monument is granite. Bronze statues of eagles stand on the lowest tier; above them are embodiments of the Navy, Infantry, Cavalry, and Artillery. Bas-relief medallions depict Lincoln, Grant, Farragut, and Sherman. Allegorical female figures embody Victory, Emancipation, History, and Union. The figure of "Emancipation" is a depiction of Sojourner Truth. At the peak stands an eleven-foot-high bronze Native American figure of "Michigan." The artist, Randolph Rogers, is best known for creating the bronze doors for the main entrance to the U.S. Capitol in Washington, D.C.

111 FIRST FEDERAL BANK BUILDING

SC SP

1001 Woodward Ave.
Smith, Hinchman, and Grylls, 1965

Daniel Burnham's Majestic Building, one of Detroit's first skyscrapers, previously stood on this site. Its replacement is a sleek modernist composition in black granite. First Federal is actually two towers, one facing Woodward and the other Michigan, joined by a central elevator core. At the time of completion, AIA's award jury saw this design as a "good use of a difficult site," although many today would relish the opportunity to make difficult use of this good site. In part, that summarizes the after-modern state of the art.

112 NATIONAL THEATER

S C

16 Monroe St.
Albert Kahn with Ernest Wilby, 1911

Kahn and his talented design associate Ernest Wilby used glazed terra cotta to sheath the exterior of this hybrid Baroque–Beaux-Arts–Moorish–amusement park design. The twin towers, deeply recessed entrance arch, and colorful Pewabic tile work add to the exotic character. Originally part of a retail streetscape that was chock full of competing signs and sights, the National was less conspicuous by day, but dominated the streetscape at night with its dramatic lighting. Sadly, and despite a public uproar, the Monroe block context was demolished a dozen years ago. The theater has been boarded up for many years and is desperately in need of restoration.

110

111

112

113

TEMPLE OF ODD FELLOWS (RANDOLPH STREET COMMERCIAL BUILDINGS)

Randolph and Monroe St.
Unknown architect, 1874

Part of a rare, surviving nineteenth-century strip of retail structures, this is a fine example of late-Victorian commercial design. While the building lost its mansard roof along the way, it's still head and shoulders above its neighbors. The red-brick façade and restrained ornament have now achieved a wonderful patina. Note the unusual staggered window heights on the second floor, which was the Odd Fellows meeting hall. Vacant and endangered, nevertheless.

114

WATER BOARD BUILDING

735 Randolph
Louis Kamper, 1928

Best known for his flamboyant work on Washington Boulevard for the Book brothers, Louis Kamper showed a surprisingly restrained departure here. This medium-height skyscraper rises from a mostly unadorned base to a clean wedge-shaped tower with spare ornament virtually confined to the penthouse level. The building's planning was quite sophisticated—note how the corners are clipped to avoid unusable acute angles at the interior. The triangular site translates to the shape of the building's elevator lobby, which is rich and memorable.

Perhaps at this late stage in his career Kamper tired of academic historicism and took a liking to Art Deco, or maybe the public agency's budget was just too tight, or perhaps his architect son was by then influencing the firm's design. In any case, it's as if Kamper was finally getting what the new skyscraper was all about. At this writing, there is talk of relocating the Water Board, which potentially would put this unique building on the endangered list.

115

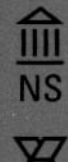

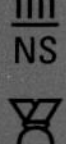

WAYNE COUNTY BUILDING (WAYNE COUNTY COURTHOUSE)

600 Randolph
John and Arthur Scott, 1897; restoration by Smith, Hinchman, and Grylls, and Quinn Evans, 1987

Listen closely and you can almost hear the strains of a Wagnerian opera. This magnificent example of Beaux-Arts Classicism was designed to anchor the eastern end of Cadillac Square and serve as a counterfoil to City Hall, unfortunately lost in 1961. Four stories of Ohio sandstone surmount a rusticated base. A monumental stone staircase leads to a pedimented pavilion with Corinthian colonnade. Massively squared "attics" hold down the corners, heavy balustrades add definition, and robust Baroque sculpture groupings enliven the sky. This is the architecture the moderns loved to hate.

113

114

115

116 BAGLEY MEMORIAL FOUNTAIN

NSC P

Campus Martius
H. H. Richardson, 1887, to be relocated ca. 2003

A most remarkable drinking fountain bequeathed to the city by local businessman and former governor John J. Bagley. This wonderful little piece of civic art is also the only known Michigan design by famed master architect Henry Hobson Richardson (1838–1886), judged by many as one of America's most important architects of the nineteenth century. The unpolished white granite structure was inspired by a vaulted canopy (ciborium) over the high altar in St. Mark's, Venice. Originally situated in Campus Martius, the fountain was later moved to the northeast corner of Woodward and Monroe. The new Campus Martius scheme moves it again, this time to the head of Cadillac Square, where it will occupy an axial placement in the median at the foot of the Wayne County Building.

117 LAWYERS BUILDING

N PR

137 Cadillac Square
Bonnah and Chaffee, 1922

One of few remaining Chicago commercial-style designs in Detroit, this handsome building was wrought by designers of the nearby Cadillac Tower (118) and the Farwell Building (83) on Capitol Square. What Kamper was to Washington Boulevard and Raseman was to Harmonie Park, Bonnah and Chaffee appear to have been to the making of Cadillac Square.

118 CADILLAC TOWER

SP

65 Cadillac Square
Bonnah and Chaffee, 1927

A somewhat unresolved stacking of current styles, this forty-story spike rises from an unremarkable base, through a Chicago-esque shaft, to a Neo-Gothic hat. The gilded crown—gold leaf protected by a terra cotta glaze—is remarkably effective under certain sun angles. The placement of the elevator core on the outside wall leaves an awkwardly blank wall, all the more empty by the loss of the abutting ten-story Gregory, Mayer, and Thom Building. A giant mural of a local sports hero didn't compensate, and proved obsolete when the player retired. We'll sidestep Downtown's emerging mural movement with a quote from modern master Louis I. Kahn (no relation to Albert Kahn), who asserted, "Paint is not architecture."

116

117

118

119 FIRST NATIONAL BUILDING

660 Woodward Ave.
Albert Kahn, 1922

By the early 1920s Kahn was developing a standardized "office module," with an efficient structural frame and floor plan dimensioned to provide natural light and ventilation. Here Kahn adapts his standard to fill an irregular site. This handsome tower's uniform pattern and clean lines are a step away from an evolving European modern style, which ironically drew heavily upon Kahn's industrial architecture. More aesthetically conservative in the city, Kahn included classical colonnades and details that he and his clients still believed more appropriately expressed commercial use and skyscraper form. The original cornices were lost along the way. See also the General Motors Building (196) of the same year.

120 VINTON BUILDING

600 Woodward Ave.
Albert Kahn, 1917

Designed for a prominent construction firm, with a bank at the ground floor, this slim twelve-story tower suggests an elegantly extended temple. In the photograph, the Vinton building is at the far right and in the shadow of First National (119), which wraps around three edges of the odd-shaped block. Burnham classicism, Arts and Crafts, Prairie, and industrial influences merge here in a solution that is uniquely Kahn. The reinforced concrete structure features vertical piers accentuated by recessed panels and topped by a gable-shaped parapet. Endangered, with great potential.

121 ONE DETROIT CENTER

Woodward Ave. and Larned
Johnson Burgee Architects, 1992

Houston-based developer Gerald Hines teamed with famed architects Philip Johnson and John Burgee to create a number of historicist skyscrapers around the United States, urban and suburban alike, during the 1980s. For Detroit the architects created a sophisticated granite-clad shaft that resolves into a memorable, Flemish-inspired silhouette. Historian Gordon Bugbee saw a more direct link to a corner tower of the Plaza Hotel in New York. In any derivation, Detroit's skyline is enriched by one of the architects' final collaborations. And as a significant footnote, the building's parking structure is one of the city's finest of its type.

119

120

121

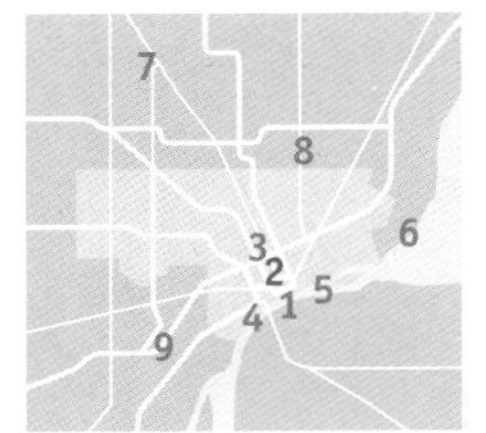

1 Downtown
2 **Midtown**
3 North
4 West
5 East
6 Grosse Pointe Lakeshore
7 Cranbrook
8 GM Technical Center
9 Ford's Dearborn

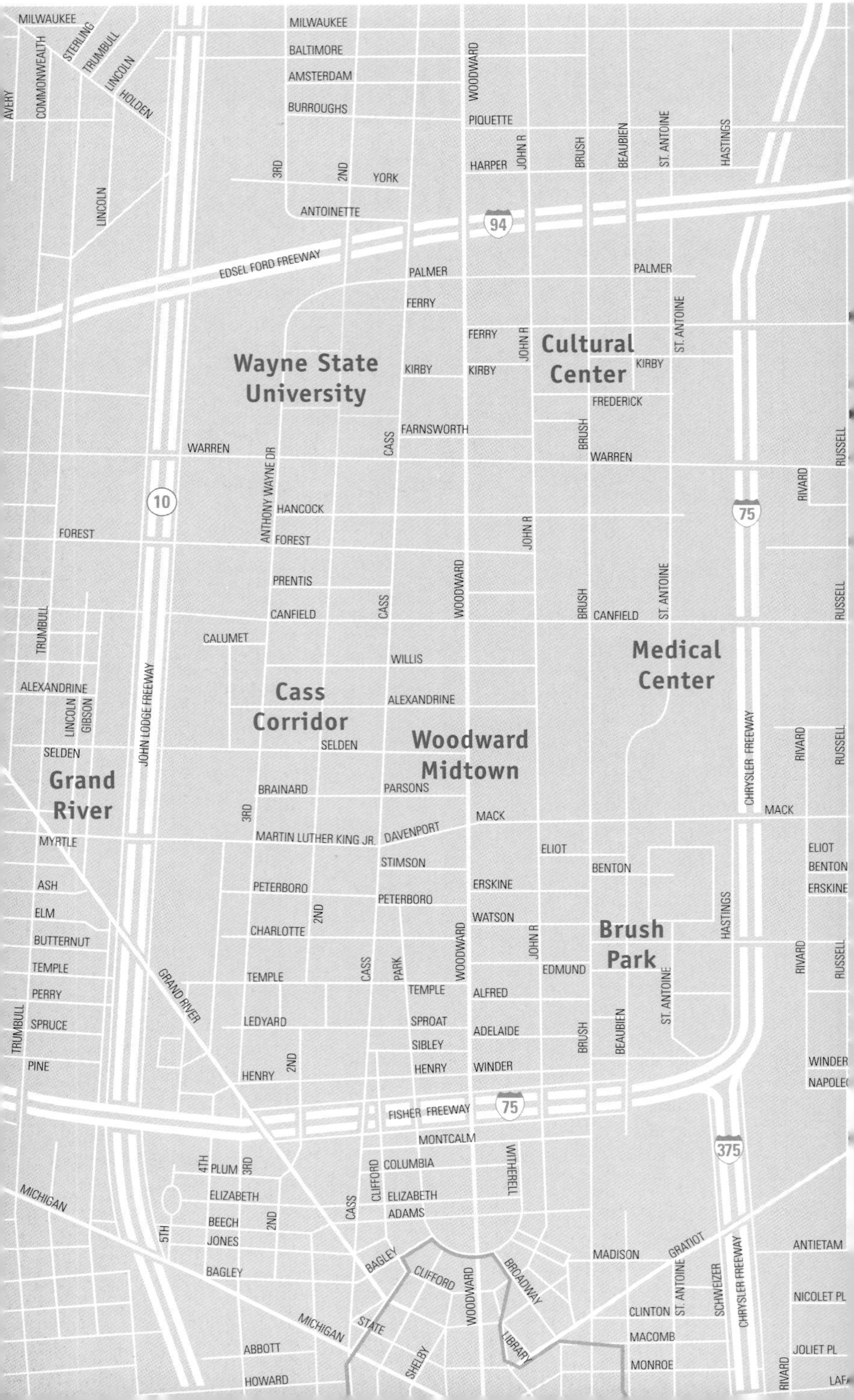

Wayne State University

Cultural Center

Medical Center

Cass Corridor

Woodward Midtown

Grand River

Brush Park

Midtown

Midtown

Our journey to Midtown follows Detroit's expansionary thrust and out-migration northward from the Downtown core. Beginning here, in the absence of practical public transit, the reader is encouraged to drive.

"Midtown," a term coined recently and gaining some acceptance, encompasses a handful of neighborhoods, districts, and corridors framed by freeways. Many of these urban geographies overlap, which is a good thing. The lower Woodward Corridor extends from I-75 to Warren, where it pauses at the Cultural Center. Brush Park, immediately to the north of Downtown on the east side of Woodward, was one of the city's first affluent neighborhoods and is now reduced to a ghost of its former self. The Cass Corridor parallels Woodward to the west and extends from Cass Park to Wayne State University. Filling out the northern third of Midtown are the University and Cultural Center areas.

Coloring outside the lines, we've here included side journeys to pick up exemplary buildings and neighborhoods nearby. These include an area of Grand River and Woodbridge to the west, and select buildings to the east of the freeway moat.

Woodward Midtown

Woodward Avenue traces its origins to an ancient Native American trail. The baroque judge and city planner Augustus Woodward dodged complaints that he named the avenue after himself by claiming the name meant "toward the forests, or wood-ward." From the mid-nineteenth century, the Midtown corridor began to rival East Jefferson as the elite place to live. Through the 1870s and 1880s, Woodward Avenue transformed at a pace second only to a contemporary subdivision build-out of McMansions. At the turn of the century, commercial and institutional uses began competing for this prized real estate, and won. For lack of civic controls to counter the laws of urban economics, the city lost a remarkable residential treasure. Remaining in its wake was a largely commercial corridor with a sprinkling of impressive churches and theaters.

WOODWARD MIDTOWN AREA

- 122 RESURRECTION PROMISE CHURCH
- 123 ECUMENICAL THEOLOGICAL SEMINARY
- 124 BONSTELLE THEATRE
- 125 ORCHESTRA PLACE
- 126 ORCHESTRA HALL
- 127 DAVID WHITNEY, JR., HOUSE
- 128 GARFIELD BUILDING
- 129 FIRST CONGREGATIONAL CHURCH
- 130 CATHEDRAL CHURCH OF SAINT PAUL

The idea of widening of Woodward was initiated in the 1920s theoretically as a means of increasing its capacity, but it resulted in nine years of combat between established commercial and religious interests, themselves usurpers of the once elite residential corridor. At stake was which side of the avenue would be pushed back, disfigured, or destroyed for the widening. In the Adams to Garfield stretch, the theaters (west) prevailed over the churches (east). Look closely at some of those commercial buildings on the east side and you'll see pre-1925 structures behind façades designed in post-1925 Art Deco styling. That's because the original fronts of these buildings were sacrificed for the sake of progress.

Looming over the Fisher Freeway at the foot of Woodward's Midtown corridor is an office building designed by Kahn (1923) and later converted to the headquarters of Motown Records. Now vacant, this structure is viewed by many as an ideal future Motown music museum. "Fill me up..."

122 RESURRECTION PROMISE CHURCH (FIRST UNITARIAN CHURCH OF DETROIT)

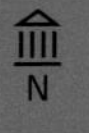

2870 Woodward Ave.
Donaldson and Meier, 1890

This ruggedly handsome rock of a church shows its age. The massing is powerfully pure and unencumbered. Unfortunately, the Woodward widening took its toll. The original open loggia, with its almost primitively sculptural colonnade, was partially removed and the remainder was enclosed. A half-round tower was removed, as well. But, importantly, the sanctuary is in a near original and quite impressive state.

123 ECUMENICAL THEOLOGICAL SEMINARY (FIRST PRESBYTERIAN CHURCH)

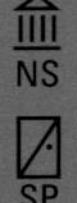

2930 Woodward Ave.
Mason and Rice, 1889

This large cruciform-plan church with walls of red rough-cut sandstone is indebted to H. H. Richardson's Romanesque—specifically his Trinity Church on Copley Square, Boston. But First Presbyterian takes Trinity to a new state here, as the massive central tower element practically becomes the church. Here, the short transept wings, topped by gabled roofs, are skillfully appended to the tower by architects George D. Mason and his partner, Zachariah Rice. When Woodward was widened in 1936, the handsome triple-arch entrance porch was moved from the west façade to the south, two engaged towers were permanently disengaged, and the sanctuary was rearranged.

124 BONSTELLE THEATRE (TEMPLE BETH-EL)

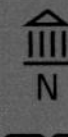

3424 Woodward Ave.
Albert Kahn, 1903; alterations by C. Howard Crane, 1925

Albert Kahn designed this domed synagogue for the Reform Congregation, of which he was a member. It was severely altered in 1925, when architect C. Howard Crane remade it as a theater. Wayne State University bought it in the 1950s and operates it today as the Bonstelle Theatre. Historically it is significant as the oldest synagogue building in Detroit. The photograph documents the building before the Woodward widening and resulting loss of its magnificent entry. The architectural lineage here extends from Beaux-Arts to French Classicism and stretches back to Roman antiquity. It may be more than coincidental that a photograph of the Pantheon hung over Kahn's desk.

122

123

124

125 ORCHESTRA PLACE

SP

3663 Woodward Ave.
Rossetti Associates, 1998

This five-story, glass-and-brick building houses administrative offices of the Detroit Symphony Orchestra and Detroit Medical Center. The dark façade is sparely yet carefully detailed, and the building's siting at the edge of the street creates a strong urban presence. The unusual top story with metal cornice seems to take a respectful bow to Orchestra Hall (126), while elevating a tried and true design motif to a higher plane.

126 ORCHESTRA HALL

NSC S P$

3711 Woodward Ave.
C. Howard Crane, 1919; restoration by Quinn Evans and Richard Frank

This is one of C. Howard Crane's early works in an impressive career as one of America's premier theater designers. If the boxy exterior and neoclassical cloak seem a bit expeditious, perhaps it's because the building was designed and built in six months. This feat was forced by conductor Ossip Gabrilovich's threat of departure for want of a proper concert hall. The maestro got his wish, as Orchestra Hall is an acoustic and decorative marvel.

The Detroit Symphony Orchestra made its home here from 1919 to 1939. The building later hosted vaudeville shows, movies, and even church services. Orchestra Hall was slated for demolition in 1970, when an enterprising bassoonist and generous patrons saved it. Over the next two decades, a careful renovation under the eye of architect Richard C. Frank restored its glory in time for the DSO to return in 1989. As this is written, a major expansion on the north end of Orchestra Hall, designed by Diamond, Schmitt, and Co. of Montreal, is in progress.

127 DAVID WHITNEY, JR., HOUSE

NS SP

4421 Woodward Ave.
Gordon W. Lloyd, 1894

Built for a lumber baron and steamship owner, this is one of the last grand mansions surviving from nineteenth-century Detroit. Here Lloyd merged the Chateauesque with an attenuated Romanesque to create a unique, some would say awkward, expression. The exterior is finished in a rough-cut pink jasper from South Dakota. The interiors, by contrast, are luxurious. Many of its more than forty rooms feature Tiffany leaded-glass windows, marble, onyx, and hand-carved woodwork. The design marked one of the enduring achievements of Gordon Lloyd (1832–1904), a British-born immigrant to Detroit who designed Dowling Hall (19) and Christ Church (254), both on East Jefferson. In recent years the house has served as an upscale restaurant, appropriately named for its first owner.

125

126

127

128 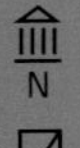

GARFIELD BUILDING (EDWIN S. GEORGE BUILDING)

4612 Woodward Ave.
Albert Kahn, 1908 and 1914; renovation by Elisabeth Knibbe Architects, 1999

This five-story, reinforced concrete framed building conveys the multiple personalities of its age. Architecturally, it strikes a formal office pose to the intersecting streets and a latent industrial demeanor on its less public sides. Edwin George, the prime developer of this section of Woodward at the turn of the century, hired Kahn to plan this speculative structure, which became home to a variety of auto-related suppliers.

Other stories are embedded in the subtext of this otherwise modest building's past. The reader will recall the circumstances of the Woodward widening and the near civil war between East and West. The commission overseeing this skirmish, the Woodward Improvement Association, was located in this building. It is perhaps more than coincidental that it is here that the taking of frontage shifts from the east side to the west side of Woodward, thereby bending to avoid this structure. More recently, through a model coalition of public agencies, nonprofit concerns, and for-profit investors, this structure was sensitively redeveloped for residential lofts.

129  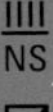

FIRST CONGREGATIONAL CHURCH

33 East Forest at Woodward Ave.
J. Lyman Faxon, 1891; addition by Albert Kahn, 1920

Boston architect John Lyman Faxon's only important building in Detroit is this richly polychromatic church that blends Romanesque massing with Byzantine detailing—a fine example of Victorian Romanesque. The centrally focusing arcade is especially handsome; so is the tall campanile topped by a winged statue of the archangel Uriel. Albert Kahn's 1924 red-brick addition to the rear respectfully defers.

130  

CATHEDRAL CHURCH OF SAINT PAUL

4800 Woodward Ave.
Cram, Goodhue, and Ferguson, 1911

St. Paul's is a large Neo-Gothic structure designed by one of the country's leading church architects, Ralph Adams Cram. In its ample proportions, smooth limestone surfaces, and historically correct details, St. Paul's recalls the architecture of large English monasteries. Cram's work here was much admired and imitated. Note that at the crossing of the nave and transepts is a massive square base designed to support a tower that has yet to be built. Over the course of his illustrious career Cram moved progressively from early to later English models, as if to retrace architectural history.

128

129

130

Brush Park

Bounded by Woodward Ave., Fisher Fwy., Mack Ave., and Beaubien
Various architects

One of Detroit's oldest neighborhoods for the wealthy is re-emerging from nearly total abandonment and disintegration. The district was developed in the 1870s on farmland owned by the prominent Brush family, with many of the streets named for family members (Alfred, Edmund, etc.) Among early residents was J. L. Hudson, founder of the eponymous department store. A rich variety of architectural styles was represented, including those popular from the mid-nineteenth century to about 1920. The Brush family developed their land carefully, imposing restrictions on the type of houses that could be built and insisting on what were then large lot widths of fifty feet. The area filled in gradually as the city grew to the north, but by 1900 some residents were already moving away, drawn to the more outlying districts of Indian Village to the east and Boston-Edison to the north. Many of the mansions were then subdivided into apartments, and commercial development replaced the elegant houses on Woodward Avenue. By the 1980s many of the houses still remaining were reduced to see-through shells, reminiscent of post-war Europe. A rear-guard action by urban pioneers and preservationists rescued some of the mansions, but these efforts were hard-pressed by serious social challenges. Today, neotraditional townhouses and senior citizen housing, within walking distance of Comerica Park and Ford Field, are bringing new life to the area.

131 ELISHA TAYLOR HOUSE

NS PR

59 Alfred
Unknown architect, 1870

Elisha Taylor was a lawyer who occupied a number of public offices, including City Attorney. The architecture here is fundamentally Victorian, including a mix of Gothic and Tudor references. The Mansard roof adds a Second Empire chapeau.

BRUSH PARK AREA

131 ELISHA TAYLOR HOUSE	133 GREATER SHILOH BAPTIST CHURCH
132 HUDSON-EVANS HOUSE	134 DETROIT URBAN LEAGUE

131

132 HUDSON-EVANS HOUSE

NS PR

79 Alfred
Unknown architect, 1874

Built for a local ship owner but known as the Hudson-Evans House after two famous residents. Grace Whitney Evans, daughter of lumber baron David Whitney, Jr., later rented it to J. L. Hudson, founder of the department store. This three-story, red-brick house, along with the Taylor House (131) next door, remarkably represent two of the few remaining buildings of Brush Park and of the Second Empire style. Surviving details include slate patterns on the roof and elaborate two-story bay windows.

133 GREATER SHILOH BAPTIST CHURCH

SC SP

557 Benton
Carlos N. Stokes, and W. W. Ahlschlager, Inc., 1926; addition by Architects International, 1978

A church with historical significance to Detroit's black community, Greater Shiloh was an outgrowth of Second Baptist (37), itself started in 1836 by former slaves. Carlos Stokes, a parishioner and draftsman, carpenter, and bricklayer, designed the present church in 1920. He is the first authenticated black designer in Detroit's architectural history. Stokes' plans were somewhat modified by the architectural firm of W. W. Ahlschlager, Inc. A 1978 addition covered up most of the original façade, as fully depicted in the drawing, 133a.

134 DETROIT URBAN LEAGUE (ALBERT KAHN HOUSE)

NS SP

208 Mack Ave.
Albert Kahn, 1906–1928

When it came time to design his own house, Albert Kahn revealed his affinity for the English Domestic Revival of the day. The floral carving on the round-arched front door and the interior woodwork reflected his love of craftsmanship. In fact, much of the furniture was designed by this prolific Renaissance man, as well. In 1928 Kahn added a spacious gallery to accommodate his library and art collection. The extensive gardens, now rather obscure, were an important part of his private world. Today the house serves as headquarters for the Detroit Urban League.

Kahn died here in 1942. Shortly before his death, the American Institute of Architects recognized his roles in shaping modern architecture and the Arsenal of Democracy. Presented in at the national convention in Detroit, the citation read: "Master of concrete and steel, master of space and time, he stands today at the forefront of our profession in meeting the colossal demands of a Government in need."

132

133 a

133 b

134 a

134 b

Medical Center

The original hospital expanded to a medical center and is now verging on district proportions. Visual variety reigns as few contributors, even within single firms, have been willing to subordinate design urges to a unifying aesthetic prescription.

135 **BRUSH BUILDING, HARPER HOSPITAL**
Detroit Medical Center
Albert Kahn, 1928

This remnant of the Medical Center's early development is a fine example of twentieth-century Neo-Romanesque applied to the tall building. Viewed best from the internal mall, its warm and vibrant face stands out among its later, more functionally driven progeny. See also Kahn's Argonaut Building (197) of the same era.

136 **DETROIT RECEIVING HOSPITAL**
4201 St. Antoine
William Kessler and Associates, Zeidler Partnership, and Giffels Associates, 1979

Prior to this time, most Detroit hospitals relied on historical allusions for architectural authority. Kessler's boldly modern design defied that precedent. His silver streak of a building, aluminum- and porcelain-clad, celebrates the modern scientific marvel of medicine. The interior, meanwhile, offers bold colors, a generous use of windows onto public spaces, and one of the most extensive art collections of any hospital in the United States.

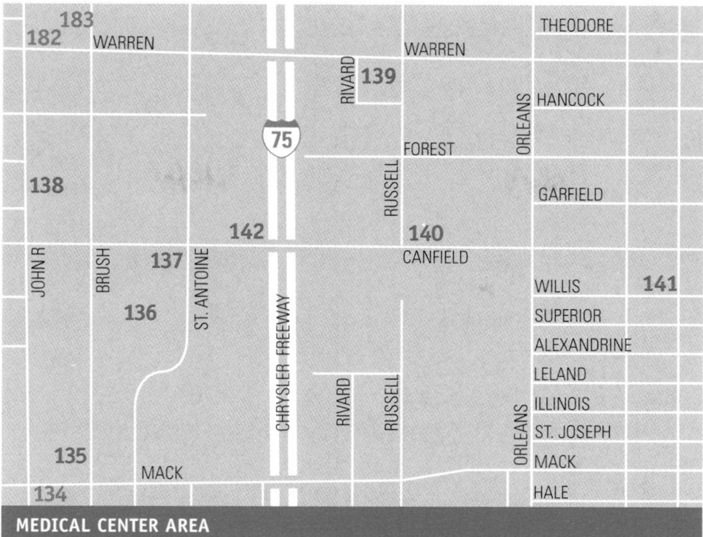

MEDICAL CENTER AREA

135 BRUSH BUILDING, HARPER HOSPITAL
136 DETROIT RECEIVING HOSPITAL
137 MEDICAL RESEARCH BUILDING
138 JOHN B. DINGELL VA HOSPITAL AND MEDICAL CENTER
139 WAYNE COUNTY MEDICAL EXAMINER'S OFFICE
140 SWEETEST HEART OF MARY ROMAN CATHOLIC CHURCH
141 SAINT ALBERTUS CATHOLIC CHURCH
142 SAINT JOSAPHAT ROMAN CATHOLIC CHURCH COMPLEX

135

136

137 MEDICAL RESEARCH BUILDING

St. Antoine and Canfield
Smith, Hinchman, and Grylls, 1965

This temple to medicine is mostly about its finely proportioned, enveloping grille wall. But for its entry canopy and stair, one would be hard-pressed to determine this building's size. It feels bigger than it is, and a visit surprises most observers. The design falls into the formalist vein of modern architecture mined deeply by Minoru Yamasaki. Yet basic maintenance is obviously a more pressing issue as to whether this modern classic stands the test of time.

138 JOHN B. DINGELL VA HOSPITAL AND MEDICAL CENTER

John R and Canfield
Smith, Hinchman, and Grylls, 1996

The architects tried to break down the overwhelming size of this hospital to fragments more human in scale. Their main device was the varied use of color on different sections of the exterior. They also articulated the massing with curved bays, partial cornices, and other evocative architectural forms. The result is a postmodern design sporting a bright enameled "wet" look, as though the building was freshly painted. The interior proves more tranquil, with medical offices grouped around a skylighted central courtyard that includes a striking, glass block vaulted chapel (138b).

139 WAYNE COUNTY MEDICAL EXAMINER'S OFFICE

1300 East Warren Ave.
Kessler Associates, 1995

Although the nature of the building's use precludes any showy architectural statement, Kessler created an efficient, modern design. The two-story brick veneer building features unique, bent glass clerestory windows, and a private meditation courtyard for workers and grieving families.

137

138 a

138 b

139 b

139 a

140 ## SWEETEST HEART OF MARY ROMAN CATHOLIC CHURCH

NSC SP

4440 Russell St. and Canfield
Spier and Rohns, 1893

This is a monumental late Gothic Revival church that, like St. Albertus (141) nearby, served Detroit's Polish Catholic community at the turn of the century. Starting with the basic cruciform plan, the architects added multiple subsidiary masses with gabled roofs. The twin towers are decorated with pinnacles and crosses. The church's transept windows, which were made in Detroit, won prizes at the 1893 Chicago Columbian Exposition.

141 ## SAINT ALBERTUS CATHOLIC CHURCH

NSC SP

4231 St. Aubin
Henry Engelbert, 1885

St. Albertus was the first Polish parish in Detroit and the center of the city's Polish community and culture at the end of the nineteenth century. This extra-large, red-brick Gothic church reflects architectural precedents found throughout Northern Europe. A set of murals at the top of the nave in fact depicts a variety of Polish church references. The massive octagonal tower unfortunately lost its spire to a lightning strike.

142 ## SAINT JOSAPHAT ROMAN CATHOLIC CHURCH COMPLEX

NSC SP

715 East Canfield
Joseph Kastler and William E. N. Hunter, 1901

St. Josaphat was designed to serve a thriving Polish community residing in the area, as its three well-balanced spires form a prominent landmark. The interiors are more Baroque—with hints of Russian influence—than the Late Victorian Romanesque exterior would suggest. From just the right angle southbound on I-75, St. Josaphat's spires align with RenCen's tower profile in the distance. As depicted here by Korab (142b), the juxtaposition forms an indelible image of Detroit's past and present.

140 a

140 b

141

142 a

142 b

Cass Corridor

For our purposes, the Cass Corridor environs extend from Cass Park to Wayne State University, and from Woodward to Third. Down but on the way up, this area is a serial study in contrasts. Its population today barely numbers four thousand, and many of these citizens are homeless. On the other hand, this is home to Cass Tech, one of Detroit's premier high schools, and the Detroit Masonic Temple, one of the nation's most remarkable lodges.

Prior to its decline, the area hosted a thriving mix of businesses, shops, churches, and schools, all supporting neighborhoods made up of apartment buildings and densely packed townhouses. Office workers walked and rode trolleys to Downtown destinations. While not on the scale of the Woodward mansions to the east, the Art Center Music School and the McAdow house hold their own. West Canfield is a virtually intact example of the area's previous incarnation as an upper-middle-class enclave in the late nineteenth century. The northern sections of Cass, Second, and Third are eminently walkable.

143 DETROIT MASONIC TEMPLE

NS C SP$

500 Temple (Cass Park)
George D. Mason, 1926

The Masonic Temple comprises three distinct elements unified by Mason's austere Neo-Gothic architecture applied to the multistory building. The architect confined a most successful decorative program to the pedestrian realm, while exploiting a more austere massing at the upper reaches. An eclectic array of architectural ornament somehow manages to form a cohesive whole under George Mason's mature hand. This ranks among the largest Masonic Temples in the world and as one of the most important venues in Detroit for civic, business, and cultural events.

HANCOCK
130
162 155 154 153
FOREST
152
129
JOHN R
PRENTIS
151
128
138
CANFIELD
150
127
CALUMET
149
CASS
WILLIS
WOODWARD
3RD
2ND
ALEXANDRINE
148
147
SELDEN
146
BRAINARD
PARSONS
126
135
125
MACK
MARTIN LUTHER KING JR.
DAVENPORT
134
ELIOT
145
STIMSON
124
PETERBORO
PETERBORO
ERSKINE
WATSON
CHARLOTTE
WOODWARD
JOHN R
123
122
EDMUND
TEMPLE
143
CASS
PARK
TEMPLE
131
132
144
Cass Park
ALFRED

CASS CORRIDOR AREA

143 DETROIT MASONIC TEMPLE
144 MICHIGAN CTR. FOR HIGH TECHNOLOGY
145 CLAY OFFICE AND CONFERENCE CENTER
146 CORONADO APARTMENTS
147 CASS AVE. UNITED METHODIST CHURCH
148 ART CENTER MUSIC SCHOOL
149 WEST CANFIELD NEIGHBORHOOD
150 CANFIELD LOFTS
151 PERRY MCADOW HOUSE
152 DAVID MACKENZIE HOUSE
153 GEORGE W. LOOMER HOUSE
154 MULFORD T. HUNTER HOUSE
155 THOMPSON HOME

143

144 NS C SP

MICHIGAN CENTER FOR HIGH TECHNOLOGY (S. S. KRESGE WORLD HEADQUARTERS)

2727 Second Ave. (Cass Park)
Albert Kahn, 1927

While its mansard roof profile may cast a Second Empire shadow, a closer look reveals that you can't judge a building by its skyline. This second Kresge headquarters design (the first headquarters was located in Grand Circus Park) is decidedly Art Deco. The articulated massing ascends with effortless grace, and the detailing reinforces the whole. Eliel Saarinen's influence is evident, but this is primarily Kahn, and the composition remains one of his most serenely powerful designs in high-style Art Deco. In recent years the building has partially served as an incubator for start-up firms, but remains today largely underused.

145 NS PR

CLAY OFFICE AND CONFERENCE CENTER (CLAY SCHOOL)

453 Martin Luther King
J. B. Tarleton, 1888

This boxy, much-used Italianate structure is the oldest public school building still standing in Detroit. The little red brick schoolhouse has been given new life as an office center. Its character-defining tower is missed.

146 NS PR

CORONADO APARTMENTS

3751–73 Second Ave.
Mortimer L. Smith and Son, 1894

Apartment living was just becoming an acceptable lifestyle for an affluent middle class when the Coronado was built. Its faint Romanesque lines include a corner turret, open loggias on the upper floors, a strong cornice, and other features that eventually would give way to more utilitarian expressions in later apartment towers. Compare this to Eyre's Detroit Club (92) completed three years earlier.

147 NSC SP

CASS AVENUE UNITED METHODIST CHURCH

3901 Cass Ave. and Selden
Malcomson and Higginbotham, 1891

This is one of several churches sculpted by Malcomson and Higginbotham in the robust Richardsonian Romanesque style. The smaller building to the west on Selden was the original 1883 chapel by Mason and Rice. Under that grime is a subtle contrast between golden limestone and pinkish sandstone.

The well-to-do congregation installed windows from Tiffany on three of the sanctuary's sides. The church also boasted a Johnsontracker church organ, thought to be the largest unaltered pipe organ existing from nineteenth-century Michigan.

144

145

146

147

148 ART CENTER MUSIC SCHOOL (ROBERT AND JENNIE BROWN HOUSE)

3975 Cass Ave.

Almon C. Varney, 1891; Hamilton Funeral Home addition, architect unknown, 1930

This double building has led three lives. The original structure is a residence designed by noted architect Almon C. Varney in the Queen Anne style, with its characteristic flurry of materials, textures, windows, and roof shapes. In 1925 the house was purchased by a funeral home, which soon added a mortuary chapel designed in an Egyptian Revival vein of the Art Deco. Both structures are fine examples of their respective vocabularies. Art Center Music School, the oldest of its kind in Detroit, bought the building(s) in 1981.

149 WEST CANFIELD NEIGHBORHOOD

Canfield between Second and Third

Various architects, 1871–1900

This neighborhood fragment was developed in the 1870s on farmland once owned by Lewis Cass, Michigan's former territorial governor. The exceptionally fine Victorian at 635 West Canfield is the street's oldest. Home to one of the first waves of attorneys, doctors, dentists, and architects who chose to live outside the city, the neighborhood was, in effect, an early suburban subdivision. The architecture encompasses a mix of popular nineteenth-century styles, including Queen Anne, Italianate, and Victorian Gothic. In order to stem deterioration in the twentieth century, the district became Detroit's first local historic district in 1970.

150 CANFIELD LOFTS (BUICK MOTOR COMPANY)

460 West Canfield

Lane, Davenport, and Patterson, 1921; renovation and addition by Archive Design Studio, 2000

From the early 1920s the Cass Corridor area was dominated by automobile-related commercial development. By 1929 some sixteen dealers and scores of suppliers and repair shops were located along Cass between Seldon and Warren. Beginning its long and useful life as the Detroit base for the Buick Motor Company, this utilitarian structure was most recently and creatively adapted for loft-style housing.

148

149

150

151 PERRY MCADOW HOUSE

4605 Cass Ave.
Scott and Company, 1891

This handsome Victorian mansion features bay windows, Corinthian-columned porches, a balustrade parapet, and elaborate period interiors. It was built for a family made wealthy by Montana gold mines. For many years it has served as a parish house for the adjacent church.

152 DAVID MACKENZIE HOUSE

4735 Cass Ave.
Malcomson and Higginbotham, 1895

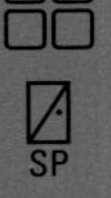

This Victorian mansion features the elements typical of a Queen Anne-style home, though quite reserved: the asymmetrical massing, picturesque conical-roofed tower, and a variety of surface treatments and decoration. David Mackenzie was a scholar who founded Detroit Junior College in 1917—the nucleus from which Wayne State University grew. Preservation Wayne, an important advocate for saving historic architecture, is one of the tenants of the house today.

153 GEORGE W. LOOMER HOUSE

71 West Hancock
Almon C. Varney, 1888

Almon C. Varney was one of Detroit's most prolific residential architects practicing in the late nineteenth century. In 1882 he coauthored *Our Homes and Their Adornments*, and in 1892 designed and built the city's first apartment building. Working here in the Richardsonian Romanesque, Varney created a robust composition of turret, entry arch, rose window, and dormer, without losing control. As an important survivor of a once-fashionable neighborhood, this masterpiece of residential architecture is richer still for the experience of its Queen Anne neighbor to the west.

151

152

153

154 N PR

MULFORD T. HUNTER HOUSE

77 West Hancock
William P. Langley, Builder, 1894

This rare Queen Anne masonry townhouse complements the Loomer House (153) next door. By contrast, this design is subtler, more genteel. Note the comparatively delicate oval window and elliptical fan light over the door. Stone base, asymmetrical brick massing, and slate roof exude quality.

155 NS SP

THOMPSON HOME (THOMPSON HOME FOR OLD LADIES)

4756 Cass Ave.
George D. Mason, 1884

A late-nineteenth-century marriage of English and French influences, this early congregate-care mansion strikes a stately pose. Mason decorated the symmetrical, anthropomorphic structure with elegant band-coursing, brackets, and pediments. Wayne State University has commendably reused the building for its School of Social Work. While common brick buildings in early Detroit were often painted, in its current makeup this lady has lost considerable allure.

154

155

Grand River

The reader is encouraged to take a side trip over the freeway to experience some firsts, mosts, and bests. Extending north from Grand River, Woodbridge is one of Detroit's first and finest streetcar suburbs. Along Grand River is perhaps our best Victorian Gothic church, our first Neo-Gothic church, and one of our most romantic buildings in the Chateauesque style.

156

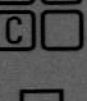

WOODBRIDGE NEIGHBORHOOD

Trumbull and Lincoln between Canfield and Grand River
Various architects, 1860–1920

Woodbridge was an early streetcar suburb of high architectural quality at the turn of the century. While much of Detroit's historic residential fabric has been lost, Woodbridge remains. Architectural styles range from elaborate Queen Anne to more modest vernacular cottages. Interestingly, corner lots tended to be developed early, and in Victorian styles, while midblocks were built out later and in more modest designs. The demarcation aligns more or less with the economic panic of the early 1890s. Above all, a pride of place sustains this traditional neighborhood and its gradual renewal.

157

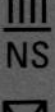

WILLIAM NORTHWOOD HOUSE

3985 Trumbull
George F. Depew, 1891

Depew indulged a variety of fantasies in this elaborate, three-story brick mansion. Massing, window, and roof treatments derive from Chateauesque, Second Empire, and Queen Anne sources. Round towers and square. Metal cresting on some roofs and absent from others. Red, white, and yellow sandstone accents are supplemented by phrases of decorative brickwork. Not by way of explanation, the owner was a cofounder of a prominent malt manufacturing company in Detroit. Nevertheless, it all seems to hang together, or separately. A most passionate and defining moment in the remarkable Woodbridge historic district.

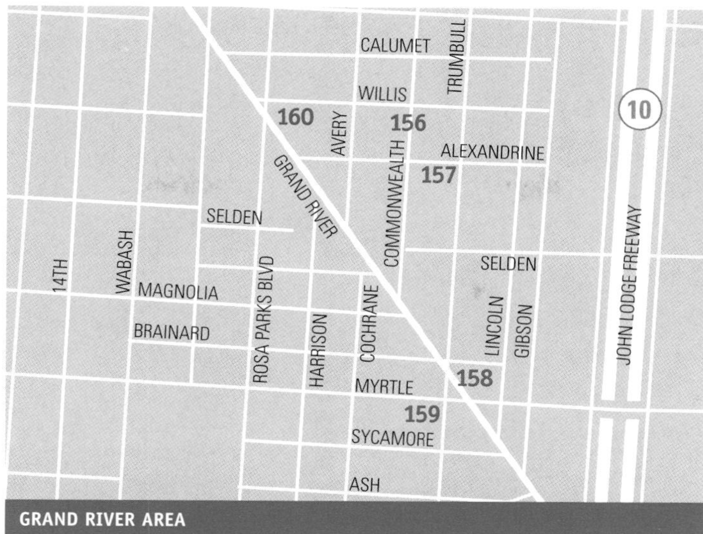

GRAND RIVER AREA

156 WOODBRIDGE NEIGHBORHOOD
157 WILLIAM NORTHWOOD HOUSE
158 TRUMBULL AVE. PRESBYTERIAN CHURCH
159 TRINITY EPISCOPAL CHURCH
160 EIGHTH PRECINCT POLICE STATION

156 a

156 b

157

158 TRUMBULL AVENUE PRESBYTERIAN CHURCH

SC SP

1435 Brainard at Trumbull
Julius Hess, 1887

One of Detroit's remaining examples of High Victorian Gothic, an effusive style that reigned briefly in the 1870s and 1880s. It was marked by a profusion of ornament and variety of color, or "polychrome." Note the remarkable corner turret. Contrast and compare with Trinity Episcopal (159) a block to the south, a more austere reproduction of English Gothic. Hess also designed the Grand Army of the Republic building (75).

159 TRINITY EPISCOPAL CHURCH

NSC 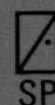 SP

1519 Myrtle and Trumbull
Mason and Rice, 1892

Trinity Episcopal marked a turning point in American church design. For decades Americans had indulged fanciful notions of medieval European design, resulting in quaint but historically unorthodox architecture. Newspaper publisher James Scripps, hoping to elevate the public's architectural consciousness, engaged Mason and Rice to produce an authentic copy of a fourteenth-century English Gothic church. Designs were based on extensive research in the English countryside. Even the tracery in the windows was archeologically correct. The late historian Gordon Bugbee, who attended and served here, believed this to be the first example of late Gothic Revival, or Neo-Gothic, by an American architect.

160 EIGHTH PRECINCT POLICE STATION

 NS PR

4150 Grand River
Louis Kamper, 1901

Louis Kamper designed this fanciful building in the French Chateau style. Even then, it was unusual to see such a picturesque assemblage of elements in a government building. The oddly shaped site most certainly influenced the romantic result. That Kamper chose this idiom, ten years after he designed the magnificent Hecker House (190) on Woodward Avenue in the same style, shows how French Renaissance architecture briefly was the rage in turn-of-the-century Detroit.

158

159

160

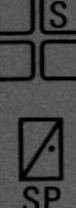

Wayne State

Wayne State University forms a substantial concentration of civic and educational buildings in the heart of the city. The evolution of the compact campus has been shaped by the need to make the most of limited available land. The university originated in Old Main, the former Central High School at Cass and Warren. Prior to World War II, the growing university expanded to nearby residences and even garages along Cass.

Recognizing the need for a plan, the Board of Education (which then ran the school) in 1942 sponsored a master plan competition, and Suren Pilafian, a young New York architect of Armenian origin, won. His plan envisioned a modern campus with large buildings grouped around open spaces. Pilafian went on to design several of the early buildings himself, including State Hall, the Library, and Fine Arts buildings.

Minoru Yamasaki updated the campus plan in 1954. He envisioned buildings of a common four-story height grouped around auto-free zones, thus taking the Pilafian plan to its logical conclusion as a superblock. Yamasaki, too, contributed several major buildings, including the stunning McGregor Memorial Conference Center.

Under President David Adamany in the 1980s and 1990s, Wayne State grew at an astonishing rate. Many new buildings were added, some of higher architectural merit than others. Today, under President Irvin Reid, Wayne State is developing a presence on Woodward Avenue to the east of the Main Campus, and is facilitating a research park and mixed-use urban village to the north of I-94. Nearly as memorable as its architecture is Wayne State's landscape design, largely the creation of Sasaki Associates. Making the most of little land, the main campus, pictured, represents to many Detroiters an "urban oasis."

EDSEL FORD FREEWAY
94
193
PALMER
171 Ferry Mall
FERRY
169
190 189
FERRY
172 170
Reuther Mall
168
10
167
KIRBY 178
KIRBY
173
ANTHONY WAYNE DR
166
164
JOHN LODGE FREEWAY
Williams Mall
165
176 177
175
Gullen Mall
163
FARNSWORTH
Ludington Mall
174
CASS
179
180
WOODWARD
181
WARREN
161
HANCOCK
130
162 155 154 153
FOREST
152
129
PRENTIS
128

WAYNE STATE AREA

161	OLD MAIN
162	HILBERRY THEATRE
163	STATE HALL
164	PURDY KRESGE LIBRARY
165	PRENTIS BUILDING AND DEROY AUDITORIUM
166	WALTER P. REUTHER LIBRARY OF LABOR AND URBAN AFFAIRS
167	HERMAN STRASBURG HOUSE
168	BELCREST APARTMENTS
169	MCGREGOR MEMORIAL CONFERENCE CTR.
170	EDUCATION BUILDING
171	NATURAL SCIENCE BUILDING
172	FACULTY/ADMINISTRATION BUILDING
173	STUDENT CENTER BUILDING
174	FREDERICK LINSELL HOUSE
175	SAINT ANDREW'S HALL

Main Campus

161 OLD MAIN

4841 Cass Ave.
Malcomson and Higginbotham, 1896;
renovation and addition by Ghafari Associates, 1997

Built initially as Central High School, Old Main is Wayne State's place of origin and now a university icon. Malcomson and Higginbotham designed many schools in Detroit, and this is one of their best. The stately Romanesque Revival composition is softened considerably by the buff-colored brick. Several subsequent additions to Old Main are barely noticeable, except for the most recent brick cube attached to the rear flank, designed by the renovation architects in a sharply modern vocabularly.

162 HILBERRY THEATRE (FIRST CHURCH OF CHRIST SCIENTIST)

4743 Cass Ave.
Field, Hinchman, and Smith, 1916

The first church built by the Christian Scientists in Detroit was designed in a frontal neoclassical style. While a departure from the more common standards of Gothic and Romanesque, classical models seem to have been a more common preference of the Christian Scientists. Wayne State bought the building in 1961 and converted the auditorium to a theater, which was then named in honor of the university's fourth president, Clarence Hilberry.

163 STATE HALL

5143 Cass Ave.
Suren Pilafian, 1948

Wayne State's first phase of serious campus building began in the late 1940s with this efficient structure designed by the university planner/architect himself. The functional L-shaped plan presents distinct personalities to different orientations. The wing facing Cass is mainstream 1940s modernism, while the northern exposure is quite exceptional. The fawn-colored, banded brick wall, minimalist window composition, and glass-and-metal entrance tower bear some resemblance to Saarinen's emerging modernism at the time, but are nevertheless highly original. Pilafian went on to design most of the university's first generation of new buildings.

161

162

163

164 ## PURDY KRESGE LIBRARY

SP

5294 (Kresge) and 5244 (Purdy) Gullen Mall
Suren Pilafian with Frank Montana, 1953 and 1954

Pilafian designed this pair of libraries in a modern idiom of lines, planes, solids, and voids. Indeed, the elemental composition is Bauhaus modern. Purdy Kresge was designed to frame a campus "room" at the former corner of Second and Kirby, but the recently added fitness center at once filled the room, reestablished the city grid, and somewhat reduced the building's energy.

165 ## PRENTIS BUILDING AND DEROY AUDITORIUM

SP

5201 (Prentis) and 5203 (DeRoy) Cass Ave.
Minoru Yamasaki and Associates, 1964 and 1965

Yamasaki's form-making derived much of its strength from the careful compositional massing of pure forms and pattern repetition of surface elements. Here, the composition of streetwall-gateway building and freestanding pavilion is perhaps a modern take on a medieval castle keep. The pleasant temple auditorium, dressed in a suggestive Gothic pattern, is surrounded by a literal moat and linked to the gateway building by an underground passage. Powerful moves and timeless references create an overall effect nearly as compelling as Yamasaki's McGregor Center (169) nearby.

166 ## WALTER P. REUTHER LIBRARY OF LABOR AND URBAN AFFAIRS

SP

5401 Cass Ave.
O'Dell, Hewlett, and Luckenbach, 1975, and addition, 1992

This angular, modern structure is home to one of the world's great archives of the modern labor movement. Seemingly carved from a larger block, this building presents a sculptural interplay of solidity and transparency, while simultaneously shaping its campus environs. A splendid four-story atrium organizes the interior spaces.

167 ## HERMAN STRASBURG HOUSE

N

PR

5415 Cass Ave.
Marcus R. Burrowes, 1915

Tightly composed and detailed, this house has long been associated with the city's performing arts. After the Strasburg family, which taught dance here, the house was occupied as a residence and music school, and since 1949 as a Wayne State Music Annex. The Arts and Crafts design derives from Burrowes' training under Stratton and Baldwin. The building's charm is in no small measure owing to melodic phrases that occasionally escape its open windows.

164

165

166

167

168 NS PR

BELCREST APARTMENTS

5440 Cass Ave.
Charles N. Agree, 1926

The Belcrest was built for an upscale clientele that demanded the services of a hotel but the long-term comfort of an apartment building. The style is essentially Neo-Romanesque, but the elaborate terra cotta cornice and other fanciful ornament edge the Belcrest toward the "exotic." Agree's fanciful side was more convincingly revealed in the Vanity Ballroom (323), designed a mere three years later in Art Deco.

169 C SP

MCGREGOR MEMORIAL CONFERENCE CENTER

495 Ferry Mall
Minoru Yamasaki and Associates, 1958

One of Yamasaki's masterpieces and believed by many to be among Detroit's finest buildings. The two-story, nearly symmetrical pavilion is sheathed in warm travertine marble. An integral sunken garden and reflecting pool nestle behind the building's podium, which is faced in Mankato stone. On the interior, two levels of conference rooms are arranged to either side of a skylighted entry hall and lounge, which has the feel of a modern gothic cathedral in miniature (169a). A triangular geometric motif forms a decorative pattern throughout the building, from window shape to balcony rail and door detail. Inside and out, Yamasaki's serenely luxurious material palette and composition recall Asian models of architecture and landscape design.

170° SP

EDUCATION BUILDING

5425 Gullen Mall
Minoru Yamasaki and Associates, 1960

Two years after designing the McGregor Memorial Conference Center (169), Yamasaki returned to Wayne State to add this symmetrical education temple in his unique style of Modern Formalism. Once again he relied on his signature geometric patterning, but here the result borders on the mundane.

168

169a

169b

170

171 C SP

NATURAL SCIENCE BUILDING (SHAPERO HALL OF PHARMACY)

5501 Gullen Mall

Paulsen, Gardner, and Associates, 1965

An inverted ziggurat, influenced perhaps by the landmark Boston City Hall, or a frontier fort. The upper-story window slits protect volatile experiments from light of day. As Hawkins Ferry noted, the structure itself seems to curiously defy the laws of gravity.

172 SP

FACULTY/ADMINISTRATION BUILDING

65 Reuther Mall

Neumann I Smith, 1990

This energetic massing of modular offices and conference spaces appeals for campus order and place. The building's atrium, brilliantly white and skylit, is an ethereal streetscape and soothing respite.

173 SP

STUDENT CENTER BUILDING

5221 Gullen Mall

Alden B. Dow and Associates, 1969

Dow studied for a time under Frank Lloyd Wright, but you would hardly know it by this design. Better known for his sprawling, ground-hugging houses, Dow here seems to self-consciously defy nature. The separation of upper and lower blocks leaves a less than usable roofscape; the cardboard model was likely more compelling. Closer examination includes hints of one master and deference to another, as the Wrightian surface patterning blends comfortably with Yamasaki's formalism. On the other hand, the unusual glass skirt at the bottom edge of the overhanging mass is an inventive Dow original.

171

172

173

174

FREDERICK LINSELL HOUSE

S PR

5104 Gullen Mall
John C. Stahl, Jr., 1904

Stahl designed this two-story brick house with a variety of historical motifs. One of the first houses that the university occupied when it began to expand in the 1930s and 1940s, Linsell and its neighbor are surviving reminders of the area's pre-university urban fabric. A pleasant, background building.

175

SAINT ANDREW'S HALL (ST. ANDREW'S EPISCOPAL CHURCH)

N SP

918 Ludington Mall
Cram, Wentworth, and Goodhue, 1902

Designed in 1890 and built in 1902, this was one of Cram's first ventures in the Perpendicular English Gothic style of church architecture. Reputedly, it was the Boston architect's first commission outside Massachusetts. The observer must look past the disfiguring effects of an early fire and expedient "restoration" to absorb the spirit of the place.

174

175

Cultural Center

Building a city takes time.

Planning for Detroit's new cultural center followed principles aligned with the City Beautiful movement, which was inspired by Chicago's Exposition of 1893. Proponents believed that urban beauty would result from the symmetrical and "hierarchical" arrangement of buildings in space. On a practical level, the Center of Arts and Letters idea was advanced to stem the rapid encroachment of commercial and light manufacturing development along the Woodward corridor. The city is forever grateful to persevering visionaries and realists alike.

In 1905 the Detroit Board of Commerce invited Frederick Law Olmsted, Jr., and Charles Robinson to propose civic improvements, and the team recommended a grouping of public buildings harmoniously designed around a "grand public space." In 1910 the art museum purchased land in an elite Woodward residential section two miles north of Downtown. The Library Board shortly followed suit. In 1913 Bennett and Day were invited to prepare a scheme for an arts center complex and in the same year Cass Gilbert won a national competition to design the new Main Library. Then in 1919 the Arts Commission, on the recommendation of member Albert Kahn, selected Philadelphia architect Paul Cret to design the Detroit Institute of Arts.

A new Orchestra Hall was included in early planning of the ensemble, but due to lack of progress in developing the library and art museum, its board abandoned the group in 1919 for a site nine blocks to the south.

The cultural center vision as built is a fraction of the plan. City politics and global economics frustrated the dream until follow-up planning in the 1940s. From the 1950s to this day, the University Cultural Center has added the Historical Museum, Science Center, and Charles H. Wright Museum of African American History, and has served as a nucleus for the development of many other cultural and institutional resources in Midtown Detroit.

ANTOINETTE
EDSEL FORD FREEWAY
94
193
PALMER
PALMER
171 Ferry Mall FERRY
169
170
190 189
FERRY
JOHN R
188
BRUSH
BEAUBIEN
ST. ANTOINE
168
167 KIRBY 178 KIRBY
187
KIRBY
173
166
164
FREDERICK
165
176 177
184
185 186
Gullen Mall
163
174
CASS
FARNSWORTH
179
180
WOODWARD
181
183
182
WARREN
161

CULTURAL CENTER AREA

176 DETROIT PUBLIC LIBRARY, MAIN BRANCH
177 DETROIT INSTITUTE OF ARTS
178 DETROIT HISTORICAL MUSEUM
179 DETROIT SCHOOL CENTER BUILDING
180 SAMUEL L. SMITH HOUSE
181 HORACE H. RACKHAM BUILDING
182 DETROIT SCIENCE CENTER
183 CHARLES H. WRIGHT MUSEUM OF AFRICAN AMERICAN HISTORY
184 SCARAB CLUB
185 JOHN OWEN HOUSE
186 CHARLES W. WARREN HOUSE
187 KRESGE-FORD BUILDING, COLLEGE FOR CREATIVE STUDIES
188 EAST FERRY AVE. HISTORIC DISTRICT
189 CHARLES LANG FREER HOUSE
190 COL. FRANK J. HECKER HOUSE

Cultural Center

176 DETROIT PUBLIC LIBRARY, MAIN BRANCH

5201 Woodward Ave.
Cass Gilbert, 1921; additions by Cass Gilbert, Jr., and Francis Keally

A beautiful piece of civic architecture, the Main Branch of the Detroit Public Library is reminiscent of the Boston Public Library, by McKim, Mead, and White, with whom Cass Gilbert had apprenticed. But working here with a more refined classical brush, Gilbert's design is lighter, more cheerful and inviting. Renaissance Revival has evolved here into twentieth-century classicism.

The gleaming white Vermont marble sheathing seemingly lifts the building above its solid limestone terraces. A delicately rusticated base supports the piano nobile's seven-bay loggia, the most prominent gesture in this otherwise quiet composition. Above is an entablature of small square windows and bas-relief panels depicting the signs of the zodiac. The interior spaces, originally arranged and finished in a classical manner, have been modernized—with mixed results.

Gilbert went on to design primarily in the classical language of architecture, most notably the U.S. Supreme Court, while restoring for his personal use an historic eighteenth-century Dutch colonial in Ridgefield, Connecticut. Gilbert's son designed later and somewhat less than sympathetic additions to this fine public building.

177 DETROIT INSTITUTE OF ARTS

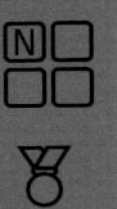

5200 Woodward Ave.
Paul P. Cret, 1927; numerous additions and renovations by others

The DIA ranks as one of Detroit's cultural jewels and an indisputable architectural landmark. Its art collection is world class, and the white-marble magnificence of Paul Cret's Renaissance-inspired building has stood as a Detroit cultural touchstone for three-quarters of a century.

Architect Cret was a French-born graduate of the Ecole des Beaux-Arts in Paris. He later settled in the United States, where he designed several major civic commissions around the nation. Cret's plan for the DIA, while monumental, was not unique. Contemporary museum design theory held that the architect would produce an outer shell of classical or Renaissance style within which large galleries would allow for flexibility in the display of art in its many forms. In the last few decades the DIA has toned down some of these palatial interiors to provide a more neutral setting for the artwork.

Ironically, the most recognizable work at the DIA, Diego Rivera's famous murals of Ford's Rouge factory and other industrial scenes, was installed over Cret's objections. The architect felt that Rivera's work defaced his building. He appealed to Albert Kahn, who served as adviser to the DIA board, but Kahn sided with Rivera.

176

177 a

177 b

That was hardly the only change made. Over the years, the DIA built more galleries to display its expanding collections. Initial additions were built behind Cret's main building so as not to conflict with it. Many notable architects contributed, including Minoru Yamasaki.

Later expansions to Cret's original included Gunnar Birkerts' black granite, modernist echo to the south of Cret's pavilion, and Harley, Ellington and Day's copy to the north. While these neutral flanks were designed to respectfully recede, their massive scale is undeniable. The high spaces at the intersections of new and old are delightful. And, as this is written, the DIA has engaged Michael Graves to encase later additions in a new/old slipcover, designed in Graves' more figural classicism.

Inside, William Kessler's interior architecture brought new order and amenity to this venerable institution. Kessler's, as well as Lou Gauci's, progressive interior modifications have garnered a number of AIA interior design awards. Skylighting the Kresge Court (177b) was a bold move yielding a memorable space. The next phase of interior makeover aspires to bring further clarity to the flow of exhibit spaces.

In and out, it's hard to say how the renovation will evolve, but some critics fear—or hope, as the case may be—that the DIA's eclectic mix of styles will be lost.

178 DETROIT HISTORICAL MUSEUM

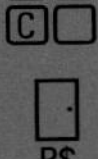

5401 Woodward Ave. at Kirby
William E. Kapp, 1951

PS

A warm and pleasant building designed by the talented Kapp, on his own after leaving Smith, Hinchman, and Grylls. The massing and sculptural eyebrows suggest stylistic influences from Frank Lloyd Wright's international style. The forecourt was recently renovated.

179 DETROIT SCHOOL CENTER BUILDING (MACCABEES BUILDING)

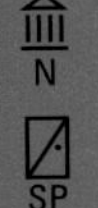

5057 Woodward Ave. at Putnam
Albert Kahn, 1927

Albert Kahn disliked the individualistic skyscrapers rising in New York City in the 1920s. "Bedlam reigns," he complained. "Everyone is trying something different." He preferred to adhere to a type of design already fairly successful. So he designed the Maccabees Building as a fourteen-story tower flanked by subordinate masses—similar to his *Free Press* Building (93) of 1923, albeit more vertically proportioned. Kahn's setback/Art Deco style, with traces of Romanesque detailing here, gradually evolved to the Fisher Building (198) and Albert Kahn Building (199) in New Center. Maccabees, a social beneficiary society, sold the building to the Detroit Public School system in 1960.

178

179

180 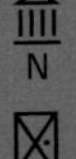

SAMUEL L. SMITH HOUSE

5035 Woodward Ave.
Rogers and MacFarlane, 1889

This three-story, cross-gabled Queen Anne house provides a glimpse of the area's elite residential character prior to the creation of the Cultural Center. Rogers and MacFarlane built an active general practice, including the design of many fine residences in Indian Village. Rare survivor or not, the Smith house held its own on the avenue once known for its mansions.

181 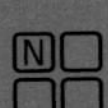

HORACE H. RACKHAM BUILDING

106 Farnsworth St.
Harley, Ellington and Day, 1941

A fine example of "stripped classicism," in which designers used classical massing while omitting the more traditional elements of academic classicism—base, column, capital, entablature, etc. Instead, and consistent with the Art Deco classicism of the day, artist Marshall Fredericks created a rich array of sculptural reliefs that indeed enliven a seemingly paper-thin façade. The building served for decades as home to the Engineering Society of Detroit. Named for a generous philanthropist, the Rackham Building forms an important southern edge to the still-evolving Cultural Center.

182

DETROIT SCIENCE CENTER

5020 John R
William Kessler and Associates, 1979; addition and renovation by Neumann|Smith, 2001

When completed in 1979, the Detroit Science Center instantly became a playful architectural landmark in the Cultural Center. Architect William Kessler had created a magical assemblage of forms expressive of their functions. Kessler's modernist gambit was recently transformed by Neumann|Smith in what appears at first glance to follow the original idea. But the new interior is remarkably different, even ironic. Within that articulated massing lies not a sequence of customized exhibit spaces, but a multilevel theme park under a vast, industrial-strength roof. This colorful and highly resonant warehouse for science will surely appeal to a generation raised on Game Boys and MTV.

180

181

182

183 CHARLES H. WRIGHT MUSEUM OF AFRICAN AMERICAN HISTORY

P$

315 East Warren Ave.
Sims-Varner, 1998

This new museum is replete with symbolic references to African art and architecture. For example, the column form is based on a traditional African rope motif. The central hall is metaphorically layered in meaning, as well. Richard Bennett's African masks and bronze doors are sincerely impressive. Sims-Varner has created an inventively rich, must-see addition to Detroit's Cultural Center.

184 SCARAB CLUB

NSC

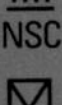
PR

217 Farnsworth St.
Lancelot Sukert, 1928

The Scarab Club is an imposing three-story romantic structure housing one of Michigan's oldest arts organizations. It was named for the scarab, an Egyptian symbol of rebirth, a name meant to symbolize the perpetual renewal of the arts in Detroit. The interior, which features studios, galleries, and classrooms, reflects Arts and Crafts philosophy. Note the club's scarab logo rendered in Pewabic tile over the entry. The bas relief on the west party wall is a later addition and brings interest to a surface presumably not originally intended for such full exposure, as captured in Korab's detail photograph through a site sculpture. (184b)

183

184 a

184 b

185 JOHN OWEN HOUSE (HANSBURY SCHOOL)

544 East Frederick
Unknown architect, 1885

This house and its neighbor to the east both share important connections to Detroit's African American history. Built in 1890 for John Owen, Jr., a prominent developer and realtor, the building later became the Hansbury School, where many young African Americans learned music from Mrs. Bertha Hansbury. A black employment agency also occupied the house for some time.

186 CHARLES W. WARREN HOUSE

580 East Frederick
Unknown architect, 1885; converted, 1919, and restored, 1970

The Warren House was designed in a hybrid of late-nineteenth-century styles, from Romanesque to Queen Anne. The heavy stone foundations, arched entrance, carved brownstone, and, especially, the transitions in scale across the composition recall the quirky scale juxtapositions of Philadelphia's Frank Furness. The roof forms and dormer almost appear to detach. In 1919 Detroit's first black hospital opened in the house, named Dunbar Hospital for the poet Paul Lawrence Dunbar. The hospital moved in 1928, and the house was purchased by Charles E. Diggs, the first African American state senator. Restored in 1970, the building came to house the Detroit Medical Society headquarters and a medical museum. This structure and the Owen House (185) next door were both built by the Vinton Company, a leading Detroit builder.

187 KRESGE-FORD BUILDING, COLLEGE FOR CREATIVE STUDIES

245 East Kirby, between John R and Brush
William Kessler and Associates, 1975

This modern icon explored the possibilities of structural expressionism and shares some affinity with the "metabolist movement" developing in Japan at the time. The thirty-two-foot square module was designed to expand horizontally and vertically with no appreciable change in appearance. While the school has grown, the building has not. Some commentators have called the virtuoso megastructure a "Tinkertoy" novelty, but it's far more than that. Winner of a national AIA design award at its inception, Kessler's monumental achievement was accorded AIA Detroit's twenty-five-year award in 2000.

185

186

187

188 EAST FERRY AVENUE HISTORIC DISTRICT

East Ferry between Woodward and Beaubien
Various architects, 1880s–1920s

This historic district encompasses the three blocks of East Ferry between Woodward and Beaubien and contains thirty-three primary structures serving commercial, residential, and institutional uses. The land was earlier developed as an experimental seed farm by Dexter Ferry, whose descendents subdivided it for higher and better returns. Building here began in the late 1880s and continued for three decades.

The Hecker and Freer mansions were among the first and most prominent, and thus followed a Detroit pattern of grander houses on the main avenues and more modest structures built farther away. All the same, this area has been a well-to-do neighborhood for the upper middle class over much of its distinguished history. From the 1940s on, buildings in this community formed important associations for Detroit's black history, with institutions such as Bailey Hospital (previously Dunbar, relocated from East Frederick and now demolished) and Lewis College, a business school for African Americans.

189 CHARLES LANG FREER HOUSE

71 East Ferry
Wilson Eyre, Jr., 1890

Charles Freer made his fortune manufacturing railroad cars with his partner, Colonel Frank Hecker. While Hecker built the extravagant Chateauesque mansion next door, Freer turned to Wilson Eyre, Jr., for a Shingle-style house. The house is a marvel of texture and line. Freer's priceless art collection included the magnificent Peacock Room by James Whistler, which he installed here in 1904 after acquiring it in London. Freer later directed that the room and his collection of Asian art be reinstalled in the Freer Gallery of Art in Washington, D.C. Even if this were not one of very few Shingle-style houses in Detroit, it might still be the finest.

190 COL. FRANK J. HECKER HOUSE

5510 Woodward Ave. at Ferry
Louis Kamper, 1891

Louis Kamper designed this sumptuous three-story mansion in the French Renaissance Chateau style for Colonel Frank J. Hecker, a Union Army officer and wealthy businessman. The lavish, forty-nine-room interior featured Italian Sienna marble, mahogany, and Nubian Egyptian marble details. The structure is one of Detroit's few examples of this Continental style; another, also by Kamper, is the Eighth Precinct Police Station (160). Both stand in contrast to Lloyd's mix of Chateau and Romanesque in the David Whitney House (127) down the avenue. The Hecker house today is occupied by law offices.

188

189

190

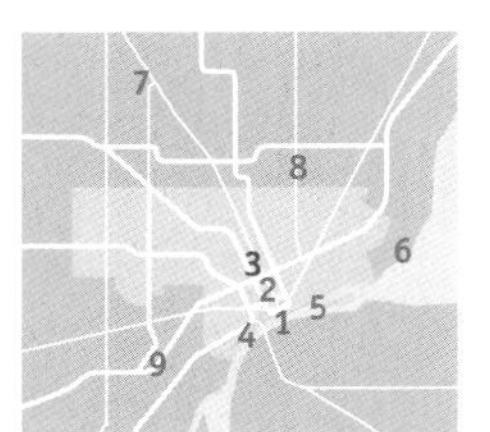

1 Downtown
2 Midtown
3 **North**
4 West
5 East
6 Grosse Pointe Lakeshore
7 Cranbrook
8 GM Technical Center
9 Ford's Dearborn

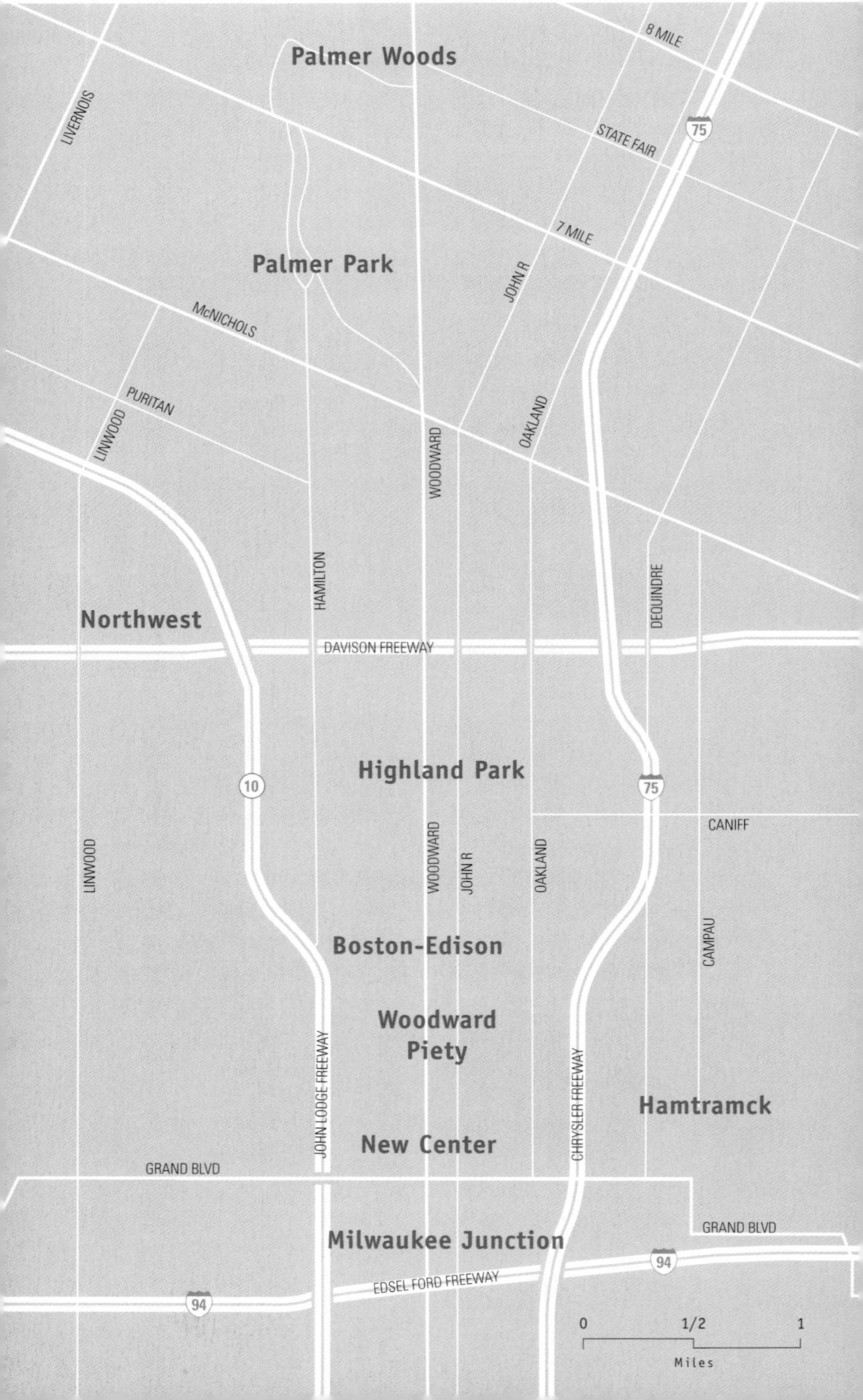

Palmer Woods

8 MILE

LIVERNOIS

75

STATE FAIR

7 MILE

Palmer Park

JOHN R

McNICHOLS

PURITAN

LINWOOD

WOODWARD

OAKLAND

HAMILTON

DEQUINDRE

Northwest

DAVISON FREEWAY

Highland Park

10

75

CANIFF

LINWOOD

WOODWARD

JOHN R

OAKLAND

Boston-Edison

CAMPAU

Woodward Piety

JOHN LODGE FREEWAY

CHRYSLER FREEWAY

Hamtramck

New Center

GRAND BLVD

GRAND BLVD

Milwaukee Junction

94

EDSEL FORD FREEWAY

94

0 1/2 1

Miles

North

North

Our northward journey follows the Woodward corridor, which serves at once as path and place of orientation. Woodward means many things to many people: ancient trail, main street, pioneer highway, dream cruise. For native Detroiters, Woodward can be a serious line of demarcation that separates East side from West. If you're born fifty feet on either side, you may be typed for life. Indeed, prior versions of this guide succumbed to its geographic clarity, if not its deep-seated connotations. We view Woodward as a connector, a uniter, an urban zipper.

As a geographic label, "North" is therefore proposed here with considerable hesitancy. As we retrace a slow but relentless ripple of suburban expansion, we follow the money, the power, and the glory, from Boston-Edison to Piety Hill. And, our focus on the Woodward corridor unquestionably omits a larger, richer story of special neighborhoods and buildings of note—east and west.

From the end of the Detroit line here, the reader could alternatively skip to the Special Environments section and continue northward to Cranbrook.

Milwaukee Junction

Milwaukee Junction was one of two major railroad interchanges built in the early 1890s to facilitate Detroit's industrial expansion. As a result, this area emerged as the cradle of Detroit's auto industry. Many of the larger plants were built to the east of Woodward. It is here that Ford built his first large-scale factory on Piquette, albeit soon eclipsed by Highland Park. Many other automotive entrepreneurs and related suppliers built plants in the area.

The concentration of early auto-related industrial and commercial buildings west of Woodward has been largely adaptively reused over the years for other purposes. Cadillac's 1905 assembly plant at 450 West Amsterdam, designed by George D. Mason, has served Westcott Paper since 1965. Beneath that modern façade of Henry Ford Health System's administrative center on Second Avenue is the massive Burroughs typewriter factory,

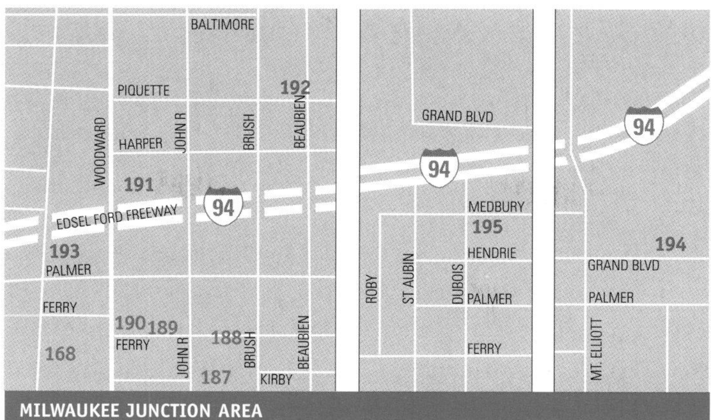

191 HOLY ROSARY ROMAN CATHOLIC CHURCH

192 FORD MOTOR CO., PIQUETTE PLANT

193 CASS MOTOR SALES

194 PACKARD MOTOR CAR CO. PLANT

195 SAINT STANISLAUS HISTORIC DISTRICT

designed by Albert Kahn in 1905. The Cadillac Sales and Service Building at 6001 Cass—Kahn again, 1927, and pictured here—was reused as classrooms for the Police Department and now serves Wayne State University. An exception is the Dalgleish Cadillac showroom at 6160 Cass, designed by Kahn in 1927 for Cadillac's siblings Buick and Pontiac.

At this writing developers are planning a new, mixed-use "urban village," which will complement Wayne State's initiative to create a research park in the area. The particularly handsome, terra cotta-faced former Graphic Arts Building at 41–47 Burroughs, designed by Murphy and Burns in 1926, is intended for residential lofts. As a cornerstone of the research park, the more nondescript former Pontiac dealership at 440 Burroughs (Kahn, 1927) is to be redeveloped as an incubator for new businesses.

Woodward again is the area's organizing central corridor. At either end are literal and figurative gates to the district's past and future. To the south, at Ford Freeway, is one of Detroit's finest Richardsonian Romanesque churches, built just at the time the emerging auto industry staked its claim on the area. To the north, at the junction of Woodward and the still active railway, will be a new inter-modal transportation center, under design at this writing. In time, Detroit will be linked to the region and Chicago via high-speed rail. Emergence, growth, decline, rebirth: what goes around comes around.

191 HOLY ROSARY ROMAN CATHOLIC CHURCH (ST. JOSEPH'S EPISCOPAL)

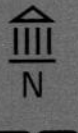

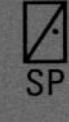

5930 Woodward Ave.
Malcomson and Higginbotham, 1896

This rugged sandstone church is a fine example of the complex massing favored by turn-of-the-century architects working in the Richardsonian Romanesque style. Note how the square tower is modulated by a two-story stair turret on the Woodward side, as well as its battlemented parapet.

Originally conceived and built for the Episcopalians, the church's Greek cross plan is quite similar to the architects' design for the Methodists on Cass Avenue some five years earlier (148). A later Catholic congregation extended the sanctuary eastward to form a more traditional Latin cross plan, except in this instance the chancel necessarily, and uniquely, resides at the foot rather than the head of the cross. The oversized, gilded statue of the Blessed Virgin Mary was added after the original Episcopal congregation sold the church in 1907. The wonderful chapel and tower composition behind (191b) are a poetic refrain of the principal massing.

192 FORD MOTOR COMPANY, PIQUETTE PLANT

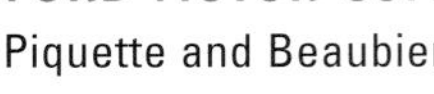

Piquette and Beaubien
Field, Hinchman, and Smith, 1904

Ford's first major automotive factory, this historic structure was also among the last he would build with a heavy timber structural frame. Analogous to the latest release of computer software, Highland Park's lighter and more fire-resistant concrete frame made Piquette obsolete in less than a decade. Beneath the white paint today is a charming and, in hindsight, quaintly romantic façade (192b). Some would call the style "industrial vernacular," which is inclusive enough to embrace a host of references, from medieval, to Palladian, to Chicago commercial. At this writing, efforts are underway to save this important piece of Detroit heritage.

193 CASS MOTOR SALES

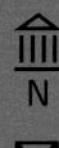

5800 Cass Ave.
Unknown architect, 1928

This three-story Art Deco building was designed as an integrated car showroom, service garage, and business office. The proto-modern, floating entry feature and detailing are handled with energy and discipline. Noticeable Art Deco styling includes the stepped-arch treatment above the front entrance and on the second-story window sections.

191 a

191 b

192 a

192 b

193

194

PACKARD MOTOR CAR COMPANY PLANT

1580 East Grand Blvd.
Albert Kahn and others, 1901–1911

The first large-scale auto plant built in Detroit, the Packard complex included ten buildings. The first nine were constructed using the venerable heavy timber system that built the mills and factories of the first industrial revolution. In Building 10 Kahn designed an efficient frame and floor structure in concrete, a material known well to the Romans but long abandoned. Kahn's innovation was the addition of steel reinforcing, which added considerable strength to the concrete. The new composite material not only could carry weight more economically than timber but was more fire resistant as well. In fact, the "Kahn trussed bar" was primarily invented by Kahn's younger brother Julius, a structural engineer whose training at the University of Michigan was underwritten by his older brother.

For the exterior the architect developed an economical system for infilling the concrete frame, including a large expanse of window sash atop a short masonry wall. As the formula evolved, the wood window installed in Buiding 10 was soon to be replaced by steel sash. The architecture developed here eventually became a factory-design standard worldwide. Historic Building 10 exists but is endangered.

195

SAINT STANISLAUS HISTORIC DISTRICT

Medbury and Dubois
Harry J. Rill; Kastler and Hunter, 1890–1920

This historic district consists of five buildings that made up the former St. Stanislaus Roman Catholic parish. They include the church on the southeast corner of Medbury and Dubois (195a), the elementary school at 2228–38 Medbury, the rectory at 5815 Dubois (195b), the former boiler house, and the high school at 2246 Medbury. This was Detroit's fifth parish established to serve the Polish community. The magnificent baroque church of 1911–1913, with its opulent Beaux-Arts interior, was designed by Harry J. Rill of Detroit. Rill was German-born and had worked in the office of noted church designer Peter Dederichs. As with other Catholic parishes of the era, the church and related buildings anchored the neighborhood for many years. The parish ceased to exist under the archdiocese's 1989 reorganization, and the property was sold. Rill also designed the exceptional Detroit Cornice and Slate Company (28) on St. Antoine.

194 a

194 b

195 a

195 b

New Center

Modern architect and planner Le Corbusier once said, "The plan is the generator." Streets, transit lines, railways, and freeways are among primary generators of city form. Just as the regional rail junction at Milwaukee was constructed to enable the early auto industry, a boulevard ring was built in the late nineteenth century to define Detroit's early limits. Grand Boulevard, the precursor to the modern beltway, was planned as an open horseshoe to the Detroit River, and later, by bridge extensions, to Belle Isle and Windsor. Actually, the route was originally "planned" by Native Americans, who cut the circuitous portage trail to avoid passing the fort on the river.

As writer Joel Garreau suggests, if you look at the intersections of major ring roads and radiating spokes, you are likely to find an "edge city," built or in progress. An edge city is defined as a subcenter remote from but related to an urban core. New Center, at the intersection of Woodward and Grand Boulevard, is just such a place. Indeed, Garreau believes that Detroit's New Center may be the original edge city. What Henry Ford initiated with the Boulevard Building in 1910, William Durant and the Fisher brothers completed just before the Great Depression.

Durant built his corporate headquarters on West Grand Boulevard in 1922 for three stratefic reasons: this location offered the emerging General Motors Corporation convenient access to both Downtown resources and outlying factories; it avoided city taxes; and it was near the new and exclusive residential subdivision Boston-Edison, less than a mile to the north. The equally impressive blockbuster planned by the Fisher brothers followed a different course to the same location. When the Fishers were unsuccessful in assembling enough land Downtown, and at the right price, they moved their urban dream to New Center. To this day New Center represents one of Detroit's most urbane big city environments and an architectural ensemble second to none.

NEW CENTER AREA

196 CADILLAC PLACE
197 ARGONAUT BUILDING
198 FISHER BUILDING
199 ALBERT KAHN BUILDING
200 NEW CENTER ONE BUILDING
201 WILLIAM CLAY FORD II CENTER FOR ATHLETIC MEDICINE
202 NEW CENTER COMMONS
203 HENRY FORD HOSPITAL
204 HENRY FORD HOSPITAL PARKING STRUCTURE
205 LEE PLAZA APARTMENTS
206 BOULEVARD TEMPLE METHODIST HOME

New Center

196  

CADILLAC PLACE (GENERAL MOTORS BUILDING)

3044 West Grand Blvd.
Albert Kahn, 1922

SP

Originally named the Durant Building after the founder of General Motors, this monumental structure is perhaps Albert Kahn's personal masterpiece in commercial architecture. Here neoclassical refinement is applied to the tall building with considerable maturity and skill. Kahn followed Sullivan's three-part skyscraper formula to be sure, with an Italian Renaissance arcade that engages the street, a finely proportioned shaft, and a Corinthian colonnaded crown. What is most impressive about the GM Building is the sheer scale of the enterprise. Upon completion, the fifteen-story structure was the second largest office building in the world, after the Equitable Building in New York. Four identical cross-wings extend from the central backbone, which is subtly expressed in the end elevations. This configuration enabled each of the hundreds of individual offices to enjoy natural light, ventilation, and views. Inside, marble finishes and coffered ceiling vaults contribute a sophisticated, if not luxurious, spaciousness to public lobbies. With General Motors' relocation to Renaissance Center, the State of Michigan has recently adapted this corporate icon to appropriately stately new purposes.

197 PR

ARGONAUT BUILDING

485 West Milwaukee
Albert Kahn, 1930

GM's research and development soon outgrew the General Motors Building Annex on Milwaukee, and Albert Kahn was called upon to design a functional box. The interiors are unremarkable, but the façade's Neo-Romanesque brickwork detailing is richly urbane, especially for its rather subordinate context. A similar handling of masonry banding enlivens Kahn's Griswold Building (84) of the prior year.

196

197

198 FISHER BUILDING

3011 West Grand Blvd. at Second
Albert Kahn, 1929

This landmark at the head of Second Avenue was recently named the "Building of the Century" by members of AIA Detroit. In 1927 the Fisher brothers commissioned Albert Kahn to design the world's finest office building, and to many, including the Architectural League of New York, he delivered. Besides the twenty-six-story tower, the mixed-use complex includes an eleven-story parking garage and a three-thousand-seat theater. An even grander design for the site included an identical twin at the opposite corner and a massive central skyscraper conceived as more than twice the height of the flanking towers. Curtailed by the Depression, the Fisher brothers' blockbuster in New Center would have competed on the area skyline with the Book brothers' seventy-story proposal on Washington, also abandoned with the Crash.

As in any high Art Deco design, multiple stylistic references are brought together under the watchful eye of a master. Besides the obvious arcades, a ground-level motif much preferred by Kahn, the exterior detailing is indebted especially to Romanesque precedents. The Fisher Building's opulent interior features a three-story vaulted arcade finished with forty different varieties of marble, solid bronze trim, and a program of ornament extolling the virtues of commerce, industry, and the arts. Cranbrook artists assisted an army of itinerant European artisans to create a stunning work of old and new world design. Kahn's observation that "architecture is ninety percent business and ten percent art" was inverted here—thanks in no small part to the Fisher brothers' largesse.

199 ALBERT KAHN BUILDING (NEW CENTER BUILDING)

7430 Second Ave.
Albert Kahn, 1931

This refined commercial building was developed by the seven Fisher brothers from material originally intended for the greater Fisher Building (198) complex. Yet, in some respects the architecture here is more consistent and original. The characteristic Art Deco, step-back profile was employed throughout, from overall massing to smaller scale detailing—for example, note the subtle window head designs. This design theme is carried inside to the main lobby's colorful ceiling vault. Kahn moved his firm to the upper floors of the ten-story building upon completion. The department store Saks occupied the lower levels for nearly forty years, until departing for the suburbs. Kahn's firm, on the other hand, has remained in the building that now bears his name, and in the city that bears his imprint.

198

199

200 SP

NEW CENTER ONE BUILDING

3031 West Grand Blvd.
Skidmore, Owings and Merrill (Bruce Graham), 1982

Later and somewhat postmodern, this building is most successful for its urban and architectural integration into the New Center ensemble. Rather than compete with the more figurative expressions of the Fisher (198) and General Motors (196) Buildings, this background foil draws form, shape, and style from its context. The arcade is an abstract quotation that brings unity to the whole. The only regrettable aspect is the wall material, which only distantly simulates stone. Synthetic pretense aside, this is good city building.

201 PR

WILLIAM CLAY FORD II CENTER FOR ATHLETIC MEDICINE

6525 Second Ave.
Neumann|Smith and Associates, 1996

The fitness center is a relatively new building type, and this one is a welcome addition to New Center. Traditional motifs, albeit composed in nontraditional ways, blend into the neoclassical surroundings. Compare the architect's more modernist take on the type several blocks south on Second Avenue/Gullen Mall, on Wayne State's central campus.

202 SP

NEW CENTER COMMONS

Bethune, Pallister, and Seward, West of Woodward Ave.
Various architects, 1900–1925

Admirably restored by General Motors, this traditional neighborhood offers a glimpse of how things once were and how they could be again. Only the decision to rearrange traffic access and patterns might be second-guessed.

203 SP

HENRY FORD HOSPITAL

2799 West Grand Blvd.
Various architects, 1912–

Henry Ford's vision for a new hospital was progressive in its day. Albert Wood's work, anchored by an octagonal entrance pavilion, was dignified and impressive. Many other architects have practiced here since, including but not limited to Malcomson and Higginbotham, Kahn, Rossetti, and Skidmore, Owings, and Merrill. However individually meritorious these later additions may be, the divergent parts seem in search of an aesthetic whole, and are forever vulnerable to sacrifice for the greater functional efficiency of the medical complex. Such is sadly the case with Kahn's imposing Nurses Education Building (1924), pictured at right (203b), which is nearing the end of its useful life.

200

201

202

203 a

203 b

204 HENRY FORD HOSPITAL PARKING STRUCTURE

2799 West Grand Blvd.
Albert Kahn Associates, 1959

The application of sculptural grilles marked a radical departure from the then standard practice of leaving parking structure design relatively unadorned. Compound curved panels of white precast concrete not only screen the cars within but also provide a finer scale to the enclosure without suggesting a human use. There can be too much of a good thing, however, as these structures stretch to near monotonous lengths.

For a remotely similar expression of modern formalism, see also the architect's Bank One headquarters building (109) Downtown. Designed and built at the same time, both appear to be under the influence of Yamasaki.

205 LEE PLAZA APARTMENTS (LEE PLAZA HOTEL)

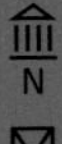

2240 West Grand Blvd.
Charles Noble, 1929

The Lee Plaza was one of Detroit's elaborate apartment hotels in the 1920s heyday of such structures. The fifteen-story, orange-glazed-brick structure is notable for its evocative decoration. This is high-style Art Deco, with a dash of Mediterranean fantasy. The steeply sloped green copper roofs make a strong statement on the skyline. In recent years the building has sat empty, with its lower entrances bricked up. At this writing thieves are making off with valuable ornament for shameful reuse out of town. Endangered, this fine piece of architecture screams for new life.

206 BOULEVARD TEMPLE METHODIST HOME (BOULEVARD TEMPLE METHODIST CHURCH)

2567 West Grand Blvd.
J. Ivan Dise, 1926; renovations by Nathan Levine, 1962, 1970

This remarkable Neo-Gothic composition consists of three contiguous elements designed by J. Ivan Dise in the 1920s, including a central church flanked by a four-story school and a nine-story apartment tower. Given the vacant surroundings today, the complex seems to have been shoehorned onto its site. In 1962 the apartments were converted to retirement units. In the 1970s Nate Levine ingeniously integrated the church and school into the retirement facility, which has been an anchor to its neighborhood for many years.

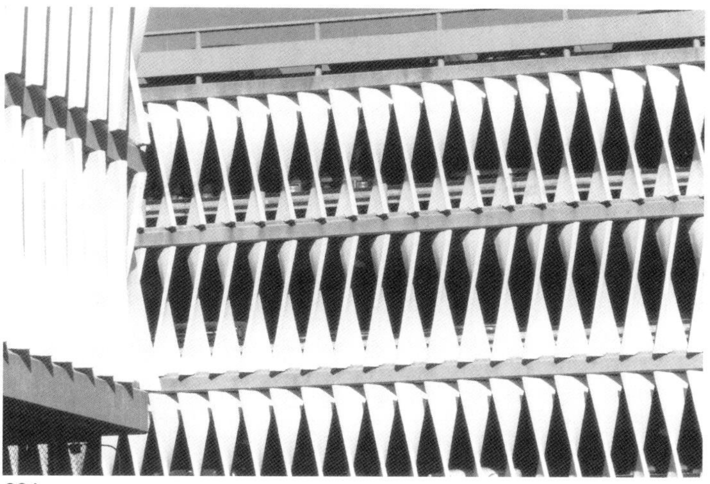
204

205

206

Woodward Piety

This segment of Woodward, from Grand Boulevard north to Highland Park, hosts a proud procession of fine churches and synagogues. The core of the district is known to some as "Piety Hill." Actually, this is the second "Piety Hill"; the first began Downtown and extended north past Brush Park and was also centered on Woodward Avenue.

207 METROPOLITAN UNITED METHODIST CHURCH

8000 Woodward Ave.
William E. N. Hunter, 1926

A fine example of Neo-Gothic, in which historical themes were synthesized with modern sensibilities. The architect, William E. N. Hunter, was a member of the congregation and a well-known Detroit church designer. Famed merchant Sebastian Kresge liberally supported this parish.

208 ABYSSINIA INTERDENOMINATIONAL CHURCH (WOODWARD AVENUE PRESBYTERIAN CHURCH)

8501 Woodward Ave.
Sidney Rose Badgley, 1911

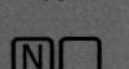

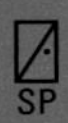

This Neo-Gothic church marks an unusual departure from the standard design fare of the day. The castellated form, developed from a Greek cross plan, is surmounted by a unique octagonal tower-turret at the crossing.

209 SAINT JOHN'S CHRISTIAN METHODIST EPISCOPAL CHURCH (NORTH WOODWARD CONGREGATIONAL CHURCH) AND ROW HOUSES

8715 Woodward Ave.
Hugh B. Clement, 1912; addition by A. R. Morison

This red-brick and limestone-trimmed church came into the world as North Woodward Congregational. Completed in an unpretentious Tudor-Gothic style, with hints of Arts and Crafts, the architecture is consistent with the Puritan roots of the denomination. Notably lacking is a large tower picturesquely massed to one side. The architect of the handsome rowhouses is unknown. Regardless of author, these Arts and Crafts dwellings splendidly complement the whole. The wing between the sanctuary and rowhouses was designed by A. R. Morison in sympathetic restraint. The original piece of the complex, which can be seen only from the alley side, was designed by Malcomson and Higginbotham in 1907. The church later sold to St. John's CME, the first African American congregation to worship on North Woodward's Piety Hill.

TAYLOR
HAZELWOOD
GLADSTONE
3RD
BLAINE
2ND
PINGREE
W. PHILADELPHIA
W. EUCLID
VIGINIA PARK
SEWARD
DELAWARE
WOODWARD
213
212
211
210
209
208
207
JOHN R.
JOSEPHINE
HOLBROOK
KING
ALGER
HAGUE
W. PHILADELPHIA
E. EUCLID
MELBOURNE
MT. VERNON
MARSTON
BRUSH
BEAUBIEN
KINGSLEY
OAKLAND

WOODWARD PIETY AREA

207 METROPOLITAN UNITED METHODIST CHURCH

208 ABYSSINIA INTERDENOMINATIONAL CHURCH

209 SAINT JOHN'S CHRISTIAN METHODIST EPISCOPAL CHURCH AND ROW HOUSES

210 THE FAMILY CENTER

211 LIGHTHOUSE CATHEDRAL

212 SAINT MATTHEW'S AND SAINT JOSEPH'S CHURCH

213 LITTLE ROCK BAPTIST CHURCH

207

208

209

210 THE FAMILY CENTER (UTLEY LIBRARY)

8726 Woodward Ave.
Gustave A. Mueller, 1936; renovated by Hamilton Anderson, 1997

This modest yet symmetrically imposing library has been happily reused for institutional purposes. The style is a mix of late Beaux-Arts Classicism and Prairie influences. The window muntin pattern is original; the teal paint is a later, fresher idea.

211 LIGHTHOUSE CATHEDRAL (TEMPLE BETH-EL)

8801 North Woodward Ave.
Albert Kahn, 1922

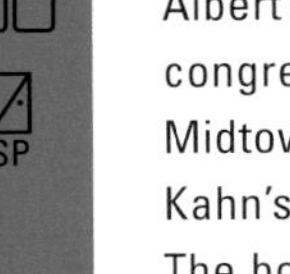

Albert Kahn designed this neoclassical temple for his Reform Jewish congregation after they left their earlier Kahn-designed temple in Midtown—now the Bonstelle Theatre (124). As in the prior work, Kahn's temple form is unchurchlike and more akin to an auditorium. The boxy form and colossal Ionic colonade are studiously impressive. Gracing the interior are ten stained glass windows dedicated to the Ten Commandments. The original congregation worshiped here until 1974, when the building was sold to the Lighthouse Tabernacle.

212 SAINT MATTHEW'S AND SAINT JOSEPH'S CHURCH (ST. JOSEPH'S EPISCOPAL CHURCH)

8850 Woodward Ave.
Nettleton and Weaver, 1926

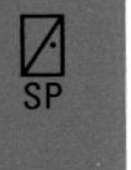

Another fine Gothic-style church, with a tall, narrow-gabled nave extending back to a crossing point with gabled transepts. The church began life as St. Joseph's Episcopal, which relocated here from 5930 Woodward (see entry 191). St. Matthew's, which merged with St. Joseph's in 1971, was Detroit's oldest Black Episcopal congregation.

213 LITTLE ROCK BAPTIST CHURCH (CENTRAL WOODWARD CHRISTIAN CHURCH)

9000 Woodward Ave.
George D. Mason, 1928

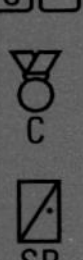

George Mason, one of Detroit's most important architects of the late nineteenth and early twentieth centuries, designed this Gothic-inspired church for a Disciples of Christ congregation. With its purchase in 1978, the Little Rock Baptist congregation began replacing the original clear windows with stained glass. Such is the nature inherent in the Gothic style to be ever enriched over time, which is also to say that a cathedral's work is never done.

210

211

212

213

Hamtramck

Technically outside but nevertheless surrounded by Detroit, Hamtramck is included here as a unique immigrant enclave built by the automotive industry. Named for a French Revolutionary War hero, Hamtramck remained a sleepy little farming village until the early twentieth century. From 1910 to 1920 the city's population grew from nearly 4,000 to 47,000, most of whom emigrated from Poland to build cars for the Dodge Brothers. Beginning in 1980, second and third generations continued the tradition of fine auto making at GM's Poletown plant.

Fewer than a half-dozen housing types are tightly packed across a grid of tree-lined streets. Walkable neighborhoods, in turn, center on important religious and educational facilities. Bringing a sense of continuity and place to the whole is the commercial cruciform of Joseph Campau and Caniff, where the architecture is mostly about an energetic and colorful array of signage.

214 **SAINT FLORIAN CHURCH**

2626 Poland Ave.
Ralph Adams Cram, Cram and Ferguson, 1928

SP

Oh, to be a mouse in the corner of Cram's office when this hearty soul was created. Reviewers may place this building in the Neo-Gothic age because of its date. As we saw at St. Albertus (141) and St. Josaphat (142), red brick is a Polish church architectural tradition. But a medieval assignment may underestimate the design's foresight. Look carefully at the imposing front, with its immense planar surface, abstracted massing and ornamentation, colossal punched opening, and floating rose window, and you might see the future. While St. Florian tips its hat to the modern, it arguably leaps to the postmodern. Korab's poetic photo, reproduced here, summarizes the timeless Gothic tale of cathedral as urban sign and symbol. The interiors are equally impressive.

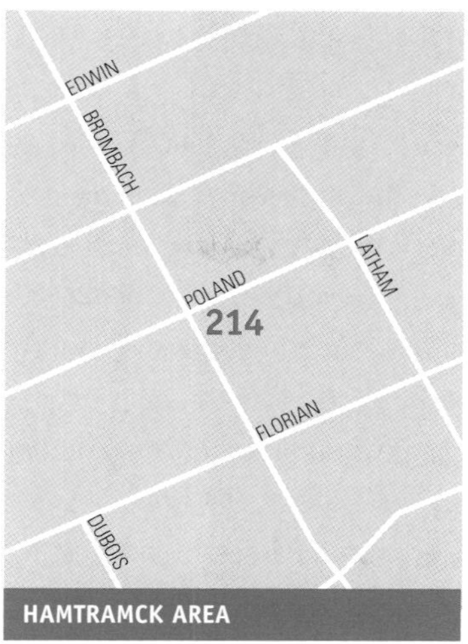

214 SAINT FLORIAN CHURCH

Hamtramck

214

SP

Boston-Edison

Suburban sprawl is nothing new. By the early 1900s Detroit's power elite had leapfrogged out from neighborhoods closer to Downtown to a new area west of Woodward along Boston, Edison, and nearby streets. For a time in the 1910s and 1920s, the clout of this neighborhood rivaled that found anywhere. The new homeowners were an entrepreneurial Who's Who of this still pre-corporate age: Ford, Kresge, Briggs, Fisher, and Siegel were just some of the company-builders who lived here. On a less attractive historic note, Jews had been precluded from Indian Village, which was first subdivided in the same year. Albert Kahn, Malcomson and Higginbotham, and other leading architects contributed designs here. With the development of Boston-Edison, builders had learned to ward off the commercial chaos spreading along Woodward by imposing strict codes; lots had to be of a certain minimum width, houses had to have full basements, and only quality materials built to last were permitted on exteriors. Commercial uses were prohibited from the Woodward lots, and, breaking with tradition, larger houses were developed on block interiors, especially on Boston and Chicago. Not that many of the wealthy families needed encouragement: Boston-Edison quickly became one of the city's grandest neighborhoods, with some of its biggest houses. But the district proved less adept than Indian Village at staving off problems of decline. Still newer enclaves beckoned, and the "first families" of Detroit industry all moved out sooner or later. Some of the larger houses were adapted for institutional or group-home uses. All five of the mansions presented here came into religious hands, at least momentarily, as first families sold or donated these fleetingly ancestral homes. Today, a new generation of urbanists is renovating many of these historic houses, and Boston-Edison remains one of the city's most impressive neighborhoods.

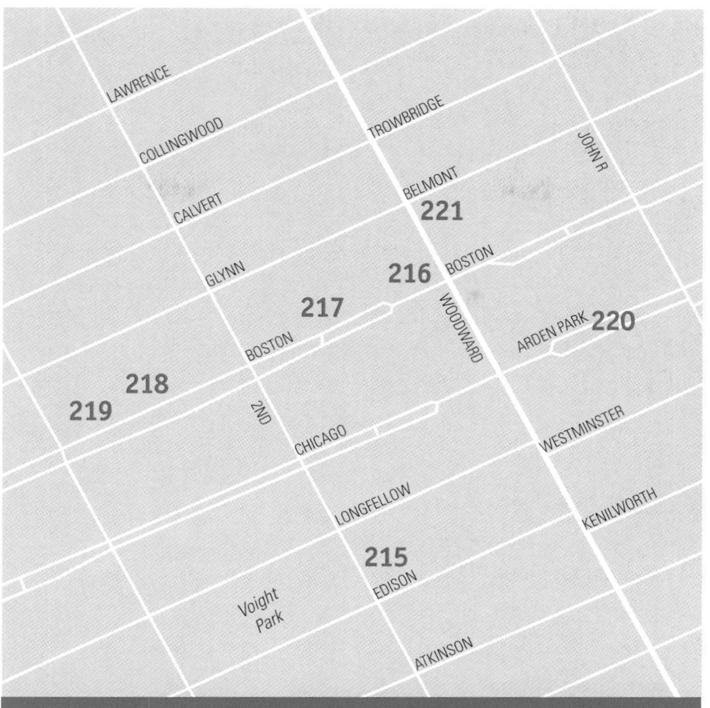

BOSTON-EDISON AREA

215 HENRY AND CLARA FORD HOUSE
216 S. S. KRESGE HOUSE
217 BENJAMIN SIEGEL HOUSE
218 CHARLES T. FISHER HOUSE
219 W. C. BRIGGS HOUSE
220 ARDEN PARK-EAST BOSTON NEIGHBORHOOD
221 CATHEDRAL OF THE MOST BLESSED SACRAMENT

Boston-Edison

215 HENRY AND CLARA FORD HOUSE

140 Edison Ave.
Malcomson, Higginbotham, and Clement, 1908

This solid and stately residence with its contiguous gardens was home to the Fords during some of Henry's most productive years, when Highland Park was the center of his growing business and the period during which he perfected the Model T. The architecture merges popular styles of the day, including Beaux-Arts Classicism and Prairie. T. Glenn Phillips designed the splendid gardens. To satisfy son Edsel's interest in automobile design, the Fords outfitted a machine shop above the garage. But the family soon moved to Dearborn, where an even more expansive estate and industrial empire awaited.

216 S. S. KRESGE HOUSE

70 W. Boston at Woodward Ave.
Meade and Hamilton, 1914

Inspired by Mediterranean villas, this mansion, with its unusual white stucco exterior, remains one of the city's most stunning houses. Like many of Boston-Edison's largest houses, this one wound up in religious hands for a time when the Kresge family donated it to the Catholic archdiocese.

217 BENJAMIN SIEGEL HOUSE

150 West Boston Blvd.
Albert Kahn, 1915

This impressive, thirteen-thousand-square-foot villa-mansion was built for the renowned founder of the B. Siegel department store. Since then the house has served both residential and institutional uses, including the site for the National Conference for Community Justice.

218 CHARLES T. FISHER HOUSE

670 West Boston Blvd.
George D. Mason, ca. 1915

This sprawling Neo-Tudor house built for one of the famed Fisher brothers shows some of the architectural extravagance that would be invested later in the Fisher Building (198). With its chimneys, gables, balconies, carvings, and other touches, this dark-brick house with lighter stone accents was (and probably still is) most people's idea of what Rich Man's Architecture should look like.

215

216

217

218

219 W. C. BRIGGS HOUSE

700 West Boston Blvd.
Chittenden and Kotting, ca. 1915

This light-colored, mottled stone house is a quieter take on an English manor home than the more flamboyant Fisher house (218) next door. As a social note, a Briggs daughter later married a Fisher son.

220 ARDEN PARK-EAST BOSTON NEIGHBORHOOD

Arden Park and East Boston between Woodward and Oakland
Various architects, 1892–1920s

This subdivision was platted, or officially planned, in 1892, predating Boston-Edison and Indian Village by two years. Houses here had to reflect a certain size, cost, and richness of material. This tightly controlled process was meant to ensure an exclusive development for Detroit's emerging entrepreneurial elite. Among residents here were Frederic Fisher, the eldest of the Fisher Body brothers, and J. L. Hudson of Hudson's department store.

The name Arden Park was given to the area in 1910 when realtor-developer Max Broock replaced the name of East Chicago Boulevard. Many prominent architects contributed designs, including George Mason, Albert Kahn, and Smith, Hinchman, and Grylls. And, typical of the early 1900s, a breadth of architectural styles is represented on Arden Park and East Boston, including Italian Renaissance, Colonial Revival, Tudor-Elizabethan, Bungalow, Prairie School, and Shingle style. Black professionals began to move here in the 1940s, including Charles Diggs, who moved from his house on East Frederick (186). The house to the east of the Cathedral (221) was built for John Dodge and has served as the residence of the Archbishop of Detroit since 1980.

221 CATHEDRAL OF THE MOST BLESSED SACRAMENT

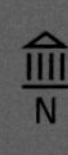

9844 Woodward Ave.
Henry A. Walsh, 1915; additions and renovations by George Diehl, 1950s; renovations by Gunnar Birkerts, 1999–

The early decades of the twentieth century saw an enormous increase in the number of Roman Catholic parishes in the city. Henry Walsh of Cleveland designed this architecturally ambitious church for the surrounding parish, but the construction was not initially completed. In the 1930s Archbishop Mooney considered Blessed Sacrament so fine that he petitioned Rome to move the Diocesan Cathedral here. And in the early 1950s Diehl and Diehl completed the towers and renovated the church to better serve its cathedral functions. One of the city's most imposing Neo-Gothic churches, the Cathedral is now undergoing a new program of restoration and renewal under the eye of Gunnar Birkerts.

219

220

221

Highland Park

Similar to neighboring Hamtramck, Highland Park was farmland until about 1900, when it was transformed virtually overnight to receive a first wave of out-migration from Detroit. The three-square-mile city was organized east and west from Woodward Avenue, and bounded north and south by the Ford and Chrysler plants, now long abandoned for greener pastures.

Housing for the upwardly mobile working class typifies residential architecture of the period. The Highland Heights historic district encompasses such notables as McGregor Library and a brilliant Art Deco apartment building on Woodward. Included also is the well-preserved Stevens' Subdivision, populated with bungalows and colonial revivals influenced by the Arts and Crafts movement. (Parenthetically, the first mile of concrete roadway was poured on a stretch of Woodward just north of the Ford plant in 1909, and to some, has hardly been resurfaced since.)

222 **MCGREGOR PUBLIC LIBRARY**
12244 Woodward Ave.
Tilton and Githens, and Burrowes and Eurich, 1926

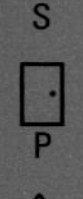

This substantial public library hails from a time of prosperity generated by Henry Ford's Model-T factory up the road. City officials toured libraries in the East and Midwest seeking the best models for their buildings. As a result they chose the New York firm of Tilton and Githens to collaborate with the local firm of Burrowes and Eurich. Classical adaptations include the colorful terra cotta frieze and the unusual coffered entrance apse. The interior saw the book stacks confined to the basement so the entire main floor could remain open to the public. At this writing the library is closed due to an operational funding crisis.

223 **TRINITY UNITED METHODIST CHURCH**
13100 Woodward Ave.
George D. Mason, 1923

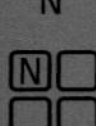

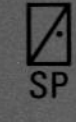

A rather austere Neo-Gothic design by the prolific Detroit architect George Mason, who is here depending more on volumetric massing than detail for architectural effect. Since 1979, the church has served the New Mt. Moriah Baptist congregation.

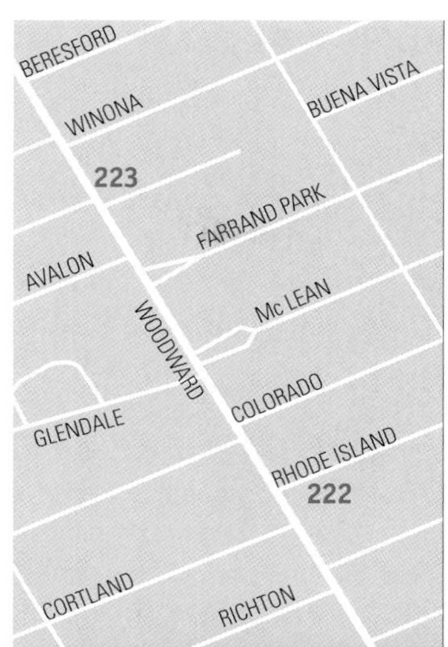

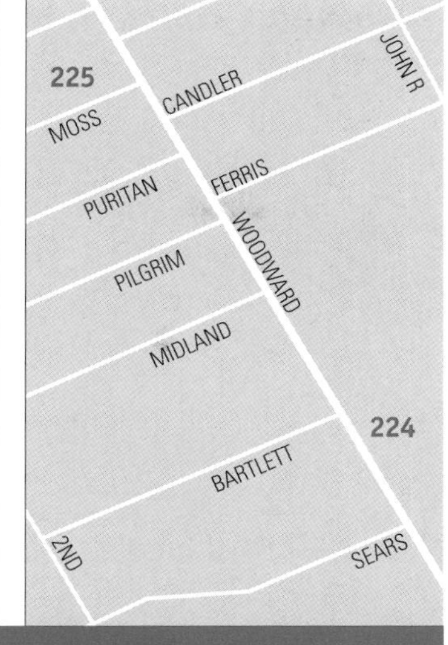

HIGHLAND PARK AREA

- 222 MCGREGOR PUBLIC LIBRARY
- 223 TRINITY UNITED METHODIST CHURCH
- 224 FORD MOTOR COMPANY, HIGHLAND PARK PLANT
- 225 MEDBURY-GROVE LAWN NEIGHBORHOOD

222

223

224 **FORD MOTOR COMPANY, HIGHLAND PARK PLANT**
15050 Woodward Ave.
Albert Kahn, 1909–1920

Highland Park was the intermediate step in Ford's revolutionary development of the modern assembly-line factory and Kahn's comparably pioneering architecture to support it. An all-concrete structure replaced the heavy timber technology employed on Piquette (192). In turn, Highland Park's more functional design was ultimately perfected in the single-story Rouge Plant in Dearborn, begun, astonishingly, less than a decade later. In his first drawings of the Highland Park site, Kahn placed the administrative building in the center, but Ford had a bigger idea. The plant, he advised his architect, would need to develop from its Woodward edge and spread eastward to entirely use the site's 180-plus acres.

At Highland Park Plant 1, Kahn and Wilby refined the wall system first explored at the Packard plant (194) on East Grand Boulevard. The concrete frame was infilled with brick panels and steel industrial window sash imported from England. The end bays were designed to create a more massive effect of corner bastions, which visually halt the repetitive modular bays. In time this pragmatic construction recipe, with artful seasoning, would be replicated hundreds of times throughout the United States and abroad.

Nicknamed the "Crystal Palace," the initial 860-foot-long plant complex fulfilled the inventor's vision of housing an entire operation under one roof, with no open courts and no dividing walls. To compensate for the reduction in perimeter walls, Kahn brought in great quantities of natural light through roof monitors. The architect firmly believed that this achieved a dual benefit of saving energy and enhancing worker morale. Kahn's functionalist interiors, especially the crane-way canyons with projecting balconies (Plants 3 and 4, 224b), inspired the early masters of modern architecture.

The administration building, built in two vertical stages, was dressed up for the Woodward frontage with studied proportions, fine brick and stone detailing, decorative glazed tiles, and a finishing cornice. While still standing, this globally historic structure is endangered.

225 **MEDBURY-GROVE LAWN NEIGHBORHOOD**
Eason, Moss, and Puritan Aves.
Various architects, 1910–1930

Believed by the State Historic Preservation Office to contain one of Michigan's most outstanding collections of single-family bungalows and variations on the type, this neighborhood includes two subdivisions developed in the period from 1910 to 1930. Craftsman detailing is much in evidence.

224 a

224 b

225

Northwest

A side trip to Focus:HOPE and the University of Detroit Mercy campus is worth the while. What's interesting about the three contemporary university buildings included here is their common departure from the eclectic underpinning of the campus. The original building and landmark tower were designed in a Spanish style that pays homage to the origins of St. Ignatius Loyola, founder of the Jesuit order. The modern idiom soon lost considerable favor yet now is enjoying some resurgence.

226 FOCUS:HOPE CENTER FOR ADVANCED TECHNOLOGIES

S SP

1355 Oakman Blvd.
Original architect unknown; renovation by Smith, Hinchman, and Grylls, 1994

An inspired adaptation of an earlier factory, this nonprofit center is now used to train a new generation of machinists under the fitting title of Focus:HOPE. The award-winning interior is exceptional.

227 FISHER ADMINISTRATIVE CENTER

SC SP

University of Detroit Mercy McNichols Campus
Gunnar Birkerts and Associates, 1966

Although few in number, Birkerts's buildings in Detroit exemplify the rich quality of his international achievement. Each of his works seems to be approached as an opportunity to explore the essence of an architectural problem, resulting in a statement that often exceeds the immediate project. That's the case here, in this seeming experiment for a taller building. Base, shaft, and crown are clearly articulated. The roof is suspended from the core with encased cables, which then translate to surface columns that support the office floors.

No small degree of Birkerts's legacy is his mastery at manipulating scale and the observer's perception of size, familiar and otherwise. For example, the size of this structure is surprisingly small and, to some, disappointingly so. In any event, Birkerts's architecture cannot be reduced to two dimensions, but forces us to visit and study his buildings firsthand.

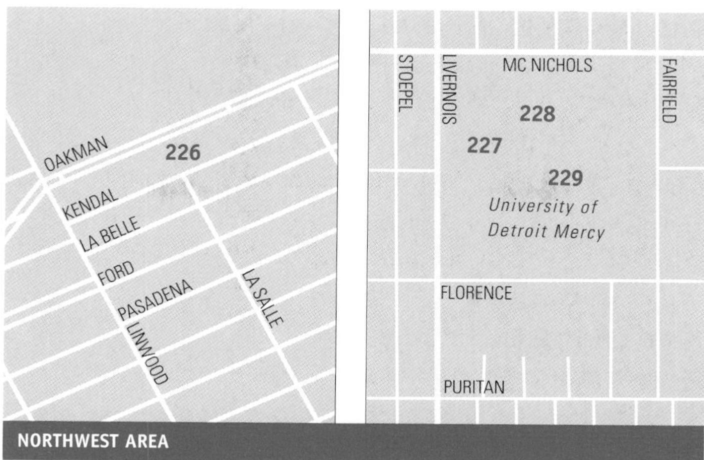

NORTHWEST AREA

226 FOCUS: HOPE CENTER FOR ADVANCED TECHNOLOGIES

227 FISHER ADMINISTRATIVE CENTER

228 UNIVERSITY CENTER ANNEX

229 FORD LIFE SCIENCES BUILDING

226

227

228 S SP

UNIVERSITY CENTER ANNEX

University of Detroit Mercy McNichols Campus
Tarapata-MacMahon-Paulsen Associates, 1970

If Birkerts's nearby office towerette is about artful structuralism, this gutsy building is about expressive construction. Practically devoid of mediating articulation, it almost appears as if the study model was built in full size.

229 SC SP

FORD LIFE SCIENCES BUILDING

University of Detroit Mercy McNichols Campus
Glen Paulsen and Associates, 1967

Monumental and abstract, this building's human scale and warmth is almost completely reduced to, and dependent on, the brick. A bold move in the modern idiom.

228

229

SP

Palmer Park

Bounded by McNichols, Pontchartrain, and Covington
Various architects, 1925–1965

By the 1920s many middle-class families had accepted the idea of living in apartments instead of houses, as evidenced by this special place. The Palmer Park Historic District includes some forty apartment buildings developed in the 1920s and 1930s, with designs ranging from the more exotic to the severely modern. Buildings from the 1920s include an eclectic mix of Egyptian, Spanish, Mediterranean, Venetian, Tudor, and Moorish revival styles, while the 1930s witnessed more modern explorations in Art Deco and International styles. Interspersed with the historically designated buildings are many other apartments built through the mid-1960s that are compatible with the character of the earlier work but not included in the historic district. A general consistency of building height, material, and craftsmanship provides a pleasing unity to the variety of architectural expression. With its relieving open space amenity, Palmer Park is a model of high-density residential planning and design.

230

P

MERRILL FOUNTAIN

Palmer Park
Carrere and Hastings, 1901; relocated, 1926

The City Beautiful "movement" was taken a bit too literally, as this ornament was moved from Campus Martius in 1926. Once beautiful, and now in need of care, the fountain was designed by a prominent New York purveyor of refined French Classicism.

231

N

PR

WHITMORE PLAZA

300 Whitmore Rd.
Weidmaier and Gay, 1928

This exceptionally fine Art Deco building with exotic Moorish accents is a focal point of Palmer Park. The popular U-shaped footprint provides an inviting forecourt, and the sculptural massing, stepping as it ascends, is a compelling idea brilliantly executed. The color palette richly reinforces the whole.

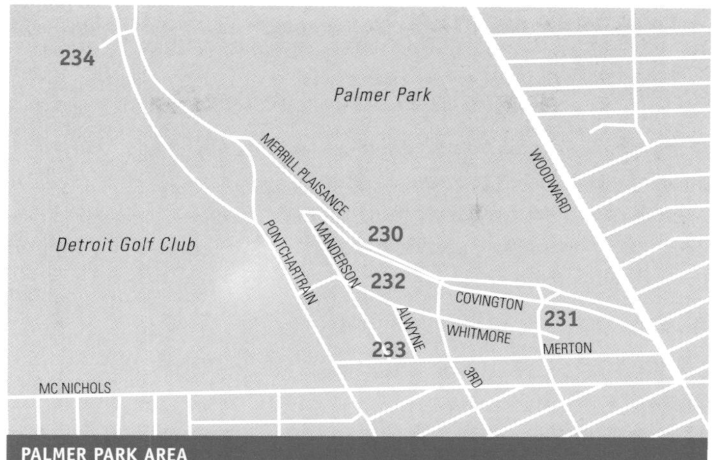

PALMER PARK AREA

230 MERRILL FOUNTAIN

231 WHITMORE PLAZA

232 PALMER PARK APARTMENTS

233 SAINT PAUL TEMPLE OF THE APOSTOLIC FAITH

234 DETROIT GOLF CLUB

230

231

232  PR

PALMER PARK APARTMENTS

900 Whitmore Rd.
Robert West, 1938

A precocious expression of Bauhaus Modern applied to apartment building design. Note the several creative variants on corner window openings. The decorative masonry panels suggest a less than total commitment to the new aesthetic, but the whole is the equal of any of its generation, here or abroad.

233 N SP

SAINT PAUL LIFE AND PRAISE CENTER CHURCH (TEMPLE ISRAEL)

17400 Manderson
William E. Kapp, 1949, 1956, 1960

Originally a Jewish temple, this striking composition fits into its neighborhood, onto its site, and around its faith. The elemental massing reveals successive building stages of sanctuary, social hall, and school. The sanctuary drum finesses the site's acute-angled corner and anchors the whole. The Egyptian temple frontispiece both dignifies and celebrates entry to the sacred realm. The Art Deco expression is at once ancient, classical, and modern, and as such is at home in Palmer Park. But this is more than Deco dubiously stretched to 1949; this is a unique statement by a creative architect searching for an appropriate response to physical contexts and ancient text, including the first books of architecture.

234 PR

DETROIT GOLF CLUB

17911 Hamilton
Albert Kahn, 1916

Kahn returned to the Arts and Crafts or English Domestic Revival style for inspiration here. The fine brickwork, interesting roof massing, and broad verandas create an atmosphere of charm and relaxation.

232

233

234

Palmer Woods

Woodward Ave. and Seven Mile Rd.
Ossian Cole Simonds, 1915; numerous architects, 1915–1970

Encompassing nearly two hundred acres and three hundred structures, Palmer Woods was designed for pleasant rural effect. Streets twist and turn and ramble like country lanes. Mini-estates picturesquely deploy on large lots to create an isolated world remote from, yet accessible to, the city. The layout can be traced to Frederick Law Olmsted's 1868 plan of Riverside, Illinois, which is credited, (or blamed), as the fountainhead of the suburban subdivision. Yet, unlike Riverside, which was planned around its hilly terrain, Palmer Woods is as flat as a pancake. In lesser hands than noted landscape architect Ossian Cole Simonds, the effect could have been more than a little contrived. What distinguishes this early sub from its seemingly inexhaustible supply of knock-offs is the quality and variety of its residential architecture. In a listing familiar to Detroit's finest neighborhoods, architectural styles range from Neo-Tudor and Neo-Georgian to Mediterranean and even modern. Many of Detroit's finest residential architects are represented here, including Marr, Dise, Crane, Halpin, O'Dell, Harley, and Day. And while the architecture generally tilts toward the past, the likes of such important modernists as Frank Lloyd Wright and Minoru Yamasaki snuck in signature pieces at mid-century. Palmer Woods today remains a thriving upscale neighborhood, home to many of the city's leaders.

235 TURKEL HOUSE

2760 West Seven Mile Rd.
Frank Lloyd Wright, 1956

Frank Lloyd Wright designed many houses in Michigan but only one within the city limits of Detroit. In 1955 Dorothy Turkel commissioned this house after reading Wright's *The Natural House*. Wright responded with an example of what he called "Usonian Automatic," a house designed with inexpensive building materials, yet invigorated with the qualities of openness he valued and preached. The L-shaped, four-thousand-square-foot house is sited perpendicularly to the street with Wright's signature low-key entry. Built entirely of concrete blocks, including more than three dozen custom designs, Turkel is a rare two-story edition in the Usonian series. Like any modernist statement in a mostly Tudor neighborhood, the new house caused some shock, if not stir, among its neighbors, but that didn't seem to bother either the client or "the master."

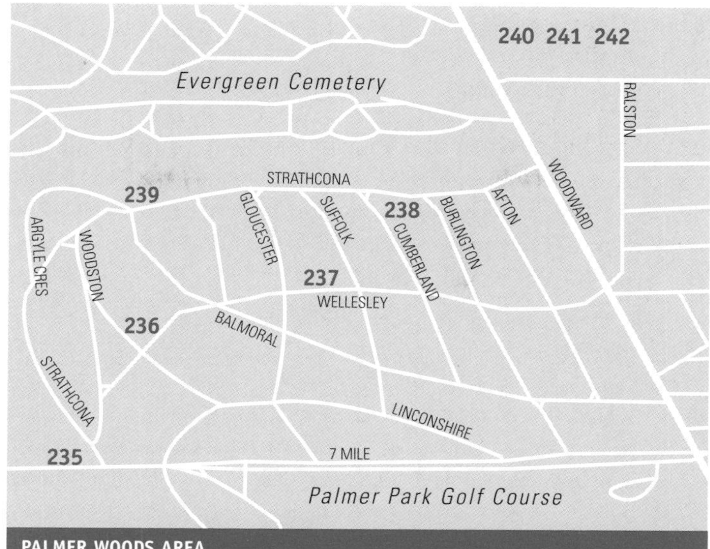

PALMER WOODS AREA

235 TURKEL HOUSE
236 BISHOP GALLAGHER HOUSE
237 JOHN KUNSKY HOUSE
238 CHESTER SOUTHER HOUSE
239 S. BROOKS BARRON HOUSE
240 MICHIGAN STATE FAIRGROUNDS MAIN BUILDINGS
241 U. S. GRANT HOUSE, MICHIGAN STATE FAIRGROUNDS
242 MICHIGAN STOVE, MICHIGAN STATE FAIRGROUNDS

Palmer Woods

235

236 BISHOP GALLAGHER HOUSE

1880 Wellesley Dr.
Maginnis and Walsh, 1925

Ecclesiastical power may have its earthly symbols. This Tudor Revival mansion was built in 1924–1925 for Bishop Michael J. Gallagher at a time when European immigration was swelling the number and influence of Detroit's Roman Catholics. Look closely at the medallions, crests, and shields on the exterior and you'll see angels, papal insignia, and other religious inspirations. The interior was among Detroit's most regal, with marble fireplaces, intricate carvings, Pewabic tile inlays, and extensive oak paneling. In 1989, in a more secular world, the archdiocese sold the house after first taking out all religious objects, including an altar and stations of the cross. Former Detroit Pistons star John Salley then owned the house for a time.

237 JOHN KUNSKY HOUSE

1630 Wellesley Dr.
C. Howard Crane, 1924

Detroit's great theater architect produced an extremely picturesque version of a Tudor cottage here. The slate roof, gables, and prominent chimneys nearly leap out. Perhaps Crane was so used to playing the showman in his movie palaces that he couldn't resist a little stage-setting. This rare venture into residential design was crafted for one of Detroit's most important theater owners and builder of the State, the Capitol, and others, all designed by Crane.

238 CHESTER SOUTHER HOUSE

19551 Burlington
Leonard B. Willeke, 1925

In an Arts and Crafts house, materials and workmanship are everything. The only house in Palmer Woods completely faced in stone is here elevated to domestic art. For all the romance of the stone, Souther lacks the picturesque massing often found in the English Domestic Revival style. Willeke's Jackson house (304), located in Indian Village and completed several years earlier, is similarly rich in surface treatment and simple, even bulky, in form.

239 S. BROOKS BARRON HOUSE

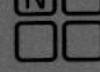

19631 Argyle Crescent
Yamasaki, Leinweber, and Associates, 1955

A rare example of International style in Palmer Woods. Rarer still, Yamasaki's serenely introverted design draws inspiration from centuries-old Asian traditions of residential design, from its disciplined geometry to its integration of house and garden.

236

237

238

239

240

MICHIGAN STATE FAIRGROUNDS MAIN BUILDINGS

Woodward Ave. and Eight Mile Rd.
Lynn W. Fry, State of Michigan Building Department, 1922–1926

NS
P$

The Fairgrounds is heir to America's oldest state agricultural fair. A complex of three monumental works in the neoclassical mode includes the Riding Coliseum, Dairy Cattle Building, and Agriculture Building, all designed by Lynn Fry with the State Building Department. Appropriately included in the national and state registers.

241

U. S. GRANT HOUSE, MICHIGAN STATE FAIRGROUNDS

Woodward Ave. and Eight Mile Rd.
Unknown architect, 1849

S
P$

A representative example of mid-nineteenth-century urban residential architecture. Yet another example of Detroit archi-mobility, this structure was moved first from Fort Street, then parked within the Fairgrounds. The Grants occupied this house from 1849 to 1850 on an early tour of duty.

242

MICHIGAN STOVE, MICHIGAN STATE FAIRGROUNDS

Woodward Ave. and Eight Mile Rd.
Unknown original designer, 1893; restoration by SmithGroup, 1998

S
S
P$

Is it sculpture, architecture, or advertisement? It is undeniably fifteen tons of stove, built (of wood) for the 1893 Columbian Exposition in Chicago to celebrate Detroit as the stove capital of the world. AIA's award jury observed, "This is a serious effort of applying architecture to a historical icon through great craft and humor. It symbolizes Detroit's rich manufacturing heritage while establishing a legacy in fantasy architecture." Detroit's legacy is indeed more than just cars, although we cannot confirm a prior subculture of "stove guys."

AGRICULTURAL BUILDING

240

241

GARLAND
GARLAND
The Michigan Stove Company
THE MICHIGAN STOVE AND THE STATE FAIR

242

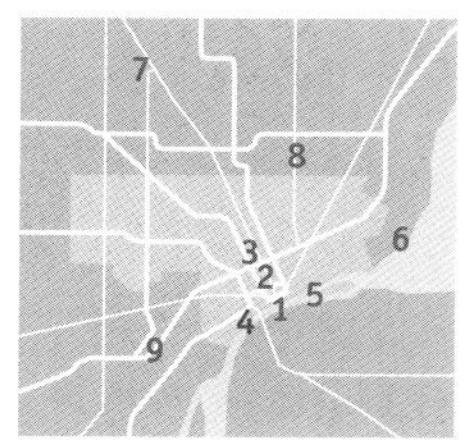

1 Downtown
2 Midtown
3 North
4 **West**
5 East
6 Grosse Pointe Lakeshore
7 Cranbrook
8 GM Technical Center
9 Ford's Dearborn

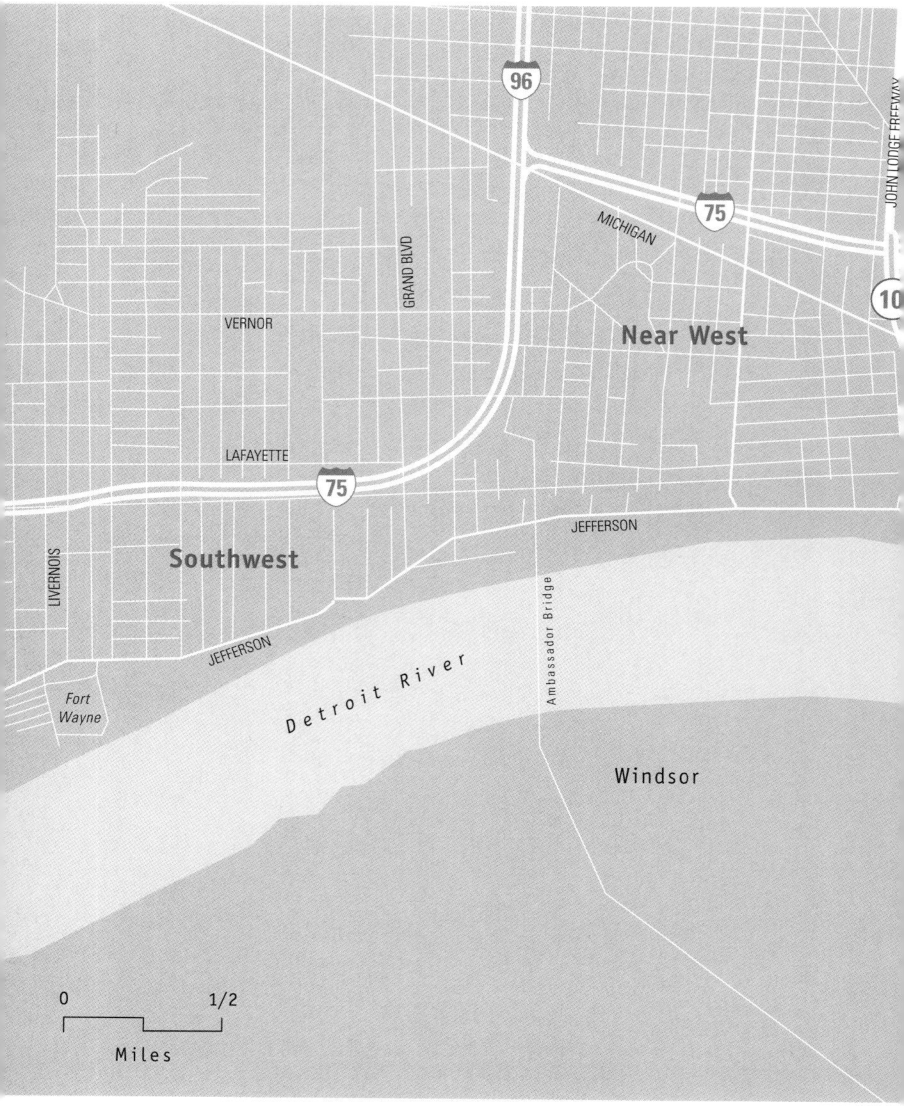

96
JOHN LODGE FREEWAY
75
MICHIGAN
10
GRAND BLVD
VERNOR
Near West
LAFAYETTE
75
JEFFERSON
Southwest
LIVERNOIS
Ambassador Bridge
JEFFERSON
Detroit River
Fort Wayne
Windsor
0 1/2
Miles

West

West

Heading west, we encounter first the near edge of Downtown and thereafter a riverfront still largely industrial. This highly diverse area boasts a proud past and promising future.

The reader is welcome to continue westward to Ford's Dearborn, as outlined in the Special Environments section. This out-of-sequence departure is perfectly acceptable and alternatively just as logical. We won't tell.

Near West

The near west side of Downtown was dislodged from the core by a freeway gash a half century ago. Today this tiny enclave presents an amazing array of big scale and small. Corktown offer hints of Detroit's rich ethnic heritage. Michigan Central Station was and is an aberration. In a sense, it's the big idea that could have spawned the first edge city, ahead of New Center by nearly a decade. Long vacant, Michigan Central is the ultimate see-through building. Equally empty and sad is the historic ballpark at Michigan and Trumbull. These big promises not kept are enough to give an area a complex. If only some enterprising developer would do just that.

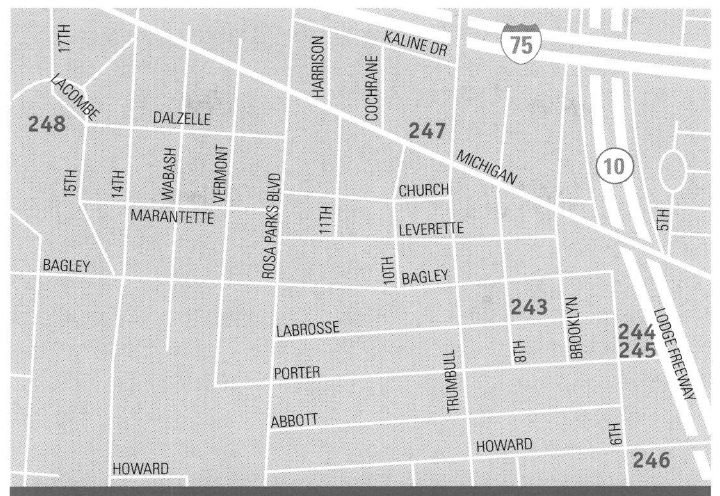

NEAR WEST AREA

243 CORKTOWN NEIGHBORHOOD

244 MOST HOLY TRINITY ROMAN CATHOLIC CHURCH

245 MOST HOLY TRINITY RECTORY

246 DETROIT BUS TERMINAL

247 TIGER STADIUM

248 MICHIGAN CENTRAL RAILROAD STATION

Most Holy Trinity in context

243 CORKTOWN NEIGHBORHOOD

Largely bounded by Lodge Fwy., Porter, Trumbull, Bagley, Rosa Parks Blvd., and Michigan Ave.
Various architects, 1849–1920

Corktown got its name from the thousands of Irish immigrants, most from County Cork—or at least embarking from Cork's port town of Cobh—who filled up the near west side in the mid-nineteenth century. Some of Corktown's houses date to the late 1830s and are thus among the oldest structures still standing in the city. Corktown contains one of the only Federal-era houses in Detroit. The architecturally unassuming little townhouse at 1430 Sixth Street was built about 1830. Styles range from simple frame cottages to more elaborate Queen Anne houses and brick structures. After the Irish moved out, immigrants from Malta and Mexico moved in. Urban renewal in the 1950s, though, reduced the once-sprawling district to a remnant spanning just a few blocks. Many houses have been renovated in recent years, and urban pioneers have added new townhouses and even a bed and breakfast. Today, Corktowners remain proud of what they call Detroit's oldest neighborhood.

244 MOST HOLY TRINITY ROMAN CATHOLIC CHURCH

1062 Porter St.
Patrick C. Keeley, 1856; renovation by Gordon Bugbee and William Worden, 1985

The opening of the Erie Canal in 1825 spurred Irish immigration to Detroit by the early 1830s. Irish Catholics became so numerous that they built their own parish, which initially was sited near what is now Campus Martius. As the Irish filled up the city's west side, the church was moved. The current building was finished and furnished over many years by a parish of few means but considerable faith. Brooklyn architect Patrick Keeley, known for designing hundreds of Catholic churches throughout the United States, designed this elegant landmark in a serenely simple Gothic style.

245 MOST HOLY TRINITY RECTORY

1050 Porter St.
Mason and Rice, 1886

Designed in the popular Romanesque Revival style of the day by one of Detroit's most prominent architectural firms, this dignified rectory is perfectly at ease with the earlier church it serves.

243

244

245

246 **DETROIT BUS TERMINAL**

1001 Howard St.
Kessler Associates, 1994

William Kessler, an accomplished modernist who has left a broadly creative mark on Detroit, here designed a small depot for a tight site. One of his signature pure forms—cylinder—sheathed in shimmering glazed blue tile provides focal interest in this highly functional design.

247 **TIGER STADIUM (NAVIN FIELD)**

Trumbull and Michigan Ave.
Osborn Engineering Co., 1912; later additions, 1923, 1938, 1983

Baseball was played at Michigan and Trumbull since before 1900. The old Bennett Park accommodated 10,000. When it became Navin Field in 1912, seating was expanded to 23,000. Upper-level grandstands were added in 1923. Two more additions in the 1930s brought seating capacity up to 54,000, and the name was changed to Briggs Stadium. Lights were added in 1948. In 1961 the name was changed to Tiger Stadium. Exterior industrial siding was added, unfortunately, in 1983.

In the early 1900s baseball fields were squeezed into crowded urban neighborhoods. Of necessity, designers kept seats close to the playing field, and this became a design virtue that was the hallmark of Tiger Stadium and other early ballparks. Unfortunately, due to the presence of obstructing columns and the absence of luxury suites, this historic site was abandoned for the new Comerica Park in 2000.

248 **MICHIGAN CENTRAL RAILROAD STATION**

Vernor and Michigan Ave.
Warren and Wetmore, and Reed and Stern, 1913

This was an early attempt to marry a magnificent Beaux-Arts terminal, inspired by Roman baths, to a functionally efficient office tower. The station's siting here was determined by the then existing rail yards tunnel to Canada. The layout of Roosevelt Park in front of the station is an example of the City Beautiful movement in planning that swept America at the turn of the twentieth century. As a set piece, Michigan Central was further intended as the terminus to a grand boulevard that would boldly link up to the Cultural Center across town.

The decline of American railroads led to the abandonment of the terminal itself in the 1980s. Vandalism has reduced this handsome landmark to a ruin. Its current see-through state has even induced a local myth that the sixteen-story tower was never occupied; but these floors were indeed used, albeit with few partitions. Architects Warren and Wetmore are better known for designing New York's Grand Central Station, whose recent preservation offers a model to which Detroit might aspire.

246

247

248

Southwest

The area farther south and west of Downtown embodies an extensive fabric of architecture without architects, ranging from monumental engineering to traditional neighborhoods that work. The landmark Ambassador Bridge lifts off from Detroit's Latino community. Centered on Bagley and extending from 17th to 25th Streets, Mexicantown includes a festive array of ethnic restaurants and shops. Holy Redeemer Church at Vernor and Junction, reputedly modeled after the Church of St. Paul in Rome, is worth a visit. In all, Southwest Detroit moves on without a second thought about elitist architecture or a guide to it.

249 STE. ANNE CATHOLIC CHURCH COMPLEX

NSC SP

1000 Ste. Anne
Albert E. French and Leon Coquard, 1887

Ste. Anne is Detroit's oldest parish and reputed to be the second oldest continuously active Roman Catholic parish in the United States. Cadillac played a role in the founding of the church in the year of his arrival in 1701. Father Gabriel Richard, the first priest to serve in the U.S. Congress, was named pastor a century later. The current church building is the parish's eighth. It was designed by Leon Coquard, a parishioner and an employee of Albert French, in a late Gothic Revival style. Later additions, including the parish hall, were designed by Coquard after he parted with French. The building's elaborate detail, twin spires, flying buttresses, and grand stained glass show influences from France, most appropriate for a French-speaking congregation. A couple of windows from the 1860s remain unaltered and are believed to be the oldest stained glass in Detroit.

250 AMBASSADOR BRIDGE

P$

Fisher Freeway, I-75, at Porter to Ontario 3
Jonathan Jones, engineer for McClintock-Marshall Co., 1929

This is the gee-whiz engineering stuff that complete cityscapes are made of. When built, "The Ambassador" was the longest suspension bridge in the world, extending 9,602 feet with approaches. The exposed cross-bracing and the graceful sweep of the cables provide aesthetic as well as structural integrity. By day or by night, this landmark structure is a dramatic gateway between great lakes and nations.

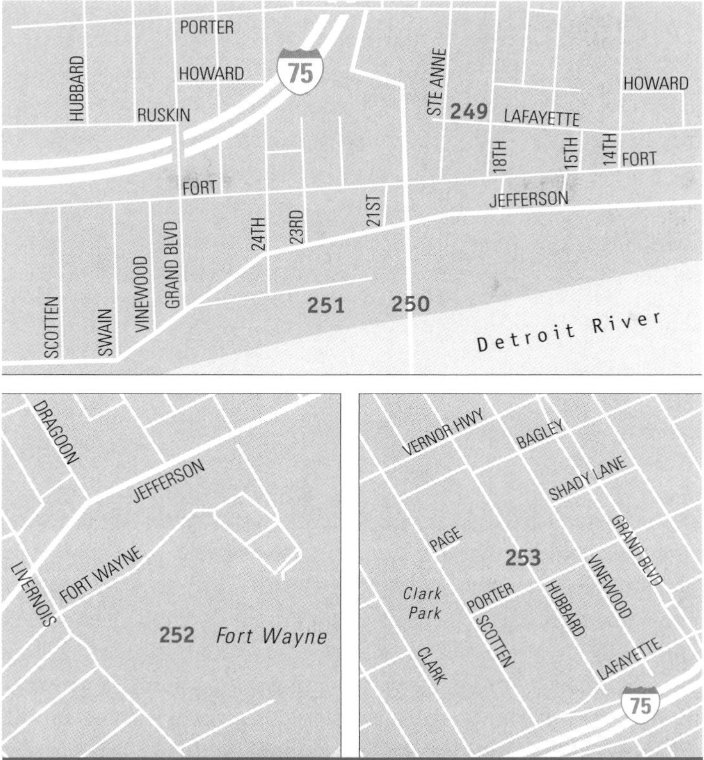

SOUTHWEST AREA

249

250

251

RIVERSIDE PARK SHELTER

Vinewood at the Detroit River
Roger Margerum, 1984

SC P

Designed by one of Detroit's pioneering African American architects, this is a small park and boat launch just downstream from the Ambassador Bridge. It includes an elegant little pavilion with a roof frame in the shape of a pinwheel. Against the bridge it's evocative of a Bauhaus coffee table. The park remains a haunt of idlers, anglers, and river-watchers.

252

FORT WAYNE

6053 West Jefferson Ave.
Lt. Montgomery C. Meigs, 1845–1850

NS SP$

Strategically positioned at a river bend, Fort Wayne was designed after the works of Sebastien Vauban, a French engineer. The original fort, prompted by concern about an impending attack from Canada, was a square bastion with sand embankments. The three-and-a-half-story barracks building follows Georgian and Federal precedents in New England institutional design. But as Hawkins Ferry noted, "the only token of Federal elegance is the elliptical window in the central pediment." Never attacked, except by architecture critics, the fort was technically obsolete before it was built. Now vacant, this immensely valuable piece of Detroit history and waterfront real estate is endangered. Fort Wayne's designing officer much later gave us the awesome National Building Museum in Washington, D.C. (1882–1887). Military design is not necessarily oxymoronic.

253

HUBBARD FARMS HISTORIC DISTRICT

Bounded by Vernor, Grand Blvd., Lafayette, and Clark
Various architects, 1870–1920s

C SP

This historic district includes about three hundred buildings built on land once largely owned by Bela Hubbard, a nineteenth-century explorer, naturalist, geologist, author, lawyer, and civic benefactor. Unlike, say, Indian Village, which was platted and developed in a unified way, property in Hubbard Farms was subdivided by different individuals and sold as house lots at different times under different restrictions. As a result, a great variety of building uses and types evolved. The area similarly possesses a rich architectural history, with styles ranging from Queen Anne and Italianate to bungalows. It is also notable as one of Detroit's most prominent pre-automobile districts, with only a handful of houses possessing driveways. A subtly enriching touch is the slight elevation of the front yards above the sidewalk and street—a thoughtful detail that can make all the difference in the world.

251

252

253

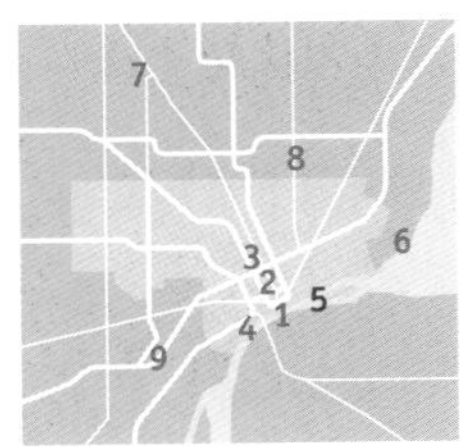

1 Downtown
2 Midtown
3 North
4 West
5 East
6 Grosse Pointe Lakeshore
7 Cranbrook
8 GM Technical Center
9 Ford's Dearborn

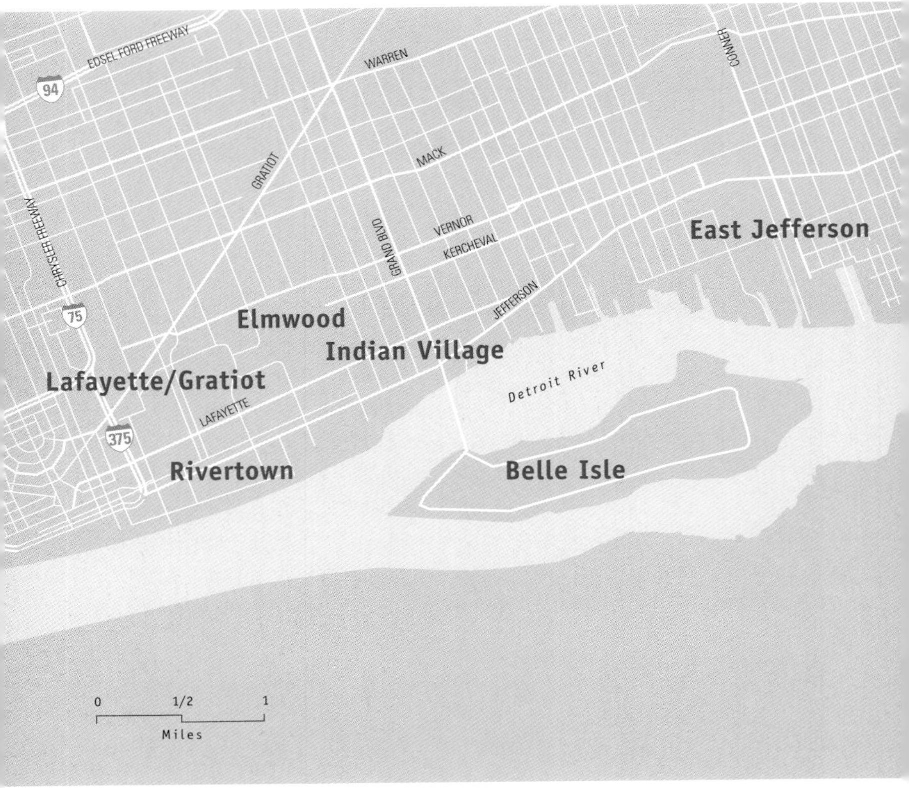

EDSEL FORD FREEWAY
94
WARREN
CONNER
MACK
GRATIOT
CHRYSLER FREEWAY
GRAND BLVD
VERNOR
KERCHEVAL
East Jefferson
JEFFERSON
75
Elmwood
Indian Village
Lafayette/Gratiot
Detroit River
LAFAYETTE
375
Rivertown
Belle Isle
0 1/2 1
Miles

East

East

Eastward ho from the Downtown core, the riverfront and Jefferson corridor vie for attention in an ongoing conversation of architectural interest and natural beauty. Through civic resolve and the power of visionary planning, the greater whole will someday reemerge as an exceptional place to live, learn, worship, work, and play. The selections here merely hint at the potential.

The reader is invited to extend this journey to its historically inevitable conclusion in the Grosse Pointes.

Rivertown

Rivertown encompasses Detroit's early expansion along Jefferson Avenue and the Detroit River, beginning at the present Renaissance Center and extending to the Belle Isle Bridge.

The Jefferson corridor has led many lives. By the late eighteenth century it was a desirable place to live outside the confines of the fort and frontier town. By the mid-nineteenth century rapidly developing industries and rail lines encroached on its quality of life. Beginning with the turn of the twentieth century, a mix of apartment buildings, institutions, clubs, and retail uses made for a vibrant, albeit short-lived, urban village.

Since the mid-twentieth century, planning and development in the area has been sporadic and unfulfilled. In the greater context, the Rivertown experience has been a Dickensian best and worst of times. Highlights include the emerging string of linked waterfront parks and the Stroh family's commitment to revitalizing the Parke-Davis complex. Points of darkness are the losses of some extremely rare pieces of architecture and history, most notably including the Chene House, the Walker House, and the Campau House.

Rivertown's long-term horizon can hardly be anything but bright, given the awesomely reliable resource of the Detroit River. The completion of a continuously green shoreline will be one of the city's defining and reaffirming moments. In the more

RIVERTOWN AREA

254 CHRIST CHURCH, DETROIT
255 THOMAS A. PARKER HOUSE
256 SIBLEY HOUSE
257 PALMS APARTMENT HOUSE
258 CHARLES TROWBRIDGE HOUSE
259 CROUL-PALMS HOUSE
260 CHRISTOPHER MOROSS HOUSE
261 YWCA
262 GREENING OF DETROIT PARK PAVILION
263 ST. AUBIN PARK AND MARINA
264 CHENE PARK AND AMPHITHEATER
265 MCGREGOR CARRIAGE HOUSE
266 PASADENA APARTMENTS
267 WAYNE STATE UNIVERSITY UPC RESEARCH CLINIC
268 JOHN N. BAGLEY HOUSE
269 WILLIAM H. WELLS HOUSE
270 GARDEN COURT APARTMENTS
271 STROH RIVER PLACE
272 UAW-GM CENTER FOR HUMAN RESOURCES
273 THE PLAYERS CLUB
274 LIGHTHOUSE SUPPLY DEPOT
275 THE LOFTS

foreseeable future, Jefferson Avenue may experience a generation or two of development opportunism before it reemerges as a vital urban place.

In the meantime, many significant Rivertown structures are in danger of extinction. Most notably, the Dry Dock Engine Works Building at Atwater and Orleans is perhaps the most important surviving nineteenth-century industrial building in Detroit, and certainly eligible to be a National Historic Landmark. Beneath that rather austere exterior is an innovative steel frame structure (see drawing below). And it was here that a young man named Henry Ford acquired machinist skills as an apprentice to naval architect and master shipbuilder Frank Kirby.

Dry Dock Engine Works interior

254 NS SP

CHRIST CHURCH, DETROIT

960 East Jefferson Ave.
Gordon W. Lloyd, 1863–1880

Christ Church is the oldest Protestant church in Michigan still located on its original site. Construction began in 1860; the chapel was consecrated in 1863; and the whole was completed about 1880. The style is English Gothic Revival, yet adapted to modern needs and constraints. Key decorative elements include the large window with tracery over the entrance, the squared tower with its Germanic wedge-shaped roof, and the pinnacles crowning the buttresses on the left side of the church. The "backside" is wonderfully picturesque (254b). Lloyd was a young English architect, classically trained, who settled in Detroit in 1858 and late in his career was the dean of Detroit architects.

255 NC PR

THOMAS A. PARKER HOUSE

975 East Jefferson Ave.
Gordon W. Lloyd, 1868

This Gothic Revival house, built for a wealthy grocer and real estate developer, typifies the sober residential work that Gordon Lloyd produced in the mid-1800s. Note similarities with the Lloyd-designed Christ Church (254) across the street. Much of Lloyd's important residential work has been lost, although the Parker House and David Whitney, Jr., House (127) on Woodward Avenue survive.

256 NS PR

SIBLEY HOUSE

976 East Jefferson Ave.
Unknown architect, 1848

Sarah Sibley, widow of Judge Solomon Sibley, built this frame house for herself and her two daughters in 1848. The style is Greek Revival, popular at the time in city and country alike. The Sibley family lived in the house until selling it to the neighboring Christ Church (254) in 1925. It became the church's rectory in 1946.

254 a

254 b

255

256

257 PALMS APARTMENT HOUSE

SC PR

1001 East Jefferson Ave.
George Mason and Albert Kahn, 1902

This six-story, upper-class apartment house was a collaborative effort of Albert Kahn and his former employer, George Mason. The building form was reputedly designed by Mason. The innovative structure is the work of Kahn and marks one of the very first applications of steel-reinforced concrete to apartment design. But the design stopped short of exploiting the aesthetic possibilities of the concrete frame, as the exterior was built with more conventional, load-bearing walls. Kahn would shortly thereafter develop the full potential of the new medium in his factory designs. Wittingly or otherwise, Palms expresses an unresolved tension between past, present, and future.

258 CHARLES TROWBRIDGE HOUSE

NSC PR

1380 East Jefferson Ave.
Unknown architect, 1826

This house is the oldest known structure in the city. The sedate Greek Revival style was later "updated" with Victorian features, such as the bay window. A banker and later mayor of the city, Trowbridge built his house as a two-story, "five-window," with a centered door. The central hall of the 1826 original was entered off both Rivard and Jefferson, then reoriented exclusively to Jefferson Avenue. Seemingly none the worse for editing to a "three-window" design, the Trowbridge evolution demonstrates the remarkable flexibility and strength of this venerable colonial pattern-model of residential design.

259 CROUL-PALMS HOUSE

NC PR

1394 East Jefferson Ave.
William Scott, 1881

The Croul-Palms House is the most significant Queen Anne-style house remaining on East Jefferson from the street's nineteenth-century glory days of grand residences. Queen Anne influence is evident in the irregular massing, contrasting surface materials, and picturesque rooflines. In the early 1980s the building was restored and refurbished to lead a new, more officious existence. William Scott was a designer-builder, and his sons became prominent Detroit architects, with Wayne County Courthouse (115) to their credit.

257

258

259 a

259 b

260 NS PR

CHRISTOPHER MOROSS HOUSE

1460 East Jefferson Ave.
Christopher Moross, 1843–1848

This handsome "three-bay" townhouse is among the oldest surviving brick houses in the city. It was one of two built on the site by local brickmaker Christopher Moross in approximately 1843 to 1848. The site comprises parts of the original Gouin and Riopelle ribbon farms. Embellishing an eighteenth-century urban vernacular form are Greek Revival-style details, including heavy stone lintels over the windows and an entry featuring delicate sidelights and transom. Thoroughly restored in the early 1970s, today it serves as headquarters of the Detroit Garden Center. There are a few other such townhouses in Corktown whose dates are uncertain.

261 SP

YWCA (UNIVERSITY CLUB)

1411 East Jefferson Ave.
Smith, Hinchman, and Grylls (William E. Kapp), 1931

By 1931 American universities were interpreting the cloistered look of Oxford and Cambridge in a style that came to be known as "Collegiate Gothic." William Kapp explored the new old vocabulary in this club for college graduates. In comparison to his earlier design of the Ross Roy Building (267), this is more seriously attentive to precedents. The romantic effect is achieved with complex massing, a picturesque roofscape, leaded glass windows, and interiors rich with paneling and carved beam ceilings. Even the exterior masonry here was a reproduction of the handmade brick common to Cambridge, England. Interestingly, this medieval statement replaced a Victorian mansion that had served as the club's first facility after a relatively brief life as the home of Michigan Senator James McMillan.

262 P

GREENING OF DETROIT PARK PAVILION

1463 East Jefferson Ave.
Zago Architecture, 2001

This unusual park shelter both playfully and seriously challenges the nature of the pavilion type itself. A tightly stacked volume of translucent tubes hovers within an open steel framework. On one level the design tips a respectful hat to Mies van der Rohe's Lafayette Park (277) nearby. More poetically, this little structure invites the observer to reconsider the basic elements of architecture, as both a noun and a verb.

260

261

262

263 ST. AUBIN PARK AND MARINA

Atwater and St. Aubin
Schervish Vogel Merz, 1989

A modest boat marina created as part of the "linked riverfront parks plan" conceived in the early 1980s. The site was previously home to the Detroit Dry Dock Company, and indeed a surviving dock can be seen at the west side of the park. The boat sculpture beside the building is a highly creative plaything.

264 CHENE PARK AND AMPHITHEATER

Atwater and Chene
Schervish Vogel Merz Cardoza, 1984, and addition with Kent Hubbell, 1990

The projects favored by Mayor Coleman Young in the 1980s to "open up" the riverfront to the public tended to be ambitious ones. The original 1,600-seat pavilion at Chene Park was replaced in 1990 with this 5,000-seat amphitheater. The superstructure consists of concrete turrets and balconies, meant to mimic the cement company silos nearby. The signature teal-colored handrails and light posts mirror the color used on Young's other riverfront projects. Kent Hubbell designed the Teflon-coated canopy. If and when Detroit creates a truly continuous public waterfront, Chene Park will be a focal point. Until then, it remains architecturally isolated.

265 MCGREGOR CARRIAGE HOUSE

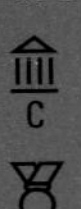

1995 East Woodbridge
Architect unknown, 1885; renovation by Schervish Vogel Merz, 1981

Originally used to shelter carriages and stable horses, this is one of only a handful of carriage houses that survive on the East Riverfront. Handsomely restored, it serves as a reminder of days when East Jefferson was lined with mansions of the wealthy. Unfortunately, the McGregor House itself, fronting on Jefferson Avenue, was demolished in 1936 due to the rapid commercialization of the street. The carriage house was renovated for the offices of Schervish Vogel Merz in 1981, but its future fate is uncertain.

263

264

265

266 PASADENA APARTMENTS

2170 East Jefferson Ave.
Mortimer L. Smith and Son, 1902

By 1900 advances in elevator technology allowed high-rise residential towers to pierce East Jefferson's wall of elegant single-family mansions. The Pasadena, built for an upper-class clientele, was a good example. The eleven-story structure is faced with yellow brick and articulated by window bays that rise from the basement to the tenth story. Over time the Pasadena lost some of its upper-story Beaux-Arts Classical ornament, including cornices and false balconies, yet it remains an imposing structure.

267 WAYNE STATE UNIVERSITY UPC RESEARCH CLINIC (ROSS ROY)

2761 East Jefferson Ave.
Smith, Hinchman, and Grylls, (William E. Kapp), 1925

As a work of the mid-1920s this Neo-Romanesque building borders on the romantic/exotic. Although somewhat late in the age of eclecticism, this work came early in William Kapp's career with Smith, Hinchman, and Grylls. The building was originally designed for G. H. Phelps Advertising and Radio Station. The emblematic town crier on the east façade was crafted by renowned architectural sculptor Corrado Parducci. Note how the chimney cap imitates the shape of the building in miniature. The Art Deco building next door was completed just two years later with a seeming disregard for its context.

268 JOHN N. BAGLEY HOUSE

2921 East Jefferson Ave.
Rogers and MacFarlane, 1889

The Bagley house is a fine example of French Renaissance Revival architecture, with overtones of H. H. Richardson's Romanesque in the handling of materials. Indeed, a few years prior to building this house, the Bagley family had hired Richardson (1838–1886) to design a memorial fountain (116). Because of this connection, the house was long believed to be the work of Shepley, Rutan, and Coolidge, which carried forward Richardson's firm after his death. But more recent evidence points to the Detroit firm of Rogers and MacFarlane as the architects. The stone entrance was carved by noted sculptor Julius Melchers. Bagley was the son of a former governor of Michigan.

266

267

268

269

WILLIAM H. WELLS HOUSE

2931 East Jefferson Ave.
William H. Miller, 1889

With the Bagley House (268) next door, this handsome Romanesque Revival house stands as one of the few survivors of Jefferson Avenue's elegant residential district of the late nineteenth century. The house is notable for its picturesque massing of turrets and projecting bays. Cornell University's first student of architecture, William H. Miller became known for such major works as Cornell's Uris Library.

270

GARDEN COURT APARTMENTS

2900 East Jefferson Ave.
Albert Kahn, 1915

Albert Kahn designed this neoclassical apartment building in 1915 for J. Harrington Walker of Hiram Walker and Sons, Distillers, whose house stood across the street. Walker moved into the building upon its completion. Originally it housed thirty-two large, luxury apartments. Two rounded bay-window units rise the full nine stories, giving depth and solidity to the façade in a massing model that was common in the early era of apartment building design. The Walker family also developed a ferry at the foot of Joseph Campau to take Walker and other Detroiters to the Walkerville distillery complex across the river.

269

270

271 STROH RIVER PLACE (PARKE-DAVIS)

Joseph Campau at the Detroit River
Various architects, 1891–1930; renovations, 1980–

The pioneering pharmaceutical manufacturing company Parke-Davis was founded in 1867 and moved to the riverfront site in 1873 to take advantage of convenient transportation offered by water and rail. Between 1891 and 1955, twenty-three buildings were erected, first in conventional mill technology and later in reinforced concrete. The first buildings were built behind the Detroit Boat Club, which was relocated to Belle Isle at the turn of the century to make way for the Research Laboratory. Designed by Donaldson and Meier, the 1902 Laboratory was notably the first pharmaceutical research building in the United States and, including its later addition by Albert Kahn, is a National Historic Landmark.

Beginning in the 1980s the Stroh family has redeveloped the complex into office, residential, and retail uses. The handsome 1927 Administration Building, designed by Smith, Hinchman, and Grylls, was respectfully renovated by the Talon Group as its corporate headquarters. A handsome bridge connects the Administration Building to the massive warehouse, which was converted to office use by New York architect James Stewart Polshek. East of the Administration Building is Albert Kahn's 1942 laboratory building, which has been sensitively adapted to hotel use. Farther inland are several fine industrial buildings dating back to the 1880s, now admirably redeveloped as residential lofts by many architects, including Redstone, Rossetti, and Schervish Vogel Merz. As initially conceived, Stroh River Place was the largest historic tax-credit project in the nation, and it represents a model of architectural revitalization.

272 UAW-GM CENTER FOR HUMAN RESOURCES

SP

200 Walker
Giffels Associates, and Sims-Varner, 2001

This complex of buildings employs forms reminiscent of Detroit's industrial past. That's appropriate given the nature of this riverfront complex, which is a joint General Motors and United Auto Workers union training center. The facade composition and curvy rooftops hark back to the early industrial architecture of Kahn.

271 a

271 b

272

273 THE PLAYERS CLUB

NS SP$

3321 East Jefferson Ave.
Smith, Hinchman, and Grylls (William E. Kapp), 1925

Don't look too closely for historic precedent in this romantic Arts and Crafts design. The general air of fantasy is more important. The gentlemen's theater club formed in 1911 and opened this clubhouse in 1925. All the roles, including the feminine ones, to this day are played by men, who at times have ranked among Detroit's leading businessmen. Women are occasionally invited to attend. Architect William Kapp, stone sculptor Corrado Parducci, and muralist Paul Honore were all members who worked on this building.

274 LIGHTHOUSE SUPPLY DEPOT

SP

3766 Wight at Mt. Elliott Park
Major Orlando M. Poe, 1874; preservation by The Albert Kahn Collaborative, 1997

A sensible and lyrical piece of public works by public architects working in a mix of Romanesque Revival and Italianate styles. Iron columns and brick barrel-vaulted ceilings distinguish lofty interior spaces and bear the influence of Ruskin. It may be our imagination, but that rose window surround surely resembles a ship's wheel. Preserved in 1996, the building is slated to be reused as a maritime interpretation center.

275 THE LOFTS (FREDERICK STEARNS BUILDING)

NS PR

6533 East Jefferson Ave.
Stratton and Baldwin, 1899; tower addition by Albert Kahn, ca. 1910; renovation and conversion by Schervish Vogel Merz, 1989

William Stratton brought his Arts and Crafts sensibilities to this large, rambling building constructed in 1899. The later eight-story reinforced concrete tower was designed by Albert Kahn. Built originally for the Frederick Stearns Company, an important pharmaceutical firm, this early industrial site was converted to residential apartments in 1989.

273

274

275

Lafayette/Gratiot

Following an ancient Native American trail branching from the city's center and serving as a primary route for trappers, Gratiot Avenue was improved to thoroughfare dimensions in 1830. About that time, the first of several waves of German immigrants settled on the near east side, from Jefferson to Gratiot. Gratiot itself became a center for the tannery industry. Beginning in 1891, Eastern Market brought a counterpoint of broad ethnic diversity to a ten-block area north of Gratiot, where it remains to this day as a multicultural success.

German heritage and pride shaped St. Joseph Catholic Church, an impressively towering hall church in the style of those native to southern Germany. It was not coincidental that Stroh's and many other brewers would later build factories here to brew proper German ales. And, in the modern era, it is at least serendipitous that two great German masters would design a modern classic in Lafayette Park.

The early 1960s was an architecturally heady time here, as no fewer than three exceptionally fine residential towers set a pace equal to any in America. Besides Mies' and Hilberseimer's Lafayette Park, Carl Koch of Boston created one of his classically elemental stacked housing blocks (pictured at right). And a few years later, Gunnar Birkerts added yet another sculptural landmark to the near eastside skyline.

276

PR

1300 LAFAYETTE EAST

Lafayette and Rivard
Birkerts and Straub, 1964

This building offers interest from many angles and distances. In this thirty-story tower, Birkerts brings structural and functional expression to high art. The tapered columns are a modern equivalent of the classical curving profile of the Greek Doric order—technically known as entasis. Unlike classical precedent, here the colonnade is spaced not equally, but in accord with the layout of two different room widths. To further accentuate the building's thinness, the two banks of apartments are offset along the line of the central corridor. This refined, cleaved slab converses effectively with Mies van der Rohe's Pavilion across the low-rise plane.

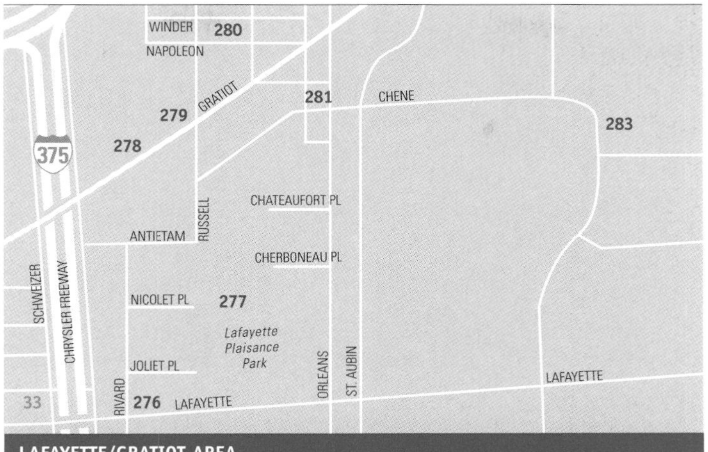

LAFAYETTE/GRATIOT AREA

276

277 LAFAYETTE PARK

1 Lafayette Plaisance
Ludwig Mies van der Rohe, and Ludwig Hilberseimer, 1959–1963

SP

Lafayette Park's Chicago developers imported modern masters of architecture and planning to design a new community for Detroit. The master plan, one of Hilberseimer's best, distributes high- and low-rise housing across expansive superblocks—large blocks created by closing streets. The Pavilion Apartments (1958) and Lafayette Towers (1963) exemplify Mies's trademark attention to form, proportion, and detail. Nearly two hundred units of two-story townhouses and one-story courtyard houses were arranged around cul-de-sacs, as the overall development frames a central municipal park. In its now mature landscape context, the modern masters' formula achieves its most engaging and timeless potential.

278 BREWERY PARK

1155 Brewery Park Blvd.
Gensler Associates, 1995

SP

This reuse of an industrial site reveals a city in search of new solutions to urban revitalization. Located on the twenty-acre former site of Stroh's Brewery, the architects drew from the industrial past. Inside, the staircase and balcony railings are direct copies of elements that once graced the Brewery. Besides this trace of history, Brewery Park represents the shape of things to come, at least in the near term, as here we see an urban application of suburban land planning and development economics.

279 TRINITY LUTHERAN CHURCH AND PARISH HOUSE

1335–1345 Gratiot Ave.
William E. N. Hunter, 1931

NSC

SP

While the congregation traces its roots to 1850, a church has occupied this site since 1866. Some believe this handsome, late Gothic-style church was primarily designed by Lewis Simpson, working with Hunter. The interior is noted for its intricately carved woodwork. The adjacent Tudor-style parish house, designed by Bernard Wetzel, was built in 1927. Hunter designed such other important works as Central United Methodist (53) on Woodward and Grosse Pointe Memorial Church (329) on Lake Shore Drive.

277

278

279

EAST

Lafayette/Gratiot

280 EASTERN MARKET

Bounded by Gratiot, Riopelle, Rivard, and Division
Various architects, 1870–

N S
P

Eastern Market is a lively commercial district comprised of several dozen structures, including large open-air sheds and many two- and three-story brick buildings with flat roofs and late Victorian detailing. The market dates to 1870, when it was established as a hay and wood market. The district was enlarged in 1921, and architectural firms such as Smith, Hinchman, and Grylls contributed designs for various buildings. Part of the district was sliced off by the construction of the Chrysler Freeway in the 1960s. Today, at its market center, displays of fresh meats, fruits, flowers, and vegetables all vie for attention. Shops, restaurants, and an occasional street musician add to the overall scene.

As an aside, the supergraphics were intended to revive interest in the market and lead to an historic rehabilitation of the structures. The gambit achieved the first goal, but architectural preservation is pending. "Kitsch" to some, the chicken has real presence all the same.

281 SAINT JOSEPH'S CATHOLIC CHURCH

1828 Jay at Orleans
Francis G. Himpler, 1873, 1883

NSC
SP

This is the only church in the region listed in the National Register at the "National" level of importance, a recognition based on the extremely fine quality of its stained glass. The German Catholic congregation hired Berlin-trained and New York-based architect Francis Himpler to design a Gothic hall church in the tradition of the venerable German model, and he delivered. With its tall windows, steep roof, and tall tower, it was different from the Victorian Gothic, such as Gordon Lloyd's designs for Protestant congregations (53, 254) in Detroit at this time. Himpler's original plans survive and are among the oldest for an extant Detroit building. Following the architect's plans, the octagonal bell house was added in 1883, and the spire was added ten years later under the supervision of Donaldson and Meier. St. Joseph's was highly regarded, well published, and led to several similar commissions for Himpler, from Grand Rapids to St. Louis. It remains the only Catholic Church in the area to offer German-language Masses.

280 a

280 b

281

282 SAINT ANTHONY CATHOLIC CHURCH

5247 Sheridan Ave. at St. Anthony Place
Donaldson and Meier, 1902

C SP

In a city blessed with many fine church buildings, St. Anthony's stands as one of the best. This impressive Romanesque structure is beautifully proportioned and finely detailed. This is one of three similar churches designed by Donaldson and Meier over a period of twenty years. An earlier church is St. Elizabeth on McDougall, and a later design is Annunciation on Parkview, off Jefferson. The design here presents a very German version of the Romanesque, with just a touch of more contemporary terra cotta trim at the entrance arch. The associated school across the street similarly infuses masterful brickwork in an otherwise economical form. In both works the subtle surface refinement is poetry in masonry. Scottish-born architect John Donaldson's firm amassed an impressively diverse portfolio of important works in Detroit in the late nineteenth and early twentieth centuries. No matter the style or context, each was approached with both skill and passion.

283 COLEMAN A. YOUNG COMMUNITY CENTER

2757 Robert Bradby Dr.
William Kessler and Associates, 1981

SC SP

To a passing motorist this city-owned recreation center may appear purely functional. But pause a moment, as the intricate and elemental setback massing belies that initial impression. A limited palette of materials, primarily concrete and glass block, are trademark modern. The glass block vaulted roof over the swimming pool sparkles.

282

283

Elmwood

Centering a district on a cemetery might appeal to an odd assortment of philosophers and clerics, or architects and planners. But Elmwood is special; so too are a handful of institutions that have formed at its edges. Three cemeteries abut here. Mt. Elliott, the earliest of the three and planned for area Catholics, includes a remarkable collection of Victorian funerary architecture. Located at the corner on Lafayette is a Jewish cemetery. Elmwood Cemetery's combination of "original" landscape and monumental city in miniature creates a profound sense of place, which on a clear day can be downright cheery. Here we find works by some of Detroit's finest architects, past and present, not to mention the remains of some of the city's best clients.

284

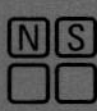

P

ELMWOOD CEMETERY

Mt. Elliott and Lafayette
Unknown planner, 1846; chapel by Albert and Octavius Jordan, 1856; gatehouse by Gordon W. Lloyd, 1870

Detroit's earliest cemeteries were located in what is now the heart of Downtown. As the city grew, new cemeteries were developed in rural outlying districts. Elmwood Cemetery was established in 1846 to serve the city's Protestant population. Albert and Octavius Jordan, architects of Fort Street Presbyterian Church (96), designed the Gothic Revival chapel in 1856. The well-known architect Gordon Lloyd designed the Gothic-inspired gatehouse in 1870, while landscape architect Frederick Law Olmsted had a hand in creating a management plan for the grounds in 1891.

Elmwood remains one of the few places in the city where visitors can glimpse a pre-Detroit terrain familiar to Native Americans. The gently rolling landscape is cut by Bloody Run Creek, named after a battle there during Pontiac's uprising of 1763. The cemetery is also notable for the large number of famous Detroiters buried there—twenty-nine Detroit mayors, at least six Michigan governors, eleven U.S. senators, and a dozen presidential cabinet members.

The cemetery is part of the Eastside Historic Cemetery District, which includes the adjacent Mt. Elliott and Lafayette Street cemeteries.

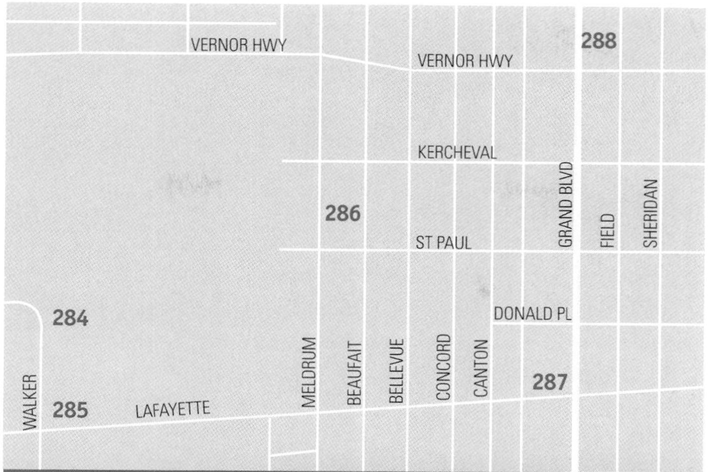

ELMWOOD AREA

284 ELMWOOD CEMETERY

285 CALVARY BAPTIST CHURCH

286 SAINT BONAVENTURE MONASTERY

287 CHURCH OF THE MESSIAH

288 FIELD HOUSE

Elmwood Cemetery

284

285

CALVARY BAPTIST CHURCH

Lafayette at Robert Bradby Dr.
Gunnar Birkerts and Associates, 1977

S SP

Jokesters may liken the orange metallic frame to a Howard Johnson's restaurant, but here Birkerts challenges our notions of church architecture. The entire structure, not just a spire, reaches for the sky. But for the entrance, there are few cues to the scale of this structure—compare to the architect's Administration Building (227) at the University of Detroit Mercy. Likely more than coincidental, the vaulted opening is a poetic recall of Lloyd's nearby gate to Elmwood, as captured in the photograph by Korab.

286

SAINT BONAVENTURE MONASTERY

1740 Mt. Elliott
Peter Dederichs, 1883–1913

N PR

This much-altered, but still handsome late Victorian complex of buildings is significant for the role it played in ministering to the poor and hungry over several decades. Father Solanus Casey, a Capuchin friar who worked here, is in line to become the first American-born man to be canonized by the Catholic Church as a saint.

285

286

287

CHURCH OF THE MESSIAH

231 East Grand Blvd. and Lafayette
Calvin N. Otis, 1852; moved and altered by William Buck Stratton, 1901

This fine example of early Gothic Revival, with its simplified detail and tall, narrow windows, was originally designed by Calvin Otis as St. Paul's Episcopal Cathedral on the northeast corner of Congress and Shelby. With the expansion of People's State Bank in 1901, the church was dismantled, significantly redesigned by William Buck Stratton, and reassembled stone by stone. The tall windows were retained to accommodate the pre-existing stained glass. Not surprisingly, Stratton added lots of Pewabic tile to an updating of the original church. St. Paul's, in turn, hired Cram, Goodhue, and Ferguson to design their new building elsewhere (130). By the way, it was Otis who also conceived Old Mariner's Church (16), which was also moved to accommodate progress. Over time, the church unfortunately lost the spire atop its tower.

While here, pause a moment to take in the church's East Grand Boulevard context, a National Historic District extending from Jefferson to Mack.

288

FIELD HOUSE

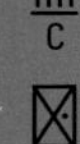

2541 Field St.
Unknown Architect, 1868

One of last remaining farm estate houses in Detroit, this Italianate house was built by Moses Field on his ribbon farm of 240 acres. Field's access road to the river became the city street that bears his name, and a road crossing the farm was named for his wife, Mary Kercheval.

287

288

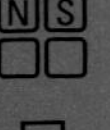

P

Belle Isle

Two-and-a-half-miles long and a half-mile wide, Belle Isle is a low, flat island rising just two feet above the level of the Detroit River. Even before the city purchased Belle Isle in 1879, the island was popular with Detroiters for hunting, fishing, bathing, and picnicking. In line with the nation's mid-nineteenth century interest in urban parks, the city hired landscape architect Frederick Law Olmsted, designer of New York's Central Park, to create a plan for the island. Olmsted's sketch called for a central road running up the island and a canal crossing one end. This struck many as too minimal. City leaders were more impressed with a scheme proposed by newspaperman Michael J. Dee, who suggested a series of canals covering the island. In the end, both Olmsted's central drive and some of Dee's canals were built. The island's original seven-hundred-plus acres were increased through land reclamation to nearly a thousand acres in 1940.

Originally forest and marsh, Belle Isle was populated with a series of individualistic buildings from the late nineteenth through the mid-twentieth century. These included two private yacht clubs, a nature conservatory, a maritime museum, a police station, an aquarium, a memorial fountain, and two editions of a casino. Also contributing to Belle Isle's character are the many picnic pavilions, foot bridges, and public statues that dot the island. Most of Belle Isle's facilities are located on the western half, as the island's eastern end remains mostly forested and in a nearly natural state. The original timber bridge to the island burned in 1915. Daniel Luton designed the graceful replacement in the classicism of the City Beautiful movement. This span was renamed for war hero General Douglas MacArthur early in World War II.

Heavily trafficked and a victim of inadequate funding, the island nevertheless remains Detroit's incomparable spot for watching sunsets and observing life on the Detroit River.

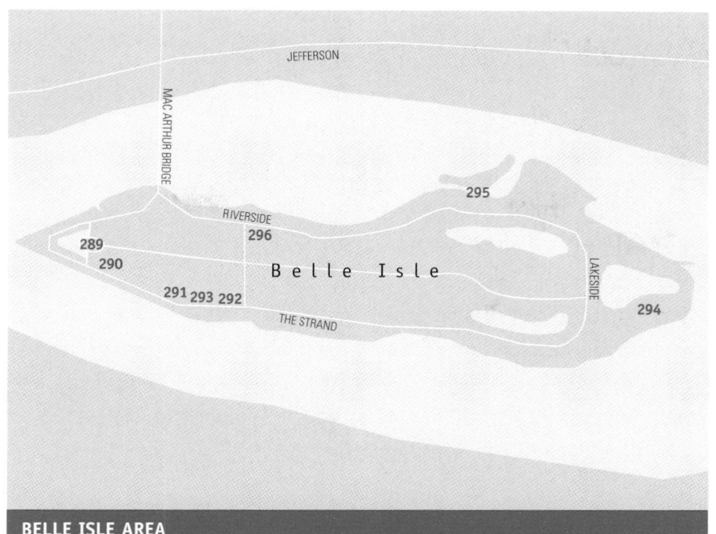

BELLE ISLE AREA

289 JAMES SCOTT FOUNTAIN	293 BELLE ISLE CONSERVATORY
290 BELLE ISLE CASINO	294 LIVINGSTONE LIGHT
291 NANCY BROWN PEACE CARILLON	295 DETROIT YACHT CLUB
292 BELLE ISLE AQUARIUM	296 BELLE ISLE POLICE STATION

Belle Isle Bridge

289

JAMES SCOTT FOUNTAIN

Belle Isle
Cass Gilbert, 1925

City leaders once planned a gargantuan marble Doric column more than twenty stories tall at the head of Belle Isle to mark Detroit's bicentennial in 1901. The idea faded in the light of financial reality. Architect Cass Gilbert, designer also of the Detroit Public Library, Main Branch (176), crafted the city's finest fountain in gleaming white marble with terraced steps and smaller collecting pools. That it was named after real estate investor James Scott proved controversial. Among the most despised men in the city, Scott had delighted in lawsuits and other disputes. In his will he left money for a memorial fountain to be named for himself. The city is richer for it.

290

BELLE ISLE CASINO

Belle Isle
Van Leyen and Schilling, 1907

The Casino often has been erroneously attributed to Albert Kahn, possibly because construction methods developed by Kahn's brother were used to build it. In fact, the architects were Van Leyen and Schilling, also known for designing local churches. The style is a Beaux-Arts free borrowing of classical motifs, including open arcades and squared towers. The word "casino" at the time meant less a gambling house than a site for public entertainments, a function the Casino still serves today.

291

NANCY BROWN PEACE CARILLON

Belle Isle
Architect unknown, 1940

Nancy Brown began writing her column for the *Detroit News* in 1919 at the age of forty-nine and continued until 1942. Her promotion in 1934 of a sunrise service on Belle Isle drew a record crowd of some fifty thousand. Perhaps consistent with its namesake, this Neo-Gothic tower strikes a pose that is at once stately and cheerfully unpretentious.

292

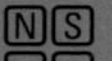

BELLE ISLE AQUARIUM

Belle Isle
Albert Kahn, 1904

A narrow brick building sited just behind the Conservatory (293) and often visited in tandem with it. The lively Baroque entry is topped by a pediment of carved dolphins. The green-glazed tile interior is original. Kahn's aquarium amazed naturalists in his day with both freshwater and saltwater marine life. Although not as high-tech as modern aquariums, it remains a delight.

289

290

291

292

293 

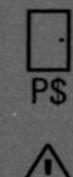

BELLE ISLE CONSERVATORY

Belle Isle

Albert Kahn, 1904

With its huge, exquisitely proportioned central dome, flanked by symmetrical wings, the Conservatory typified the lofty idealism of the City Beautiful movement at the turn of the century. The design idea was indebted to garden pavilions and architectural exhibitions of the later nineteenth century, from London to Philadelphia, Chicago, and St. Louis. Named for Anna Scripps Whitcomb, the building was very much simplified when rebuilt in the 1950s.

294 

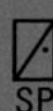

LIVINGSTONE LIGHT

Belle Isle

Albert Kahn, 1930

A sophisticated lighthouse and appropriate monument for a prominent Detroiter who owned lake freighters, this structure is an elegant ode to the possibilities of Art Deco applied to the tall building. Ornamental reliefs were designed by Giza Maroti, a Hungarian architect and sculptor brought to Detroit by Eliel Saarinen. Timelessly attractive at any scale, and thoughtfully restored by the Detroit Recreation Department.

295 

DETROIT YACHT CLUB

Belle Isle

George D. Mason, 1923

One of the city's most prolific architects, Mason borrowed Mediterranean themes for this spacious stucco and tile-roofed clubhouse. (Much of the original stucco is now unfortunately covered.) Architecturally informal and even rambling, the clubhouse suits perfectly the character of a boating community. Of special note are the magnificent wood-paneled ballroom on the second floor and two grand stairways, one on the exterior facing the main dock, the other in the main lobby. Unlike the endangered Boat Club, the DYC remains active.

296 

BELLE ISLE POLICE STATION

Belle Isle

Mason and Rice, 1893

This wonderful small police station merges Richardsonian Romanesque with the Shingle style of the same era. Some see the robust look of a Norman farmhouse. The exterior is clad in rough-dressed fieldstone.

293

294

295

296

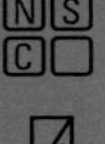

Indian Village

Burns, Iroquois, and Seminole from East Jefferson to Mack Aves.; 1894–1920

When subdivided in 1894, Indian Village extended to the river and maintained a Detroit tradition of building the most prestigious houses on the main streets. Unfortunately, many of the larger houses between the river and East Jefferson were later sacrificed for gold-coast apartment complexes. With the first boom of the suburbs in the years before World War II, many residents moved out, and Indian Village was threatened with decline. Residents formed the Indian Village Association in 1937 to enforce single-family zoning and to resist the subdivision of mansions into apartments. Over the years, the Association has succeeded in keeping Indian Village one of Detroit's finest neighborhoods. For our purposes, the Indian Village area includes West Village as well as a few nearby institutional resources of note. But it should be observed that Indian Villagers are more precisely conscious, if not fiercely protective, of their geographic identity.

297 SAINT CHARLES BORROMEO CHURCH

1515 Baldwin

Peter Dederichs, 1919; rectory and school by Van Leyen and Schilling, 1912

A hearty example of an early-twentieth-century Roman Catholic parish complex, and the anchor of Detroit's late-nineteenth- and early-twentieth-century Belgian community. Completed in 1919, the building was a late work of noted architect Peter Dederichs. Borromeo's plan follows Dederich's earlier design for St. Mary's Church (32) in Greektown. The exterior is Beaux-Arts with a bit of Prairie style, and the interior is quite Baroque. Note how the window tracery has been reduced to a simple geometry of repeated circles. The firm Van Leyen and Schilling designed the rectory and parish school in 1912.

298 WEST VILLAGE NEIGHBORHOOD

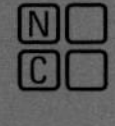

Bounded by Kercheval, Parker, East Jefferson, and Seyburn Aves.

Various architects, 1890–1920

A highly walkable neighborhood with a remarkable range of residential styles and types, including single manses, duplexes, townhouse rows, and multifamily apartments. English vernacular styles and colonial revivals blend comfortably in a mature streetscape setting to create an overall sense of place.

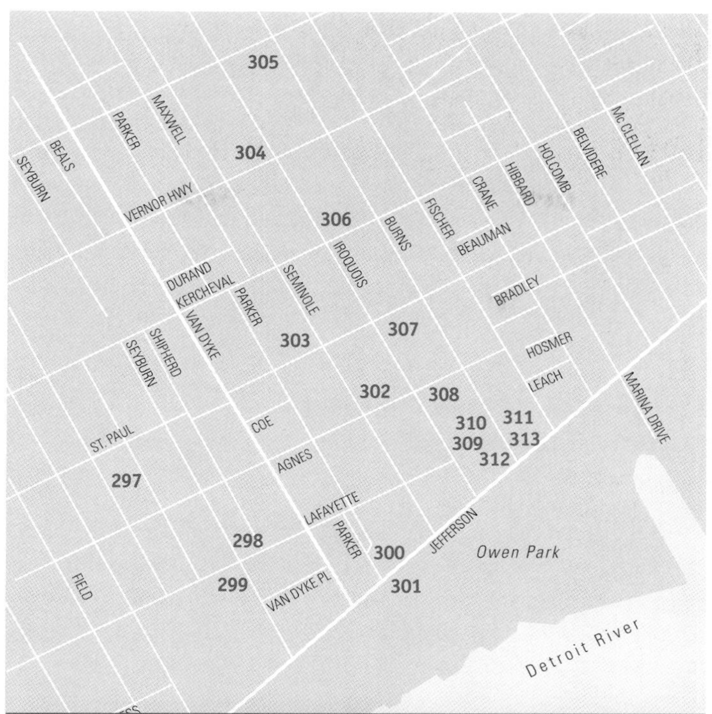

INDIAN VILLAGE AREA

297 SAINT CHARLES BORROMEO CHURCH	306 LOUIS KAMPER HOUSE
298 WEST VILLAGE NEIGHBORHOOD	307 HUPP HOUSE
299 JULIUS T. MELCHERS HOUSE	308 ARTHUR AND CLARA BUHL HOUSE
300 FREDERICK K. STEARNS HOUSE	309 MARY G. EDGAR HOUSE
301 ALDEN PARK TOWERS	310 RUSSELL HOUSE
302 CORNELIUS RAY HOUSE	311 PERCY D. DWIGHT HOUSE
303 BINGLEY FALES HOUSE	312 JAMES BURGESS BOOK, JR., HOUSE
304 ROSCOE JACKSON HOUSE	313 JEFFERSON AVENUE PRESBYTERIAN CHURCH
305 WALDORF SCHOOL	

297

298

299 JULIUS T. MELCHERS HOUSE

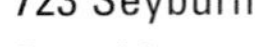

723 Seyburn
Donaldson and Meier, 1897

Viewed in the context of eighteenth-century precedent, this lively design suggests a Colonial on steroids. It was Melchers, a sculptor of great renown in the Detroit area, who recognized that the young Albert Kahn, being color-blind, stood a better chance as an architect than as an artist. Melchers himself carved the elaborate gable of the central dormer.

300 FREDERICK K. STEARNS HOUSE

8209 East Jefferson Ave.
Stratton and Baldwin, 1902

William Stratton, husband of Pewabic Pottery founder Mary Chase Perry, and his partner designed a number of Indian Village houses, many of which include creative splashes of Pewabic tile. This half-timbered mansion is a splendid blend of medieval tradition and English Arts and Crafts design. Stearns built the first phase of his pharmaceutical company a few years earlier just to the west on Jefferson and also in an Arts and Crafts vein (275). That entrepreneurial success enabled Stearns to amass an impressive collection of Asian art, which was eventually given to the Detroit Institute of Arts.

301 ALDEN PARK TOWERS

8100 East Jefferson Ave.
Unknown architect, 1923

With more than 350 apartments, Alden Park was one of the largest of the many residential complexes built between Jefferson Ave. and the Detroit River in the 1920s. It is robustly Tudor in its ornamentation—the limestone crenelations give the appearance of roof-line battlements.

302 CORNELIUS RAY HOUSE

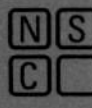

1500 Seminole
Louis Kamper, 1910

This house is turned side-on to the street to provide more privacy. The style is inspired by French Classicism with some inescapable indebtedness to American colonial architecture. The fanlight (semicircular window) and sidelights (narrow strip windows) at the door are designed in an authentic Federal fashion. The original wrap-around porch was unfortunately removed.

299

300

301

302

303
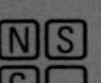
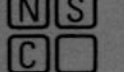

BINGLEY FALES HOUSE

1771 Seminole
Chittenden and Kotting, 1907

The stately house was built for a wealthy electric utility executive in a well-balanced Neo-Georgian style. A later owner, Mr. Poole, tripled its size to about 15,000 square feet and distinction as the largest residence in Indian Village. The carriage house alone would satisfy most people.

304
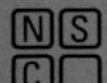
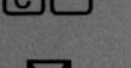

ROSCOE JACKSON HOUSE

2505 Iroquois Ave.
Leonard B. Willeke, 1917

A remarkably fine Arts and Crafts house thoroughly designed by noted residential architect Leonard Willeke, who also created the two houses immediately to the south.

305
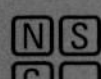

WALDORF SCHOOL (LIGGETT SCHOOL)

2555 Burns Ave.
Albert Kahn, 1913

Kahn designed this school in the English Domestic Revival style, which had gained considerable currency in Britain at the turn of the century. Kahn's love of natural light, so important in his factory designs, is evident here, too. Interesting comparisons, and contrasts, can be drawn to Saarinen's early work at Cranbrook a decade later.

306

LOUIS KAMPER HOUSE

2150 Iroquois Ave.
Louis Kamper, 1917

Designed by and for one of Detroit's most famous architects in a revival of eighteenth-century French Classicism. This elegant house demonstrates Kamper's exceeding talents at the residential scale—in contrast, see his less confident Book Tower (76). Each of the exterior stones was individually cut and numbered in Indiana before being shipped to Detroit.

303

304

305

306

307 HUPP HOUSE

1516 Iroquois Ave.
George Valentine Pottle, 1911

Built for early auto baron Robert Hupp of Huppmobile fame, this is one of a few, and some believe one of the finest, extant Detroit houses designed in the Prairie style. The Prairie sense of shelter is surely here, and the refined detailing is among its most distinguishing features.

308 ARTHUR AND CLARA BUHL HOUSE

1116 Iroquois Ave.
John Scott, 1908

Gothic and Tudor themes fuse for a rather assertive appearance. It was built for a member of the Detroit family whose fortune would later build the Buhl Building (107) Downtown.

309 MARY G. EDGAR HOUSE

1020 Iroquois Ave.
Chittenden and Kotting, 1913

With its three stories, windows suggesting a piano nobile, and entrance pavilion straight out of Vignola, this very large house on a small lot is as close as Detroit gets to a New York Fifth Avenue town-house. Chittenden and Kotting here abandoned their more usual Neo-Georgian precedents in designing a "continental" house for a wealthy widow who collected French furniture. Mrs. Edgar's son built a larger estate house in Grosse Pointe (340), but his "town" house was located only three doors from his mother's.

310 RUSSELL HOUSE

1075 Burns Ave.
Walter S. Russell, 1890

This fieldstone Richardsonian Romanesque house was dismantled and moved in 1921 to its present site from the corner of Jefferson and Jos. Campau. Although it was rebuilt in reverse image, the house is one of the few survivors of Jefferson Avenue's many nineteenth-century mansions. Reconstructing the staircase as a mirror image of its former self was quite the carpentry challenge!

307

308

309

310

311 PERCY D. DWIGHT HOUSE

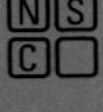
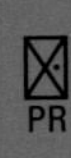
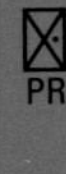

1012 Burns Ave.
Grylls and Gies, 1906

An authentically Georgian house by Maxwell Grylls, a native of England, and most likely inspired by the famous Mount Pleasant house of Philadelphia. Shortly after designing this house Grylls would join in the formation of Smith, Hinchman, and Grylls.

312 JAMES BURGESS BOOK, JR., HOUSE

8469 Jefferson Ave. at Burns
Louis Kamper, 1911

Architect Kamper and real estate developer Book created some of Downtown's most memorable skyscrapers of the 1920s, including the Book Tower (76) and the Book-Cadillac Hotel (81). For Book's mansion, Kamper borrowed freely from the Petit Trianon at Versailles, employing a Renaissance Revival style suited to sumptuous mansions. In more recent years the house has lost its balustrade on the roof and has been subdivided for commercial uses.

313 JEFFERSON AVENUE PRESBYTERIAN CHURCH

8625 East Jefferson Ave.
Smith, Hinchman, and Grylls (Wirt Rowland), 1925

A beautiful example of late Neo-Gothic church architecture designed by Smith, Hinchman, and Grylls' Wirt Rowland and built for a well-to-do congregation. The picturesque massing, rugged masonry, deeply cut central arch, and graceful window tracery transport the observer to a prosperous English monastic ensemble.

311

312 a

312 b

313

East Jefferson

"East Jefferson" is a geographic catchall that encompasses the greater riverfront corridor between the Belle Isle Bridge and the Grosse Pointes. It is more a term of convenience than representative of any commonly held usage. Indeed, some would view this zone as only episodically coherent.

At first blush the area's architectural significance is primarily residential, from a variety of high-rise apartment buildings to one of Detroit's best-kept neighborhood secrets in the Berry Subdivision, and residence of the mayor nearby. As an outlier to the north the historic house of Ossian Sweet is included here to represent Detroit's tried-and-true bungalow style, and more.

And there are some wonderful surprises here for the looking, as well. One of the city's best Beaux-Arts Classical pieces celebrates entry to the Waterworks. And if you haven't heard the name enough, Mary Chase Perry Stratton's Pewabic factory is charming. Heading into the sunrise, we conclude with the deliciously Art Deco and now vacant Vanity Ballroom, which summarizes more about the city's past glories, present state, and future possibilities than words can possibly say.

314 **KEAN APARTMENTS**

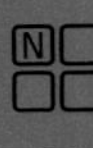

8925 East Jefferson Ave.
Charles Noble, 1931

The sixteen-story Kean is an outstanding example of free-Art Deco as applied to apartment tower design. The entrance is framed in orange terra cotta with Corinthian columns that are a bit academic even for Deco, which originated as a classical style. A playful checkerboard pattern highlights the upper façade. Don't miss the gargoyles projecting from the roof line. Completed in 1931, the Kean was the last of the large-scale residential projects to be built along East Jefferson for many years. It was designed by the same Charles Noble who designed the Lee Plaza Apartment tower (205) on West Grand Boulevard and the Elwood Bar and Grill (57).

EAST JEFFERSON AREA

314 KEAN APARTMENTS
315 JEFFERSONIAN APARTMENTS
316 BERRY SUBDIVISION AND ENVIRONS
317 HURLBUT MEMORIAL GATE
318 WATERWORKS PARK
319 PEWABIC POTTERY COMPANY
320 HANNAN MEMORIAL YMCA
321 OSSIAN SWEET HOUSE
322 LAWRENCE FISHER MANSION
323 VANITY BALLROOM

314

315 JEFFERSONIAN APARTMENTS

PR

9000 East Jefferson Ave.
Giffels and Rossetti, 1965

Over the past half century, amid a massive migration to the suburbs, Detroit has been sporadically revived by new residential projects offering an urban lifestyle. One of the most notable from the 1960s was the Jeffersonian. Instead of allusions to past architectures, the Jeffersonian's functionalist, wrap-around balconies and minimalist detailing offered a high modern "machine for living." A potentially overbearing thirty-story mass is significantly relieved by the floating floor edges and delicate railings, from which residents enjoy spectacular views of the Detroit River. With Kean (314), Jeffersonian serves as a large-scale gatepost to the East Jefferson corridor.

316 BERRY SUBDIVISION AND ENVIRONS

Bounded by Jefferson Ave., the Detroit River, Parkview, and Fiske
Various architects, 1898–1929

SP

In 1898 a building permit was issued to Louis Kamper to construct a new house for clothing manufacturer Marvin Stanton. Soon after Stanton's house was completed, and next door to it, Kamper produced a fantastic assemblage of towers, turrets, crenelations, and roofs now known popularly as "The Castle." Then in 1914 daughters of Joseph Berry petitioned City Council to develop a subdivision of high-quality single-family houses. Covenants called for houses of at least two stories in height and built of brick or stone, with setbacks and side yard spaces. Building began in 1916; the majority of houses date from the 1920s.

The seven houses on Dwight are of special interest. In 1927 General Charles W. Harrah built a mansion on the river that was later owned by Alex Manoogian. Now known as the Manoogian Mansion, the Harrah house is the official residence of the mayor of Detroit.

The Great Depression ended hopes here for the unified quality of an Indian Village or Boston-Edison. About a third of the lots were never developed, and about a quarter of the houses that were built rose only after World War II. A stylistic potpourri including Mediterranean, Medieval, Prairie School, and Neo-Colonial under a mature canopy of trees makes for an exceptional neighborhood, nonetheless.

315

316

317

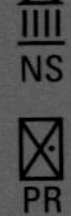

HURLBUT MEMORIAL GATE

East Jefferson Ave. at Cadillac Blvd. (Waterworks Park)
Brede and Mueller, 1894

Formal entry to Waterworks Park and one of Detroit's best examples of Beaux-Arts Classicism, this sculptural piece was erected in honor of Chauncey Hurlbut (1803–1885), longtime president of the Board of Water Commissioners. Hurlbut had left his entire estate for the beautification of the waterworks grounds and a library, which was located in this structure. The architects, classically trained Herman Brede and Gustave Mueller, bedecked the gate with florid details and triumphal statuary piercing the skyline.

318

WATERWORKS PARK

10100 East Jefferson Ave.
Field, Hinchman, and Smith, 1910–1931

The Lift Buildings, High (1910) and Low (1924), are appropriately reminiscent of Roman antecedents, particularly ancient masterworks of civil engineering.

319

PEWABIC POTTERY COMPANY

10125 East Jefferson Ave.
Stratton and Baldwin, 1907

Mary Chase Perry, one of the leaders of Detroit's turn-of-the-century Arts and Crafts movement, founded the Pewabic Pottery Company in 1904 to pursue her interest in ceramics. Her friend, architect William B. Stratton, designed Pewabic's new home, and the couple were later married. Indebted to the work of English Arts and Crafts master Charles Voysey, Stratton's design is current with the times and perfectly suited as home to a small crafts industry. Pewabic Pottery has produced decorative tiles for numerous important buildings, including the Guardian Building (108) and the Detroit Institute of Arts (177). Pewabic's influence on Detroit architecture has been profound.

320

HANNAN MEMORIAL YMCA

19401 East Jefferson Ave.
Robert O. Derrick, 1927

Built with a legacy from a Detroit real estate mogul, this tastefully poised composition was designed by an architect quite at home with the sophisticated, Neo-Georgian vocabulary. See also Derrick's Henry Ford Museum (367).

317

318

319

320

321 OSSIAN SWEET HOUSE

NS PR

2905 Garland
Maurice Finkel, 1919

This modest bungalow, and the street upon which it resides, typifies many in Detroit's working-class neighborhoods. But it stands out in the city's history for another reason. In 1925 Dr. Ossian Sweet, a black gynecologist, moved his family into this house in what had been an all-white neighborhood. A crowd of rowdy whites gathered outside to protest. A shot fired from the house killed a man. Sweet, along with his brother, Henry, and nine others, was charged with murder. Clarence Darrow defended them, and eventually all defendants were either acquitted or freed after a jury failed to reach verdicts. The bungalow thus became an early symbol in Detroit's long fractious history.

322 LAWRENCE FISHER MANSION

SP$

383 Lenox
C. Howard Crane, 1927

The elaborate Fisher mansion was one of few residences designed by noted theater architect C. Howard Crane. (See also Crane's house for John Kunsky in Palmer Woods, 237.) Built for the most flamboyant of the Fisher brothers, this house evokes the Mediterranean Revival style common to south Florida but less common to Southeast Michigan. The interior offers an assortment of stage sets ranging from Art Deco to Swiss Chalet. The mansion is now owned by the Hare Krishna group, which conducts public tours on weekends and operates a restaurant on site.

323 VANITY BALLROOM

N C

1024 Newport Ave.
Charles N. Agree, 1929

This Art Deco dance hall, with its ornamentation inspired by Aztec and Toltec motifs, enlivened Detroit's east side through the Depression and war years, hosting such band leaders as Duke Ellington, Benny Goodman, and Tommy Dorsey. It closed many years ago and is now endangered.

321

322

323

1 Downtown
2 Midtown
3 North
4 West
5 East
6 **Grosse Pointe Lakeshore**
7 **Cranbrook**
8 **GM Technical Center**
9 **Ford's Dearborn**

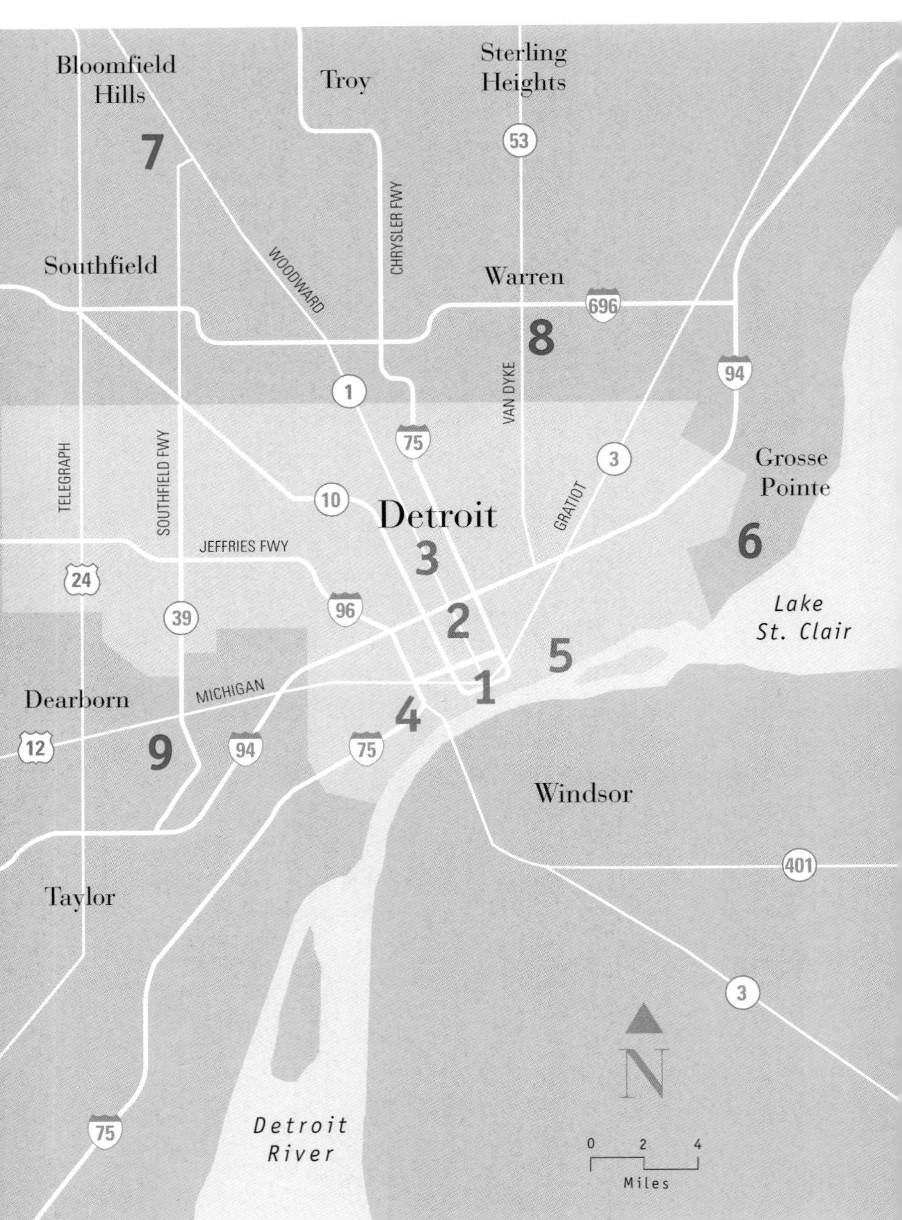

Special Environments

Special Environments

Were we to include all the significant architecture of the greater Detroit metropolitan area, this guide would be much larger. Where to define the city's limits is the challenge not only for this effort, but for larger considerations of livable community and urban sustainability. The suburbs (which deserve their own volume someday) contain a handful of key environments so special, so influential in the world of architecture, that any Detroit guidebook would be incomplete without them.

We choose to focus on four such environments, running from east to west: Grosse Pointe Lakeshore, the General Motors Technical Center in Warren, Cranbrook Educational Community in Bloomfield Hills, and Henry Ford's Dearborn. Collectively, these unique environments cover a spectrum of uses from residential to office and from institutional to industrial. Each in its way has contributed to both Detroit's identity and the world's architecture.

In their heyday, the now-vanished mansions of Lake Shore Drive brought the belle époque to the Midwest. The GM Tech Center dazzled the world with its space-age sleekness. Cranbrook evolved from a boys' school into an exemplar of art, landscape, architecture, and design. Ford's Rouge Complex taught the world how to build factories.

Sadly, two of our four environments might not make the cut today were it not for their illustrious pasts. Most of the glorious Lake Shore Drive mansions barely survived their original owners; in their place, expensive but much-diminished mansions line the once proud boulevard. In Dearborn Albert Kahn's pioneering work at the Ford Rouge Complex has been so modified over time that big chunks of the original vision have been lost. Nonetheless, we include these two areas here both for the remnants of greatness still there and because one cannot imagine a Detroit architectural guidebook without them. This is where the guide's role as time-capsule plays a trump card. Happily, both Cranbrook and the GM Technical Center will retain their original grandeur. In fact, each has been busily preserving and adding on to its heritage with several new buildings in the past decade. How well the new blends with the old is a matter we leave to each reader to decide, at least until a future edition of the guide is able to evaluate these works with greater hindsight.

Cranbrook

Grosse Pointe Lakeshore

Wealthy Detroiters had recognized Grosse Pointe's Lake St. Clair shoreline as a pleasant spot for summer cottages well back into the nineteenth century. The advent of the trolley line in the 1880s and the automobile in the early 1900s transformed it into a year-round suburb. Property boundaries still followed the long, narrow profile of the French ribbon farms. By the early 1900s mansions began replacing wood cottages, a trend that would continue uninterrupted for thirty years.

It was America's Gilded Age, a time before the income tax, an era when vast fortunes were made. Society encouraged the wealthy to spend those fortunes on highly visible houses. With few local precedents for such grand displays, well-to-do clients and their architects traveled to Europe in search of Old World inspiration. Lake Shore Drive soon sprouted one mansion after the next dressed as English manor house, Italian villa, and French chateau. Set far back on sloping lawns overlooking Lake St. Clair, these estates became repositories of art and wealth, and Lake Shore Drive one of America's enduring images of the good life.

One of the greatest of the mansions was Rose Terrace, a magnificent villa built for Mrs. Horace E. Dodge and filled with imported riches from the imperial palaces of Russia. Looking back, Gustav Muth, a staff architect with Albert Kahn Associates, recalled in the 1960s what the era was like: "The architects had carte blanche. Money was no object and decoration was essential. Usually the client had some idea of what he wanted generally. The basic design and size was most often decided by the owner, but the details were left up to the architect, and he took full advantage of the opportunity."

Such an opulent era could not last. By the 1950s higher taxes and real estate assessments, plus a dwindling pool of servants, made the great houses too expensive. One after the other closed, its wealth of furnishings sold. The mansions were razed, and their ten-acre grounds subdivided for smaller houses. "This one will go when I go," Mrs. Henry B. Joy, owner of one estate, Fair Acres, said shortly before her death in 1959. "It just breaks my heart to see them all go," another owner, Mrs. Joseph B. Schlotman, said a few years later. "The beautiful old homes with all their warmth

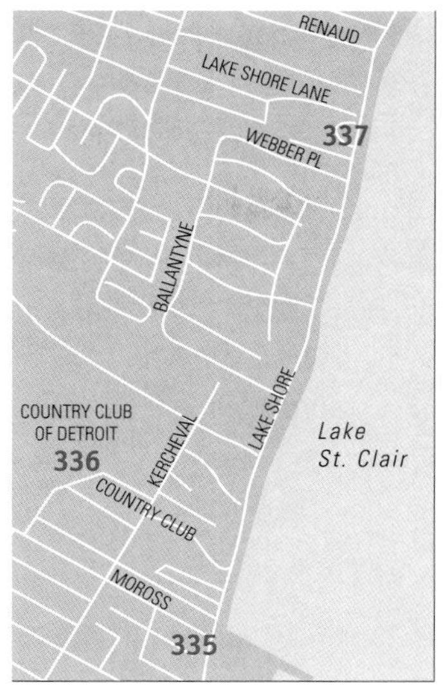

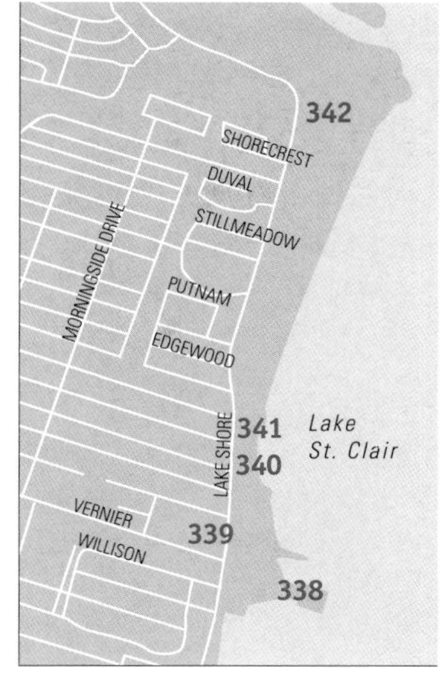

GROSSE POINTE AREA

324 DARRYL FINKEN HOUSE
325 WILLIAM B. STRATTON HOUSE
326 FRANK AND ANNE PARCELLS HOUSE
327 WILLIAM KESSLER HOUSE
328 GROSSE POINTE PUBLIC LIBRARY
329 GROSSE POINTE MEMORIAL CHURCH
330 GROSSE POINTE WAR MEMORIAL
331 BEVERLY ROAD HISTORIC DISTRICT
332 CHRIST CHURCH
333 SAINT PAUL ROMAN CATHOLIC CHURCH COMPLEX
334 GROSSE POINTE ACADEMY
335 GROSSE POINTE FARMS WATER FILTRATION PLANT
336 COUNTRY CLUB OF DETROIT
337 EMORY W. CLARK HOUSE
338 GROSSE POINTE YACHT CLUB
339 GROSSE POINTE SHORES VILLAGE HALL
340 C. GOODLEE EDGAR HOUSE
341 W. HAWKINS FERRY HOUSE
342 EDSEL B. AND ELEANOR FORD HOUSE

and dignity gone—or going—one after another. And all the old estates, full of little ranch houses." Windmill Point Drive provides a relatively intact, smaller scale representation of earlier times.

The modern era has produced mixed results. A number of houses added since the 1930s are among the best early- to late-Modern designs in the region. Gino Rossetti's Bon Secours Hospital, pictured, is a most successful example of nestling a large-scale institution into a quiet residential context. More than a few of the Postmodern replacements of earlier mansions on Lake Shore Drive, though still appearing luxurious, somehow lack the material presence of the vanished estates.

While Grosse Pointe Lakeshore may no longer be the showcase that once was, this special environment remains one of greater Detroit's defining moments in architecture, not to mention a compelling place for a leisurely drive.

324 DARRYL FINKEN HOUSE

C PR

15114 Kercheval
Swanson and Swanson, and William Hartman consultant, 1994

Remote in place, time, and ethos from Lake Shore Drive, this bold example of modernism presents another face of the Pointes, however in the extreme minority. Designed by a team that included Saarinen's great-granddaughter, this addition was honored by AIA Detroit.

Grosse Pointe

Bon Secours Hospital

324

325 WILLIAM B. STRATTON HOUSE

N PR

938 Three Mile Dr.
William B. Stratton, 1927

Stratton and his wife, Mary Chase Perry Stratton, founder of Pewabic Pottery (319), moved from East Grand Boulevard to the Grosse Pointes in the late 1920s. It is no surprise that the interior includes a wealth of Pewabic tile. A unique combination of modern massing and an eye for romantic Arts and Crafts materiality, including superb brickwork, sets this house apart from more obviously historicist models popular at the time. The reader is invited to draw comparisons to the contemporaneous work of Eliel Saarinen at Cranbrook, which also emerged at least in part from Arts and Crafts.

326 FRANK AND ANNE PARCELLS HOUSE

PR

3 Cameron Pl.
Paul Rudolph, 1970

A rare—if not the only—house in the area designed by Paul Rudolph (1918–1997), one of the masters of modern architecture. The architect rotated the three-story house on the site to maximize both the panoramic lake view and neighboring privacy. The sculptural design follows Rudolph's earlier Florida houses, exhibiting a light and open transparency. Major interior spaces are separated by changes in level, five in all, as the interior flows without interruption to exterior spaces. The original redwood siding was stained a natural gray.

327 WILLIAM KESSLER HOUSE

PR

1013 Cadieux
Meathe, Kessler, and Associates, 1959

A thoughtful modernist, architect Kessler designed his own house as a light, ethereal ranch that emphasizes privacy even on a busy street. Indeed, the street façade is practically all garden wall and easily missed at that.

325

326

327

328

GROSSE POINTE PUBLIC LIBRARY

P

10 Kercheval at Fisher
Marcel Breuer, 1953

This library shows how a modernist building can fit smoothly into the Colonial and Tudor landscape of the Pointes. Philanthropist Dexter M. Ferry, Jr., donated the money for the library, and the local school system gave the prominent site. Ferry suggested that famed Bauhaus-trained architect Marcel Breuer (1902–1981) of New York design the building. The most prominent feature of Breuer's rectangular plan is the two-story glass wall running the length of the main reading room. Breuer thus achieved his aim of symbolically opening up the library to the public and making learning and culture more accessible. An Alexander Calder mobile graces the interior.

329

GROSSE POINTE MEMORIAL CHURCH

NS
SP

16 Lake Shore Dr.
William E. N. Hunter, 1927

By the 1920s the Grosse Pointes were booming, and the wealthy Grosse Pointe Presbyterian Church needed a new sanctuary. Two brothers, John and Truman Newberry, offered to underwrite the entire budget of nearly $300,000 at the time if the name was changed to Grosse Pointe Memorial Church. The church hired W. E. N. Hunter, a noted church designer who had also designed Detroit's Metropolitan United Methodist Church (207). Hunter's late Gothic Revival design recalls noble English village fare, eminently suited to the needs of a prominent Grosse Pointe congregation.

330

GROSSE POINTE WAR MEMORIAL (RUSSELL A. ALGER, JR., HOUSE)

NS
SP

32 Lake Shore Dr.
Charles A. Platt, 1910

By the early 1900s wealthy Detroiters had joined the trend toward creating large suburban estates. Many turned to architect Charles A. Platt of New York, who had studied at the Ecole des Beaux-Arts in Paris. Impressed with Italian gardens, Platt took to creating houses and gardens as integrated wholes. One of his best was "The Moorings," a mansion for Russell A. Alger, Jr., heir to a lumber fortune and one of the early investors in the Packard Motor Car Company. Platt's free adaptation of Italian Renaissance themes to the bluffs overlooking Lake St. Clair joined masterfully with the house's formal gardens and lake frontage. In 1949 the Alger family donated the house to the Grosse Pointe War Memorial Association for use as a community cultural center. The later auditorium, while sympathetic in design, unfortunately blocks the view of the lake from the gardens.

328

329

330

331 BEVERLY ROAD HISTORIC DISTRICT

Beverly, north of Lake Shore Dr.
Various architects, 1910–1945

Developed by Henry Joy, this is one of the earliest subdivisions in Grosse Pointe catering to wealth, new and old, and represents a milestone in the Pointes' transformation from summer resort to prestigious suburb. Extending from Lake Shore Drive to Grosse Pointe Boulevard, the national historic district includes fifteen exceptional houses in a variety of period revival styles. The elegant limestone and iron gateway is by Albert Kahn, and the houses were designed by many prominent residential architects of the day, including Derrick, Carey, and Burrowes. All the ingredients valued by today's New Urbanists were in place to maximize the neighborhood's quality and the developer's return on investment. In a gesture of ultimate privacy from busy Lake Shore Drive the gates were later permanently closed.

332 CHRIST CHURCH

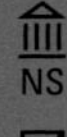

Christ Church Lane at Grosse Pointe Blvd.
Bertram G. Goodhue Associates, 1930

Like Grosse Pointe Memorial Church (329), this is an elegant Neo-Gothic structure designed for one of the Grosse Pointes' wealthy congregations. Note how the tower merges with the pediment of the façade. The Goodhue firm also created the magnificent Christ Church Cranbrook (354) in Bloomfield Hills.

333 SAINT PAUL ROMAN CATHOLIC CHURCH COMPLEX

157 Lake Shore Dr.
Harry J. Rill, 1899; additions by Smith, Hinchman, and Grylls, 1927

Set back from Lake Shore Drive, this somewhat self-consciously country French Gothic church was designed in brick with an unusual fieldstone base. The interior is more surely developed in decorous simplicity. To put this work in perspective, it was Rill who designed the Detroit Cornice and Slate Company building (28), completed a year earlier. Smith, Hinchman, and Grylls added the relatively more comfortable Neo-Tudor school and convent in 1927.

331

332

333 a

333 b

334
GROSSE POINTE ACADEMY (ACADEMY OF THE SACRED HEART)

NS PR

171 Lake Shore Dr.
William Schickel, Maginnis and Walsh, 1928

The first Catholic boarding school for girls, the then Sacred Heart Academy was designed by nationally prominent architects Schickel, Maginnis, and Walsh in a Tudor Revival style. Providing a trace of seventeenth-century history, the site is a remnant of an original French ribbon farm that once extended to Lake St. Clair.

335
GROSSE POINTE FARMS WATER FILTRATION PLANT

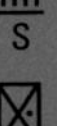

S PR

29 Moross
Robert O. Derrick, 1931

This classy Neo-Georgian utility structure was designed by noted Detroit architect Derrick to conceal its identity. Or, put another way, the design respects its residential context while setting a high standard of quality in public works architecture.

336
COUNTRY CLUB OF DETROIT

PR

220 Country Club Dr.
Smith, Hinchman, and Grylls, 1926, including earlier wing by Albert Kahn

The original Albert Kahn-designed clubhouse was substantially destroyed by fire in 1925, and the replacement by Smith, Hinchman, and Grylls followed the same Tudor English Cottage style. The result is a rambling storybook clubhouse with large rooms set amid attractive grounds—a cheerful and pleasant gathering place for social activities. (Kahn's kitchen wing, incredibly, survived the fire.)

334

335

336

337 **EMORY W. CLARK HOUSE**

PR

635 Lake Shore Dr.
Hugh T. Keyes, 1934

Architect Keyes adopted a Georgian/Regency style with bow-fronted wings and delicate iron grillwork. The result is a house in the style of an English country manor. In its day this may have been among the more modest of the great mansions on Lake Shore Drive. Today it's one of the few original survivors from the Gilded Age.

338 **GROSSE POINTE YACHT CLUB**

PR

Lake Shore Dr. at Vernier
Guy Lowell, and Henry and Richmond, 1929

Here we see the full flowering of 1920s romanticism. Based on Venetian motifs, with the slim shaft of the campanile rising 187 feet, the yacht club was designed to be the most magnificent of the many boat clubs lining the Lake St. Clair shoreline. With Edsel Ford an early Commodore, the Club could afford to pay for it. Architects Henry and Richmond, who took over after Lowell's death, said they wanted to create a dramatically vertical counterpoint to the flat terrain. They succeeded. The spire of the Club has remained a navigational landmark for boaters for decades.

339 **GROSSE POINTE SHORES VILLAGE HALL**

SC

P

795 Lake Shore Dr. at Vernier
Albert Kahn, 1915; addition by Wakely Associates, 1984

Kahn was a master at bringing out decorative design possibilities in brick masonry, and this is an excellent example. The scale is small, almost domestic, no doubt designed to fit in with the mansions that stood nearby. This inventive design is among a handful of Kahn's works inspired by Chicago's Prairie School of Sullivan, Wright, et al. The later addition at once extends and dematerializes the original in a transparent wall of considerable finesse and integrity. The massive tower, however, intended as a visual anchor, unfortunately comes off as discordantly out of scale and place.

337

338

339

340 PR

C. GOODLEE EDGAR HOUSE

880 Lake Shore Dr.
Albert Kahn, 1910

A balustraded terrace symmetrically flanked by two loggias allowed a beautiful and serene panorama of the formal garden and Lake St. Clair. Compare to Kahn's Siegel house (217) on West Boston.

341 PR

W. HAWKINS FERRY HOUSE

874 Lake Shore Dr.
Meathe, Kessler, and Associates, 1964

This spacious house was designed for the dean of Detroit architectural historians in an unabashedly modern mode. Planned on a rigorous fifteen-foot-square module, the house opens several two-story spaces to Lake St. Clair. Best viewed from the water.

342 NS C SP$

EDSEL B. AND ELEANOR FORD HOUSE

1100 Lake Shore Dr.
Albert Kahn, 1927

It is ironic that while many of Albert Kahn's most influential modern industrial works largely have been lost, his most admired surviving buildings are predominantly commercial and residential in use, and eclectic in architectural expression. Witness this loving and sprawling take on a Cotswold cottage designed for the Fords. The owners and architect purchased many of the interior decorative elements from older English houses and shipped them to Grosse Pointe for reinterpretation and reuse. Cotswold stonemasons and roofers were also brought over to ensure authentic results.

The Detroit architect built to last, regardless of context and scale. Beneath the Ford house's romantic massing are reinforced concrete floors and steel roof trusses. Impressively situated on grounds designed by noted landscape architect Jens Jensen, the building's loggias and terraces take full advantage of sweeping views of Lake St. Clair from Gaulker Point. This delightful and compelling house is now maintained as a museum, which is periodically open to the public.

340

341

342

Cranbrook

In 1904 Detroit publisher George Booth bought a large tract of virgin terrain in Bloomfield Hills that bore the geologically rich imprint of the last ice age. In the ensuing years Booth marshalled an international cadre of creative talent to carefully build upon this natural legacy. Named for the English village from which the Booth family emigrated, Cranbrook remains one of America's most exceptional designed environments.

Beginning with Cranbrook House in 1908, Booth developed his family estate through the 1910s. In 1925 he hired Finnish architect Eliel Saarinen to help him design a school for boys, thus beginning one of architecture's great collaborations. Booth had founded Detroit's Arts and Crafts Society, and Saarinen was a leader in the emerging Finnish school of architecture that sought authenticity in a return to traditional forms and materials. For two decades the men merged their complementary visions to create the Cranbrook Educational Community.

The Cranbrook achievement is universally acclaimed as a world-class collection of buildings and landscapes. Saarinen endowed each of his schools, museums, and residences with its own original character. But all breathed the essence of the Cranbrook ideal—that every creation, from the simplest detail to the largest building and gardens, should contribute to an overall sense of beauty. The code of the craftsman was honored everywhere. Materials were chosen not only for visual but also for tactile character, with an emphasis on the man-made.

Booth and Saarinen agreed that artists should play a major role at Cranbrook, and many journeyed from Europe for the opportunity to grow individually and collaboratively in residence. Wrought iron was worked by Oscar Bach, sculpture formed by Geza Maroti, and bronzes cast by Paul Manship and Carl Milles. This tradition continues to this day, as many of Cranbrook's newest works of art, as well as its smaller structures and fixtures, have been crafted on-site by teams of faculty and students.

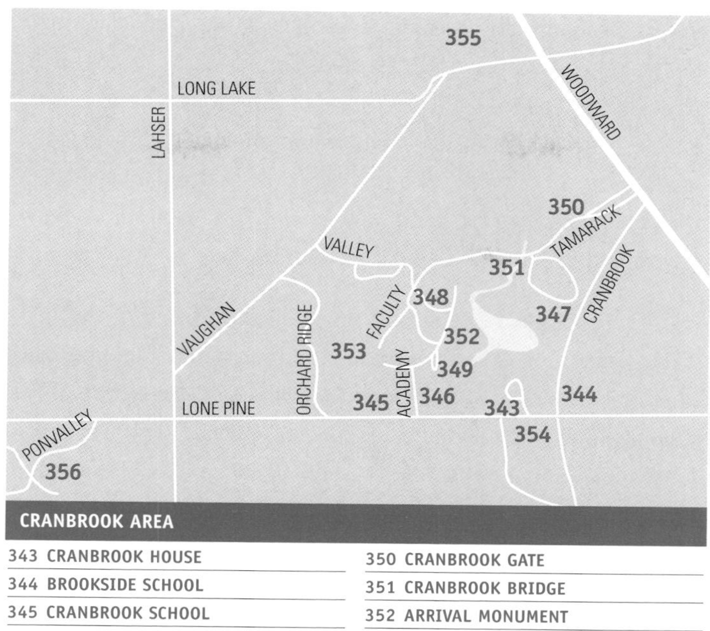

CRANBROOK AREA

343 CRANBROOK HOUSE	350 CRANBROOK GATE
344 BROOKSIDE SCHOOL	351 CRANBROOK BRIDGE
345 CRANBROOK SCHOOL	352 ARRIVAL MONUMENT
346 CRANBROOK ACADEMY OF ART	353 CRANBROOK NATATORIUM
347 KINGSWOOD SCHOOL	354 CHRIST CHURCH CRANBROOK
348 CRANBROOK INSTITUTE OF SCIENCE	355 GREGOR AFFLECK HOUSE
349 CRANBROOK MUSEUM AND LIBRARY	356 MARVIN SMITH HOUSE

The Booth-Saarinen aesthetic evolved with each building, from the traditional forms at Brookside School through the more severely modern lines of the Cranbrook Art Museum and Library. Yet the overall look of the campus has melded into a pleasing whole. So successful was Cranbrook's distinctive tan Wyandotte brick that it became the material of choice for numerous imitative suburban designs throughout the suburban region.

With the completion of the art museum and library in the mid-1940s, Cranbrook entered a dormant period when little new was added for decades. Beginning in the mid-1980s, the needs of the growing school demanded an expansion. Under Cranbrook presidents Lillian Bauder and Robert Gavin, Jr., several talented architects have added new buildings of note. In keeping with the spirit of the Saarinen legacy, these newer works have emphasized creativity in form and material. Each subordinates to the whole, and, while there are no "signature" designs that redefine the campus, as a group they breath new life into an already remarkable environment.

The Institute of Science, Art Museum, and Cranbrook House and Gardens are open to the public on a regular basis. Eliel Saarinen's house, which provides insights into the breadth and depth of his design genius, is open in warm weather months. In all, this special place in American planning and design adds immeasurably to the greater Detroit story. Departing from a locational rationale, the Cranbrook entries are presented in more or less the chronology of their completion.

Art Museum and Library

Eliel Saarinen House

343

CRANBROOK HOUSE

380 Lone Pine Rd.

Albert Kahn, 1907; additions by Marcus Burrowes and others

SP$

The vision began here, as Cranbrook House set standards that would guide a century of subsequent planning and design. In 1907 George Booth asked Albert Kahn to infuse Arts and Crafts sensibility into a traditional English manor house. Kahn's own house on Mack Avenue (134) was a prototype for the grander mansion, which today serves as Cranbrook's headquarters.

The house was sited atop a hill overlooking a landscape panorama as beautiful as any in the region. Beginning in the 1920s George Booth introduced subtle axial cuts through the forest, as the estate was brought into a greater community plan. Today, the dramatic sweep of lush gardens, artificial pond, and distant vistas create a symbiosis of man and nature that is integral to Cranbrook's identity.

Inside as well, a virtual army of artists and artisans merged their considerable talents to create a seamlessly crafted whole. Among others, Mary Chase Perry Stratton contributed her art of Pewabic Pottery (319), and Johann Kirchmayer provided extraordinary craftsmanship in wood.

In the 1910s Booth commissioned a number of supplementary outbuildings on the estate. Because Kahn's expanding practice prevented him from personally attending to every detail, Booth turned to Detroit architect Marcus Burrowes to design a garage, a cottage, a greenhouse, and an open-air theater. Burrowes's Lone Pine entrance of 1917 was embellished by Samuel Yellin's handsome wrought-iron gates. Booth returned to Kahn for later additions to Cranbrook House, including the library wing to the west in 1918 and the family wing to the east in 1920. Two years later, as the grander scheme was evolving in Booth's imagination, Kahn enthusiastically recommended that his client hire a talented Michigan professor by the name of Saarinen to oversee the next phase of Cranbrook's development.

Outside and in, Cranbrook House set the tone and example for the greater vision. This rare piece of Old World charm is open to the public.

343 a

343 b

344 BROOKSIDE SCHOOL

550 Cranbrook Rd.

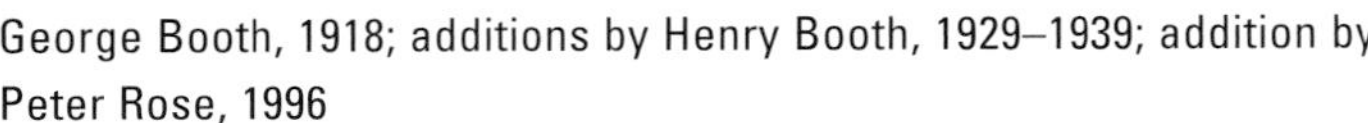

George Booth, 1918; additions by Henry Booth, 1929–1939; addition by Peter Rose, 1996

PR

George Booth himself designed the original building as an auditorium and meeting house. Booth's son Henry, who had introduced his father to Saarinen and thus sparked their relationship, designed the first additions a decade later. He, too, favored the slate roofs and brick trim of his father's Arts and Crafts design. In 1996 Peter Rose of Montreal designed the latest addition to Cranbrook's elementary school and Booths' rambling collection of country cottage-style buildings. Rose produced an interesting variant on the theme with a lively two-story wing, faced with mottled concrete block and roofed in tile to match the original building.

345 CRANBROOK SCHOOL

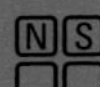

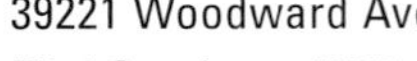

39221 Woodward Ave.

Eliel Saarinen, 1927–1930

SP

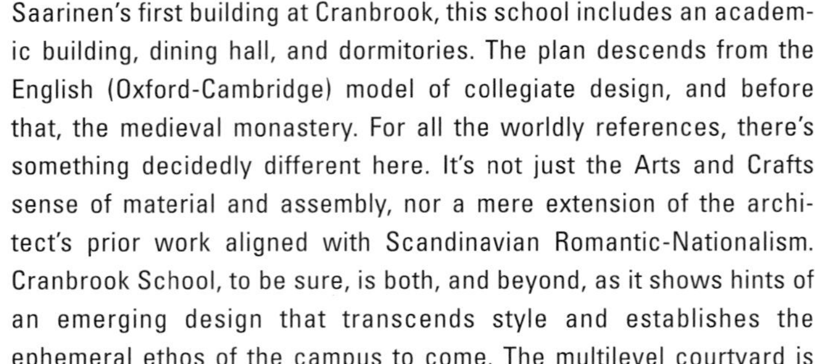

Saarinen's first building at Cranbrook, this school includes an academic building, dining hall, and dormitories. The plan descends from the English (Oxford-Cambridge) model of collegiate design, and before that, the medieval monastery. For all the worldly references, there's something decidedly different here. It's not just the Arts and Crafts sense of material and assembly, nor a mere extension of the architect's prior work aligned with Scandinavian Romantic-Nationalism. Cranbrook School, to be sure, is both, and beyond, as it shows hints of an emerging design that transcends style and establishes the ephemeral ethos of the campus to come. The multilevel courtyard is one of America's greatest outdoor rooms.

344

345 a

345 b

346 **CRANBROOK ACADEMY OF ART**

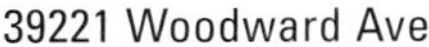

39221 Woodward Ave.
Swanson and Booth, 1926; studio and houses by Eliel Saarinen, 1927–1930

In this background ensemble Saarinen blended medieval, Arts and Crafts, and Art Moderne to create a unique and wholly original statement. The Architectural Office (1925–1926) was designed by Robert F. Swanson and George Booth. Eliel Saarinen designed the Studios (1927–1929), the Arts and Crafts Building, including studios and dormitories (1928–1929), and houses for himself and Carl Milles (1928–1930). Saarinen's own house interior is a consummate Art Moderne/Deco statement. In today's emerging "public" Cranbrook, which focuses on the new public entrance and the heavily trafficked museum and science institute, these quieter, earlier buildings remain at the heart of the Cranbrook legacy.

347 **KINGSWOOD SCHOOL**

39221 Woodward Ave.
Eliel Saarinen, 1931

For Kingswood, Cranbrook's school for girls, Saarinen and Booth chose the edge of a small lake with a wooded hill in the background. The result is among the most pleasing of Cranbrook's many delights. The horizontal massing conforms to the lakeshore, while the copper roofs, brick, and stone blend with nearby natural surroundings. The influence of Frank Lloyd Wright can be seen in the banks of windows and the overhanging eaves, but Saarinen made these motifs his own, as he did the array of Art Deco elements and detailing. The entire Saarinen family got involved. Saarinen's wife, Loja, designed the rugs, draperies, and fabrics for Kingswood; his daughter, Pipsan, designed some of the interiors; and his son, Eero, designed the furniture.

346

347

SPECIAL Cranbrook

348 CRANBROOK INSTITUTE OF SCIENCE

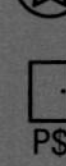

39221 Woodward Ave.
Eliel Saarinen, 1935–38; addtion by Steven Holl, 1998

Saarinen's flat roofs and horizontal lines here mark a stylistic midpoint between the evocatively rich details of Kingswood (347) and the more abstract modernism of the Museum and Library (349) to come. The planetarium was sensitively added by architect William Kapp in 1955. In the 1990s Steven Holl of New York designed the massive addition, which respectfully tucks behind Saarinen's original, even though it is now the more important of the two connected parts. Holl's entrance space doubles as a forty-two-foot-tall "light laboratory" in which different colored and shaped pieces of glass refract sunlight in ever-changing ways. The most technically demanding of Cranbrook's new buildings, with a host of scientific displays built around the themes of water and "natural connection," Holl's addition was designed to handle a throng of visitors each year. Perhaps because of that heavy usage, the new Institute features fewer of those Arts and Crafts touches that define the campus elsewhere. Time will tell if this addition struck a new vein worth further mining.

349 CRANBROOK MUSEUM AND LIBRARY

39221 Woodward Ave.
Eliel Saarinen, 1942; addition by Robert Saarinen Swanson, 1986

Saarinen's final building at Cranbrook achieved a stylistic zenith in a modernism that is remarkably at once minimalist and humanist. The Peristyle—open-air columned pavilion—connects the Museum and Library and serves as a ceremonial heart of the campus, framing the much-photographed Triton Pool court and the Orpheus Fountain by Carl Milles.

In 1986 the Albert and Peggy deSalle Auditorium was built beneath Saarinen's building and the court. This technical achievement was notably designed by Saarinen's grandson, Robert Saarinen Swanson.

At this writing, work has begun on a new wing designed by Pritzker Prize-winning architect Rafael Moneo of Spain. Moneo's wing will add much-needed studio and exhibit space, which will present something of a split personality that is responsive to the dual nature of its context. The side facing the grounds will be a strongly horizontal building covered in dark brick and roofed in copper, thus tying in to the early work. The side facing the museum courtyard will be more transparent and abstractly sculptural.

348 a

348 b

349

SPECIAL Cranbrook

350 **CRANBROOK GATE**

39221 Woodward Ave.
Dan Hoffman, 1994

P

With uplifted wings, Hoffman's gatehouse could be a bird alighting on campus—indeed, a multilayered and metaphorical reference to "Crane Brook." Impressive as this sculptural gate may be, the addition of a place of arrival off Woodward was a planning tour de force. For decades, visitors, students, and staff drove onto campus from Lone Pine Road, which was not designed to bear the burden of Cranbrook's modern popularity. The new winding road off Woodward, opened in 1992 and perhaps unnecessarily generous in width, languorously funnels the hundreds of thousands of annual visitors to Cranbrook's most public resources.

351 **CRANBROOK BRIDGE**

39221 Woodward Ave.
Dan Hoffman and Ted Galante, 1993

P

Even the most modest fixture at Cranbrook becomes special. Working with his design students, Hoffman took the assignment to build a footbridge as an opportunity to create this structural delight.

352 **ARRIVAL MONUMENT**

39221 Woodward Ave.
Juhani Pallasmaa, 1995

P

The modern Finnish architect's sculptural grouping, including a range of stone pushed to the area by the last glacier, is poetically situated and hauntingly beautiful.

353 **CRANBROOK NATATORIUM**

39221 Woodward Ave.
Tod Williams Billie Tsien and Associates, 2000

N

SP

Recently awarded a national design honor from the AIA, the new indoor swim facility by Tod Williams and Billie Tsien is the most remarkable of the new works. Tucked into the trees on a sloping hillside, the modest plum-colored exterior does little to prepare the observer for the stunning natatorium itself. Williams, a Cranbrook graduate, and Tsien added inventive features to cool, ventilate, and illuminate the space. A series of vertical baffles on the walls open to let breezes in, and two oversized oculi, or cylinder-like chutes, open to the sky. Together they are visually, as well as functionally, exquisite. The light pattern on the ceiling has been left random to mimic a starry night, and the pool surface flanks a glass curtain-wall, which enables lap swimmers to measure their progress against the outdoor landscape.

350

351

352

353

354 CHRIST CHURCH CRANBROOK

470 Church Rd.
Bertram G. Goodhue Associates, and Oscar H. Murray, 1928 and 1938

George Booth sought out the best architects and artisans to design a church based on his beloved English country parish Gothic style. The result was one of the finest collaborations of architects and artisans in the Detroit area. The church and rectory were finished in 1928; the parish house and educational wing a decade later. Among the many artisans who contributed their skills was Mary Chase Perry Stratton of Pewabic Pottery (319), who crafted the ceiling of Pewabic mosaics in the baptistery.

355 GREGOR AFFLECK HOUSE

1925 North Woodward Ave.
Frank Lloyd Wright, 1941

Wright's Affleck House has been called a small-scale Fallingwater, perhaps the most universally recognized house design of the twentieth century. Like Fallingwater, the Affleck House was designed to meld into its wooded ravine setting. The house is L-shaped in plan, with the bedroom wing perpendicular to the spacious living area. The most prominent feature is the projecting deck off the living/dining room that seems to thrust the house into nature. The house is now owned by Lawrence Technological University. Having had thousands of visitors, the Affleck House remains the best-known and most accessible of Wright's works in Southeast Michigan.

356 MARVIN SMITH HOUSE

5045 Ponvalley Rd.
Frank Lloyd Wright, 1951

After the lean years of the Depression and World War II, Wright had still one more career chapter remaining in his ambition to be the world's greatest architect. By this time, compellingly beautiful architecture seemed to fall out of the master's sleeve. Poetically captured here by Korab, this modest L-shaped Usonian house nestles into its Bloomfield Hills site with natural ease.

354

355

356

GM Technical Center

It may be difficult to recapture today just how profoundly revolutionary Eero Saarinen's General Motors Technical Center was when new. The dedication on May 16, 1956, was broadcast on nationwide television, and President Dwight D. Eisenhower spoke to the multitudes via radio. Some experts still consider the Tech Center to be the Detroit region's last indisputably great work of architecture and a rival even of the Cranbrook campus. Like the Brooklyn Bridge and the Eiffel Tower, this marriage of technology and art remains as vital today as when it was built. Indeed, the maturing landscape that Saarinen planned has enhanced his initial vision, as he knew it would.

When GM emerged from World War II as an industrial powerhouse, it sought to consolidate its widely scattered design work at a single location. Harley Earl, GM's longtime head of styling, enthusiastically recommended the firm of Saarinen, Saarinen, and Associates. The elder Saarinen had won fame for his Cranbrook work, but son Eero had yet to make his own mark on the profession. He sensed intuitively that the romantic styles of the past were clearly out of place in modern Detroit, and he threw himself into the work of creating something entirely new in Warren.

From the beginning, the younger Saarinen wanted the Tech Center's architecture to express and celebrate the technical ethic of the automotive industry. The twenty-six buildings he designed were, like automobiles themselves, built mainly of glass, steel, and aluminum standardized products. Neoprene gaskets were used instead of caulking to hold windows and wall panels in place. A light triangular steel roof truss with a span of fifty feet permitted open rooms below and maximum flexibility in space planning. Instead of thick masonry walls, Saarinen employed two-inch-thick wall panels, a sandwich with a porcelain enamel steel skin bonded to a heavy Kraft paper honeycomb core completely filled with granular insulation. The thinness of this method vastly increased usable space.

Yet all this technical advancement was set with an artist's eye in a superbly organized landscape. Saarinen grouped the buildings campus-like, low and horizontal, around a man-made lake in which he sited four islands planted with willow trees. Some 13,000

trees were planted, 60,000 plants and shrubs, 155 acres of lawn—or roughly half the total acreage of the Tech Center. Like Olmsted's famed parks, the Tech Center was designed to look its best only a generation after its initial opening.

Two of the Tech Center's most photographed icons came from the mind of architect Kevin Roche, who worked in Saarinen's office then. These are the "floating staircases" in the lobbies of the Research and Development and Design buildings. The circular staircase in R&D is supported by thin cylindrical rods anchored at top and bottom. Each stair tread is three-quarters of a ton of Norwegian granite—a total of more than twenty-five tons. Yet the staircase seems to float in space, concealing in plain sight the stainless steel suspension rods that form a converging cone at top and bottom. The stair treads in the Design building are seven-foot terrazzo slabs that overlap each other. Each tread is caught in tension between pencil-thin stainless steel rods. The handrail is made of teak.

The fountain just outside the R&D Center on the north end of the lake is a water ballet designed by Alexander Calder. He named the elements of the fountain Fantails, Seven Sisters, Scissors, and Plops. The main fountain located on the west side of the lake pumps 6,000 gallons of water per minute to create a 115-foot-wide, 55-foot-high wall of water. The space-age water tower on the north end of the lake rises 140 feet. Saarinen scoffed at the idea of trying to hide the tower on the back end of the property and instead made it something worth looking at.

One of the Tech Center's most endearing legacies is the use of ceramic glazed brick on the exteriors. Saarinen said he wanted the Tech Center to resemble autumn leaves reflected in the afternoon sun, so he chose brick colors of crimson, orange, yellow, blue, and other tones. This brightly distinctive and widely imitated look was chosen characteristically only after much initial experimentation by Saarinen and Cranbrook ceramist Maija Grotell.

So successful was the Tech Center that the younger Saarinen stepped forever out of the shadow of his famous father. In his all too brief life, he went on to design other icons of modern architecture: Dulles Airport outside Washington, D.C., the TWA Terminal at Kennedy International Airport, and the Gateway Arch in St. Louis. Small-minded critics came to chide Saarinen for his boldness; he was too much the individual, they would say, his designs too embarrassingly expressive. As the echoes of these design wars fade into history, Saarinen's work stands today as some of the best of the age.

To its credit, GM has handled this legacy with gentleness and care. Saarinen's original buildings appear much today as when he left them. For its later buildings to the east and north on the campus, GM (still adding on today) stuck to the low-rise, horizontal model Saarinen began. But there was no replacing the master architect or one-upping his master plan. Much of the newer work seems ungainly after the serene splendor of the original.

Unfortunately, this landmark of Modern architecture is not, at this writing, accessible to the public. The observer can only catch glimpses from the perimeter streets. While we must apologize for this look-but-don't-touch tease, perhaps GM will modify its policy at some future date.

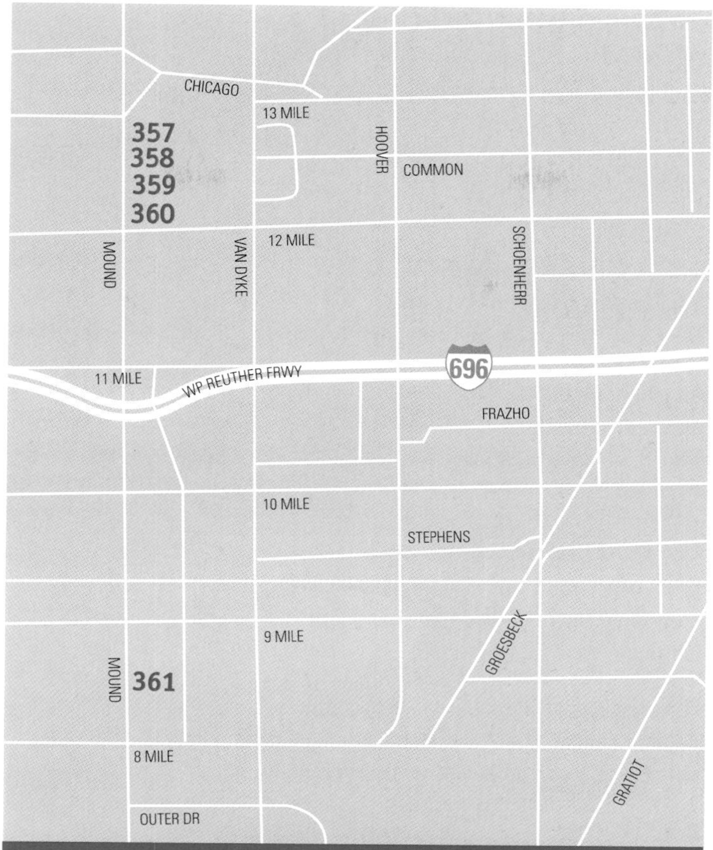

GM TECHNICAL CENTER AREA

357 STYLING BUILDINGS

358 GM TECH CENTER DESIGN DOME

359 CENTRAL RESTAURANT BUILDING

360 GM TECH CENTER TOWER AND FOUNTAIN

361 CHRYSLER-DODGE HALF-TON TRUCK PLANT

Water tower

Interior stair

357 STYLING BUILDINGS

General Motors Technical Center
Eero Saarinen and Associates, and Smith, Hinchman, and Grylls, 1956

The floating staircase remains one of industry's most potent corporate symbols.

358 GM TECH CENTER DESIGN DOME

General Motors Technical Center
Eero Saarinen and Associates, and Smith, Hinchman, and Grylls, 1956

As super-secret as a CIA bunker, the design dome remains an iconic place maker.

359 CENTRAL RESTAURANT BUILDING

General Motors Technical Center
Eero Saarinen and Associates, and Smith, Hinchman, and Grylls, with screen by Harry Bertoia, 1956

Saarinen cared about social as well as architectural cohesion. The cafeteria created a venue in which ideas could blossom. The remarkable Bertoia screen has recently been restored.

357

358

359

360 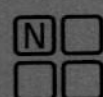 

GM TECH CENTER TOWER AND FOUNTAIN

General Motors Technical Center
Eero Saarinen and Associates, and Smith, Hinchman, and Grylls, with fountain by Alexander Calder, 1956

A memorable collaboration of architect and artist, Calder's fountain is ideally viewed in the context of Saarinen's tower. Considered a necessary evil at first, the water tower is one of the Center's signature pieces.

361 

CHRYSLER-DODGE HALF-TON TRUCK PLANT

21500 Mound Rd.
Albert Kahn, 1937

A poignant footnote to our excursion to the GM Tech Center is this masterpiece of industrial architecture located downstream on Mound Road and upstream in the evolution of modern architecture. Completed toward the end of Albert Kahn's illustrious career, this unassuming design for industry was an instant classic that reverberated across space and time. Saarinen's later achievement at the nearby Tech Center was indebted at least in spirit if not in fact to such precedents, proving the axiom that great architecture often draws on great sources.

With Half-Ton, Kahn streamlined the three-part composition of sturdy base, window wall, and roof monitor to its essential expression, at once massive and transparent.

Not uncommonly, the shelf life of industrial architecture is fleetingly short. The more manufacturing processes change, the less these buildings remain the same. Most are modified, appended if not surrounded, and otherwise altered beyond recognition. While Half-Ton is an exception, its present condition suggests that it is endangered (361b), and its preservation is a cultural imperative.

360

361 a

361 b

Ford's Dearborn

Almost before the concrete had cured at Highland Park, Ford was off to the banks of Dearborn's Rouge River to build the world's prototypical factory. Some historians believe Ford's achievement at "the Rouge" is perhaps the seminal building enterprise, if not culture-defining moment, of the twentieth century. The automobile soon revolutionized the city, invented the suburb, and forever changed the world. Unfortunately, this assessment embraces a darker side, including Ford's anti-urban sentiment: "The modern city has been prodigal, it is today bankrupt, and tomorrow will cease to be" (quoted in Bucci, 1993).

Ford's Rotunda Building, designed by Kahn for the 1933 Chicago Exhibition (rendered at right by Hugh Ferris) summarized the automaker's global ambition and reach. On a different influential plane, Kahn's architecture inspired the Bauhaus and the Modern Movement as a futurist dream. In more recent decades, the creation of Henry Ford Museum and Greenfield Village, as well as the famous Glass House that serves as Ford Motor Company's world headquarters, deepens and broadens the architectural legacy of this special environment.

362 **FAIR LANE**

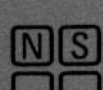

4901 Evergreen Rd.
William Van Tine, and Van Holst and Fyfe, with Jens Jensen, 1909–1915

After a decade of strategic purchases, Ford had amassed more than two thousand acres along the Rouge River in Dearborn to build his empire, including this country estate. In so doing Ford replaced the Highland Park plant (224) and West Boston Avenue residence (215) as the centers of his entrepreneurial and personal worlds. From the outset a sizable portion of land set aside for his new house was left in its natural state as wetlands, woodlands, and bird sanctuary.

The Fords hired Marion Mahoney Griffin of the Chicago firm Van Holst and Fyfe to design a Prairie-style house. But the firm was dismissed by Ford during a construction dispute and replaced by William Van Tine, who altered Griffin's plans to give the design an English baronial Gothic flavor. The result is a unique Prairie-Gothic villa.

Noted landscape architect Jens Jensen, who also designed the grounds for the Eleanor and Edsel Ford house (342) in Grosse Pointe Shores, designed the immediate site and gardens. The estate's house and grounds are presently under restoration.

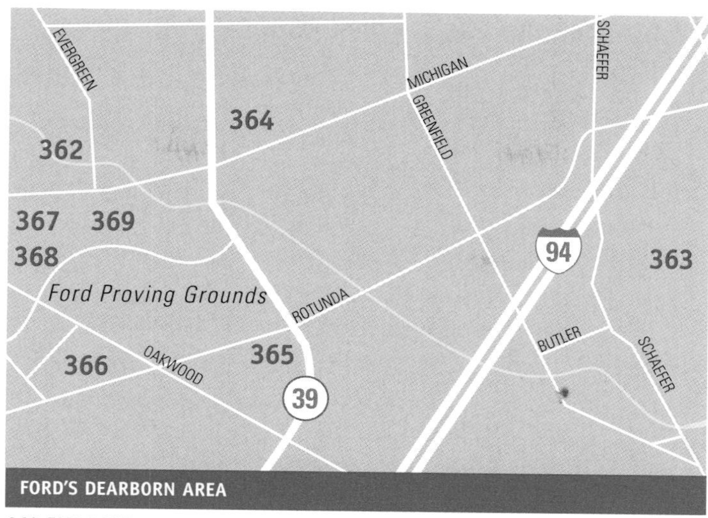

FORD'S DEARBORN AREA

362 FAIR LANE

363 FORD MOTOR CO., RIVER ROUGE PLANT

364 FORD MOTOR CO. WORLD HEADQUARTERS

365 FORD MOTOR CO., FORD DIVISION BUILDING

366 THE DEARBORN INN

367 HENRY FORD MUSEUM AND GREENFIELD VILLAGE

368 DYMAXION HOUSE, HENRY FORD MUSEUM

369 HENRY FORD BIRTHPLACE, GREENFIELD VILLAGE

Rotunda interior

362

363 FORD MOTOR COMPANY, RIVER ROUGE PLANT

3001 Miller Rd.
Albert Kahn, 1917–1941

NS

PR

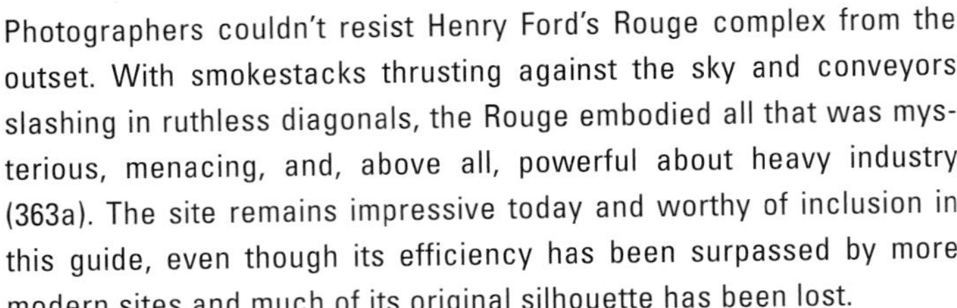

Photographers couldn't resist Henry Ford's Rouge complex from the outset. With smokestacks thrusting against the sky and conveyors slashing in ruthless diagonals, the Rouge embodied all that was mysterious, menacing, and, above all, powerful about heavy industry (363a). The site remains impressive today and worthy of inclusion in this guide, even though its efficiency has been surpassed by more modern sites and much of its original silhouette has been lost.

Historians rightly cite the Rouge as the culmination of Henry Ford's drive to increase production and cut costs to sell more cars. By 1915 Ford saw that his innovative Highland Park plant was already growing obsolete and began amassing enough land along the Rouge River in Dearborn to realize a vastly bigger and more complex operation. The more than one-thousand-acre manufacturing site that evolved between 1917 and 1927 proved to be the world's most important industrial operation. It was here that Ford and Albert Kahn would integrate their ideas about streamlined production methods in buildings ideally suited to house them.

First came the Dearborn Assembly Plant in 1917 (363b). World War I interrupted Ford's plans for the plant; he began by building subchasers, or Eagle Boats, for the U.S. Navy and then switched to cars after the war. Some 1,700 feet long and 350 feet wide, the building was divided into five huge bays, two of which had railroad tracks for parts and materials while the other three were used for assembly. With its single-story steel-frame design, the vast Dearborn Assembly Plant pioneered the new building type that soon rose up around the world.

Kahn's Glass Manufacturing Plant of 1922 carried the innovations even further and blazed a new understanding of functionalist architecture (363c). Matching the structure and design to the specific needs of glass making, Kahn put the highest part of the roof over the glass furnaces and installed huge workable sashes to carry the heat up and away. The grinding and polishing areas, which required workers to be on-hand, were kept free of columns for ease of movement. The overall construction used lightweight steel, and the broad expanses of the exterior surfaces were kept free of structural columns to simplify construction and reduce costs. Eerily photogenic and instantly influential, no other factory of the day carried the integration of architecture and industrial process more into the future than the Glass Plant. Accordingly, it is regarded by many as Albert Kahn's industrial masterpiece.

363 a

363 b

363 c

More buildings followed—power plant (363d), paper mill, cement plant, steel mill, coke ovens, open hearth mill (363e), a couple dozen major buildings in all, plus ninety miles of railroad tracks. By 1927, when final assembly shifted form the Highland Park plant, some 75,000 men and women worked at the Rouge, including 5,000 whose job was simply to keep it clean. Over the years, Ford built tractors here, Model-Ts, Model-As, and, later, Mustangs.

The spirit of innovation kindled at the Rouge never died, but it did move on. In time, newer and better production processes and the factories built around them would surpass the Rouge. As Ford and Kahn passed on, their buildings at the Rouge were modified, expanded, or demolished. Of those retained, many have been refaced in tacky corrugated siding. The Glass Plant long ago lost its smokestacks and its butterfly-roof line, and recently has been reduced to a few representative bays. The invasion of imports in the 1960s and 1970s made the Rouge less important in the scheme of things. Employment today is only a fraction of what it once was.

Yet Ford's company remains committed to the Rouge in the twenty-first century, not only as a place to build cars but as a monument to the environmental passion of the current chairman, William Clay Ford, Jr., great-grandson of the founder. A new grass-topped assembly plant is under construction at the Rouge, the greenery designed to help cool and insulate the plant. A clean-up of the river itself is underway. William McDonough, noted environmental planner and architect, is working with Ford's designers to oversee the remake of the complex.

As with the General Motors Technical Center, admittance to the Rouge complex is by security pass only. Yet the casual viewer can drive Miller Road, along the eastern edge of the Rouge complex, and see what is now Rouge Steel, spun off by Ford some years ago, in much like its original form. And a quick glimpse of the complex from the I-75 Rouge Bridge is breathtaking. To a newcomer, the vista can be unnerving, so colossal is its indifference to ordinary human scale. Even today, with the raw power of the American industrial juggernaut tamed by time and losses, the Rouge still packs a punch.

Turning now from the production core, we consider the greater reach of Ford's Dearborn, encompassing administration, design, and testing facilities, as well as public amenities that aspire to a global vision. Kahn's 1925 Engineering Laboratory (located on Oakwood near Michigan Avenue) epitomizes the transition from manufacturing to "non-manufacturing" and the architect's profoundly dual design persona. Here the emerging master wrapped a perfectly polite neoclassical collar around a spectacularly innovative workplace environment (363f). Practically universal in its application, this thoroughly modern achievement was soon replicated in the exhibit halls of Henry Ford Museum—see 368.

363 d

363 e

363 f

364 PR

FORD MOTOR COMPANY WORLD HEADQUARTERS

American Rd. near Michigan Ave.
Skidmore, Owings, and Merrill, 1956

With this world headquarters building Skidmore, Owings, and Merrill took a step beyond the glassy curtain-wall they initiated for Lever Brothers four years earlier on Manhattan's Park Avenue. Here, the columns were placed on the exterior to free up interior planning. The floor plates were so immense the architects introduced escalators to reduce congestion. Rolled out in the year of the T-Bird, this Ford is a modern classic in its own right.

365 PR

FORD MOTOR COMPANY, FORD DIVISION BUILDING

17101 Rotunda Dr.
Welton Becket and Associates, and Albert Kahn Associates, 1954

Like a corporate organization chart, the front pavilion expresses its functional distinction from the office mass behind. Cantilevered floor slabs provide sun shading for continuous bands of windows. Sophisticated modern architecture for its time.

366 NS SP$

THE DEARBORN INN

20301 Oakwood Blvd.
Albert Kahn, 1931; houses by Charles M. Hart, 1937

Built by Henry Ford in 1931, this is the first airport hotel in the country. It was designed to serve Ford Airport, which was located directly across Oakwood and later converted to Ford Motor Company's proving grounds. Although only briefly active, Ford Airport was one of the most modern airfields in the land. (The runways are still visible from the air, but the serpentine brick walls are designed to keep company secrets.)

The Inn was designed to serve the new air traveler and to further attract visitors to the Edison Institute nearby. The relatively modern plan is cloaked in Neo-Georgian, Ford's style of choice, and includes elements of buildings the auto maker admired. The Alexandria Ballroom is a copy of a colonial Virginia room. From detailing to furnishings the Inn is filled with Colonial Americana.

A most charming surprise is the miniature colonial village built behind the hotel in 1937, pictured. The idea is a foretaste of Ford's more expansive Greenfield Village. Included in the picturesque array are reconstructions of houses of famous Americans. Walt Whitman's farmhouse, Edgar Allan Poe's cottage, and Patrick Henry's Federal-style house were all interpreted and updated by architect Charles Hart of New York.

364

365

366

367 HENRY FORD MUSEUM AND GREENFIELD VILLAGE

Village Rd. and Oakwood Blvd.
Robert O. Derrick, 1929; numerous contributors to the village

This enormous museum is itself a serial display of historic Philadelphia buildings, including Independence Hall, Congress Hall, and Old City Hall. As replicas, they are technically Georgian and Federal, or Neo-Georgian and Neo-Federal, depending on your point of view. This architecture is a welcome addition to an area nearly devoid of either Georgian or Federal styles, whether in original or reproduction form. Inside, the long-span exhibition halls resemble the light monitors Albert Kahn designed for Ford's Engineering Laboratories (363f), completed nearby in 1925.

Greenfield Village, one of the first open-air architectural museums in the United States, includes a wide representative range of building types and architectural styles, spanning over several hundred years of history on eighty-plus acres. Included are houses, public buildings, and industrial shops from near and far, including Thomas Edison's Menlo Park laboratory. Despite its sometimes contrived atmosphere, Greenfield Village fills in some gaps in the Detroit architectural story, including episodes erased by time, natural causes, or human carelessness. In all, Ford rounded out a remarkable legacy in architecture here.

368 DYMAXION HOUSE, HENRY FORD MUSEUM

Village Rd. and Oakwood Blvd.
R. Buckminster Fuller, 1929

From the inventive genius who gave us "synergy," this aluminum house was designed to be mass-produced, easily reused, and completely recyclable. Dymaxion, which stands for "dynamic maximum tension," was theoretically erectable in two days and available for the price of a large automobile. To minimize the use of building materials, the house hangs from a central mast. In contrast to the more poetic expressions of machine age aesthetic by the European masters, Dymaxion was more literally "a machine for living." While this futuristic house fell short of market expectations, the museum is richer for the acquisition, ironically designed about the same time as Robert Derrick's historicist design of the museum itself.

369 HENRY FORD BIRTHPLACE, GREENFIELD VILLAGE

Village Rd. and Oakwood Blvd.
Unknown architect, 1860

A good place to conclude, Ford's childhood home is a fine example of rural Michigan's vernacular residential architecture in the mid-nineteenth century. Symmetrical massing and quiet classical details align this wholly unpretentious structure with the Greek Revival style, popular at the time, in city and country alike.

367

368

369

Timeline of Architects

Thousands of talented designers have shaped the look of Detroit. Those we highlight here produced work so distinctive that they merit special notice. Even this handful of names demonstrates the breadth of the city's architectural heritage. The earliest work represented by these architects dates to the 1860s, and the most recent was still under construction as we wrote these words in mid-2001.

Notice that very few of our highlighted architects were native to Detroit. The city has always drawn outsiders. The canvas here was so broad, the opportunities so great, that generations of architects gave their creative lives to the city. But if immigration is one connecting theme to our list, even more important is energy—a restless creative urge to remake the city in a new vision. Add to this an increasing regard for our architectural legacy and its preservation, and you have the makings of a culturally sustainable city.

Let's not forget that architects alone do not make a city. Mayors, clergy, business leaders, and builders play equally important roles. We would be remiss in a guidebook to Detroit's architecture not to mention the city's planners, most particularly the post-World War II chief of planning, Charles Blessing; or such energetic businessmen as Henry Ford II and Michael Ilitch; or farsighted institutional leaders, such as Wayne State University president David Adamany; or the dozens of individual entrepreneurs who have courageously made a difference, from Chuck Forbes to David DiChiera. But these are just a few names among thousands.

We must also mention the growing contributions of African American designers in Detroit. Until about World War II, racism kept people of color out of the ranks of many professions, including architecture. The first firm to be headed by black architects in Detroit was a partnership of Francis Griffin and Don White, which employed such young black designers as Howard Sims and Nathan Johnson, who later would play a significant role in the city as heads of their own firms. Most of the African American firms at mid-century were small, and subsisted, as do most firms in general, on the everyday trade of architecture—houses, churches, small stores, and the like. The successes of the civil rights movement in the 1960s opened up new avenues for black designers. Today, three generations of African American architects work in Detroit, some as heads of their own firms, and their accomplishments dot the skyline.

Equally at issue for the architectural profession is the history of unequal opportunities for women. In an industry long dominated by males, architecture schools are becoming increasingly balanced in numbers, and women are enjoying comparable success. While female architects make up increasingly significant shares of area firms, and are assuming positions of leadership in the profession, female-owned Detroit practices are disappointingly few in number at this writing.

Progress in diversity in all respects has been made, but there is much to do in expanding the professional tent to an all-inclusive representation of society at large. It is hoped that by the next edition of this Guide, this issue will have receded.

A young Albert Kahn (foreground)
in office of Mason and Rice, ca. 1890

GORDON W. LLOYD (1832–1904)

Born in England, Lloyd spent his boyhood in Canada but returned to Britain for a formal education and an apprenticeship with his uncle, who specialized in the design and restoration of churches. Steeped in the romantic Gothic of northern Europe, Lloyd brought a sketchbook full of medieval details with him when he settled in the boom town of Detroit in 1858. The young classically trained Englishman immediately won several important church commissions, including Christ Church on East Jefferson and Central Methodist Episcopal at Woodward and Adams. Although much of his late-nineteenth-century work has been lost, his Whitney House (now a restaurant) and his Detroit College (now Dowling Hall of the University of Detroit Mercy) stand as important reminders of his influence. Besides his reverence for the past, Lloyd also courted the new in many forms, including investing in newfangled schemes like electric lights. He died in 1904 while boarding a ship in San Francisco for his first trip to the South Seas.

JOHN DONALDSON (1854–1941)

Born in Stirling, Scotland, Donaldson's parents emigrated to Detroit when he was an infant. A graduate of Detroit High School, he received his professional training at the Polytechnic and Art Academy in Munich, and the Ecole des Beaux-Arts in Paris. He returned to Detroit and formed a partnership with Henry Brush, until the latter died in 1879. Donaldson and Meier was founded in 1880, with Henry J. Meier. Upon his death in 1917, Meier was succeeded by his son Walter. Over these several decades, Donaldson and Meier produced a remarkably rich portfolio. Consider the following from the prolific and multilingual Donaldson: Julius Melchers House, St. Aloysius Parish Church and Chancery on Washington Boulevard, Sacred Heart Seminary, addition to People's State Savings Bank, St. Anthony Catholic Church and School, and the David Stott Building.

GEORGE D. MASON (1856–1948)

If for nothing else, we thank Mason for spotting the promise in a teenaged Albert Kahn and mentoring him to early greatness. But Mason's impact on Detroit goes far beyond giving young Albert his first job. Arriving with his parents from Syracuse, New York, in 1870, Mason went on to succeed Gordon Lloyd as a dean of Detroit architecture in a career spanning a half-century. Much of his late-nineteenth- and early-twentieth-century work has been regrettably demolished, but enough remains to demonstrate his greatness: the Masonic Temple, Trinity Episcopal Church at Trumbull and Myrtle, First Presbyterian at Woodward and Edmund, the Gem Theatre and Century Club, and many more. On Mackinac Island in northern Michigan, the graceful sweeping lines of the Grand Hotel came from Mason's drawing board.

WILLIAM E. HIGGINBOTHAM (1858–1923)

From 1894 to 1923, native Detroiter Higginbotham and his partner William Malcomson designed three-quarters of the city's schools, including Central High School, now Wayne State University's Old Main. The firm's high school portfolio spans the Detroit compass: Northern, Eastern, Northwestern, Southeastern, Southwestern, Cass Tech, and the Roosevelt schools, which were won in competition. Higginbotham also developed quite a significant practice in religious architecture, notably including Cass Avenue Methodist Church and Holy Rosary Church on Woodward. His residential works ranged from the Queen Anne-style David Mackenzie House to the Neo-Georgian-style mansion for Henry and Clara Ford on Edison.

LOUIS KAMPER (1861–1953)

Trained in the office of legendary New York architect Stanford White, Kamper left a rich imprint on the architecture of Detroit. For the Book brothers he created the thirteen-story Book Building in 1917, followed by the Book-Cadillac Hotel in 1924 and the thirty-six-story Book Tower in 1926. Plans for a monumental seventy-story Book Tower were set aside when the Great Depression ended the city-building careers of brothers J. Burgess, Herbert, and Frank Book. During his long life, Kamper became one of Detroit's most ubiquitous architects, and many of his important works survive, including the Hecker House on Woodward, the J. Burgess Book mansion at Jefferson and Burns, and his own house at 2150 Iroquois. To a modern eye, much of Kamper's work seems stuck in the nineteenth century. His Book Tower, for example, struggled to apply Beaux-Arts Classicism to the tall building. Yet his Water Board Building Downtown is a cleaner and more assured skyscraper design touched only lightly by an historical brush. While his large-scale commercial work was a bit uneven, Kamper was in his element in residential design, leaving a profound legacy rivaling that of Lloyd, Malcomson, Willeke, and Kahn.

FRED L. SMITH (1862–1941)

Fred Smith's father Mortimer and grandfather Sheldon brought their architecture firm to Detroit from Ohio in 1855. Fred joined the firm as a draftsman at the age of eighteen. Their partnership, Mortimer L. Smith and Son, ended with the senior Smith's passing in 1896, whereupon Fred ventured on his own until he partnered with Field and Hinchman in 1903. With the founding of Smith, Hinchman, and Grylls in 1907, Smith assumed the role of its first president. Tracing the SmithGroup family tree to Sheldon Smith, the present firm is the oldest architectural practice in the country. Over ensuing decades SH&G contributed many of the city's most notable works, encompassing a variety and volume comparable to that of Albert Kahn. The SmithGroup is today the largest architectural practice in the state.

MARY CHASE PERRY STRATTON (1867–1961)

Founder (with Horace J. Caulkins) of Pewabic Pottery in 1903, and one of America's most important ceramists, she named Pewabic after a copper mine in her native Upper Peninsula. In 1907 she moved the operation to its present site on East Jefferson and a half-timbered English cottage designed by architect William (Buck) Stratton, whom she later married. Over many years, she systematically advanced the techniques of ceramics, and was nationally famous for her iridescent glazes and tile installations. Under her guiding hand, Pewabic contributed artwork to numerous important buildings in the Detroit area and throughout the United States, including the Guardian Building and the Cranbrook Educational Community.

ALBERT KAHN (1869–1942)

German-born Albert Kahn came to Detroit as a youth. He showed a remarkable talent for freehand sketching of buildings, but his color blindness led him from painting to architecture. As the chosen designer of Henry Ford, Kahn brilliantly remade the cramped, dingy, nineteenth-century workhouse into the modern factory. Using reinforced concrete (then a new material), steel, glass, and brick, Kahn produced efficient, well-lit factories that enabled Ford to bring his vision of modern mass production to life. Kahn's streamlined factories so impressed Europeans like Gropius and Mies van der Rohe that his work had a seminal influence on their modernism. Ironically, most of his early factories have been lost or abandoned, and the surviving work Kahn is best known for today are his less innovative yet still pleasing residential and commercial works. His Fisher Building skyscraper remains an incomparable Detroit masterpiece; his Edsel and Eleanor Ford estate in Grosse Pointe Shores is an intelligent adaptation of the Cotswold English manor house. Industrious to his very core, Kahn worked even on his death bed. Yet there was never anything coarse or slapdash in his output. There is a refinement in everything Kahn did, and his best buildings will continue to define Detroit for years to come.

ELIEL SAARINEN (1873–1950)

Eliel Saarinen's name will ever be linked with the modern skyscraper, so influential was his sleek and soaring entry in the 1922 competition to design the *Chicago Tribune* tower—the second place that kept on winning by exerting more influence than the selected design. The Finnish-born and trained architect then came to teach at the University of Michigan, where he instructed Henry Booth, son of *Detroit News* publisher George Booth. Shortly thereafter Eliel was invited to submit a design for an art academy at Cranbrook, which began Saarinen's lifework in creating the Cranbrook Educational Community. Working closely with George Booth and inspired by the publisher's leadership in the Arts and Crafts movement in Detroit, Saarinen masterfully attended to making every element of the campus a thing of beauty, from the simplest doorknob and light fixture to the largest building and ensemble. The result is a campus world renowned for the consummate quality of its art and architecture. The American Institute of Architects Detroit chapter recently named Cranbrook the best and most influential built environment created in metropolitan Detroit in the twentieth century.

WIRT ROWLAND (1878–1946)

Not every notable architect lives in fame's spotlight. Rowland was a journeyman designer who served most of Detroit's notable architectural companies during a career spanning more than four decades. Harvard-educated, he worked in turn for George Mason (1901–1909), Albert Kahn (1909–1911), Malcomson and Higginbotham (1911–1914), Kahn again (1914–1922), Smith, Hinchman, and Grylls (1922–1930), then finally got his name on the door at O'Dell and Rowland (1930–1938). He later worked with Giffels and Vallet. Thus shielded from personal fame, he nonetheless designed some of

Detroit's greatest buildings, including the Buhl, Penobscot, and Guardian skyscrapers while at SH&G in the 1920s. Clearly, submerging one's own personality within a larger firm is not always bad, if it produces the kind of opportunities for creativity that Rowland enjoyed.

C. HOWARD CRANE (1885–1952)

Detroit's great theater architect was born in Hartford, Connecticut, and came to Detroit in 1904 after apprenticing as a draftsman in Hartford. He worked briefly in the Detroit architecture office of Albert Kahn before becoming chief draftsman in 1905 for Field, Hinchman, and Smith. In 1907 he worked as chief draftsman for the architecture office of Gustave A. Mueller and by 1909 opened his own office. He designed small offices and residences and eventually came to specialize in theaters after successfully designing the conversions of many small stores into nickelodeons.

Starting with the Columbia Theatre on Monroe Street in 1911, John Kunsky, Detroit's premiere theater owner and movie exhibitor, became Crane's most important client. By the early 1920s Grand Circus Park was dubbed by Detroiters as "Kunsky Circle," because of the predominance of Kunsky-owned and built theaters, all of which were designed by Crane. They included the Madison Theatre (1917), the Adams Theatre (1917), the Capitol Theatre (today's Detroit Opera House) (1922), and the State Theatre (1925). While Crane primarily designed theaters for vaudeville and motion pictures, his designs for legitimate theaters such as Orchestra Hall (1919), the Music Box on 45th Street and Broadway in New York City (1921), and the Harris and Selwyn in Chicago (1922) won equal praise.

By the late 1920s Crane was at the height of his career, designing high-style movie palaces for United Artists and Twentieth Century Fox, two of the largest Hollywood motion picture studios. He designed the United Artists theaters in Los Angeles, Detroit, and Chicago (1927–1929) and the Fox Theaters in Detroit, St. Louis, and Brooklyn (1928–1929).

With the onset of the Depression, Crane moved to London, England, where he designed factories during World War II as well as skyscrapers elsewhere in Europe. He died in England the day after his sixty-seventh birthday. Not the least reason for his success was his charm. "The architect was always in demand for a game of golf," says preservationist Lisa DiChiera, who wrote her master's thesis on Crane.

WILLIAM E. KAPP (1891–1969)

A graduate of the University of Pennsylvania and another of the many talented designers to work for Smith, Hinchman, and Grylls, Kapp headed the firm's architectural department in the 1920s. While he undoubtedly influenced Wirt Rowland's most important skyscraper designs of the time, Kapp's personal contributions ranged from Music Hall, University Club, and Ross Roy in the city, to the famed Meadowbrook Hall in Auburn Hills. On his own from 1941, he designed such works as the Detroit Historical Society in the Cultural Center and Temple Israel in Palmer Park.

MINORU YAMASAKI (1912–1986)

Born in Seattle, Yamasaki was a second-generation Japanese American who struggled in his youth against poverty and racism. As a young architect, his tours of Japan and Europe gave him a broader frame of reference with which to adapt the orthodox glass-box modernism of his day. After working for various firms in New York City, ranging from Wallace Harrison to Raymond Loewy, "Yama" served as chief designer at Smith, Hinchman, and Grylls until starting his own firm in 1949. Using skylights, reflecting pools, pearl-white exteriors, and the repeated use of diamond or triangular motifs, Yamasaki softened modernism, creating an atmosphere of serenity and human scale in his architecture. His commissions in Detroit include some of the city's finest buildings. Among them are the incomparable McGregor Memorial Conference

Center at Wayne State University and the One Woodward Avenue office tower Downtown. Yamasaki was awarded the gold medal from both AIA Detroit and AIA Michigan.

EERO SAARINEN (1910–1961)

Son of Eliel Saarinen, Eero boldly broke with his father's Arts and Crafts-based architecture to design the much-imitated General Motors Tech Center in Warren. A monument to glass-and-steel efficiency, the Tech Center dazzled visitors with minimalist forms, colorful planes of glazed ceramic brick, and suspended staircases. Eero went on to create the TWA Terminal at New York's Kennedy Airport, Dulles Airport outside Washington, D.C., and the iconic St. Louis Arch. These highly individualistic designs were so far outside the glass-box mainstream that many critics shunned Eero as an intellectual stuntman. With the passing of modernism's rigid orthodoxy, Eero's reputation has justifiably risen. Eero Saarinen was awarded the gold medal from both AIA Detroit and AIA Michigan.

WILLIAM KESSLER (1924–)

Trained at Harvard during the heyday of modernism, Kessler has enriched Detroit and its suburbs with many clean, brisk, and meticulously crafted designs. His Detroit Receiving Hospital delivered a shock of the new to the Medical Center; his playful Detroit Science Center upended our notions of what a museum should look like. True to his modernist roots but far from a glass-box architect, Kessler's architecture has the sleekness and finish of a jet fighter. And as a trademark, Kessler enlivens his Miesian precision with a Corbusian panache, introducing strategic splashes of color on pure forms, revealed in light. Kessler was awarded the gold medal from both AIA Detroit and AIA Michigan.

Bibliography

Andrews, Wayne. *Architecture in Michigan.* Wayne State University Press, 1967.

Bak, Richard. *Detroit: A Postcard Album.* Arcadia, 1998.

Blumenson, John J.-G. *Identifying American Architecture.* American Association for State and Local History, 1977.

Bucci, Federico. *Albert Kahn: Architect of Ford.* Princeton Architectural Press, 1993.

Burden, Ernest. *Illustrated Dictionary of Architecture.* McGraw-Hill, 1998.

Burton, Clarence M. *The City of Detroit, Michigan.* S. J. Clarke Publishing Co., 1922.

Curl, James Stevens. *A Dictionary of Architecture.* Oxford University Press, 1999.

Eckert, Kathryn Bishop. *Buildings of Michigan.* Oxford University Press, 1993.

Ferry, W. Hawkins. *The Buildings of Detroit.* Wayne State University Press, 1968.

———. *The Legacy of Albert Kahn.* Detroit Institute of Arts, 1970.

Fleming, John, Hugh Honour, and Nikolaus Pevsner. *The Penguin Dictionary of Architecture.* Penguin Books, 1980.

Grossman, Elizabeth Greenwell. *The Civic Architecture of Paul Cret.* Cambridge University Press, 1996.

Hildebrand, Grant. *Designing for Industry: The Architecture of Albert Kahn.* The MIT Press, 1974.

Kaiser, Kay. *The Architecture of Gunnar Birkerts.* American Institute of Architects Press, 1989.

Lutz, William. *The News of Detroit.* Little, Brown and Co., 1973.

Marquis, Albert Nelson. *The Book of Detroiters.* A. N. Marquis and Co., 1914.

Nevins, Allan, and Frank E. Hill. *Ford: Expansion and Challenge, 1915–1933.* Charles Scribner's Sons, 1957.

Packard, Robert, and Balthazar Korab. *Encyclopedia of American Architecture.* 2nd ed. McGraw-Hill, Inc., 1995.

Parkins, A. E. *The Historical Geography of Detroit.* Kennikat Press, 1918, reissued 1980.

Poppeliers, John, S. Allen Chambers, and Nancy B. Schwartz. *What Style Is It?* The Preservation Press of the National Trust for Historic Preservation, 1977.

Pound, Arthur. *The Only Thing Worth Finding: The Life and Legacies of George Gough Booth.* Wayne State University Press, 1964.

Sexton, R. W., *American Commercial Buildings of Today.* Architectural Book Publishing Co., 1928.

Whiffen, Marcus. *American Architecture since 1780.* The MIT Press, 1992.

Woodford, Arthur M. *Tonnancour: Life in Grosse Pointe and along the Shores of Lake St. Clair.* 2 vols. Omnigraphics, Inc., 1994–1997.

Woodford, Frank B. *Parnassus on Main Street: A History of the Detroit Public Library.* Wayne State University Press, 1965.

Index to Buildings

Note: The index refers to entry numbers rather than page numbers. Sites are listed by their complete names, in normal order. Cross references will guide readers to the name under which a site is listed. Both current and original names are listed.

Index to Architects

Note: The index refers to entry numbers rather than page numbers. Individuals are indexed under last name; architectural firms are indexed by company name in normal order.

Photography Credits

AIA Detroit: architects' photos p. 340 (Gordon Lloyd, John Donaldson), p. 341 (George Mason, Louis Kamper), p. 344 (Wirt Rowland), p. 345 (C. Howard Crane), p. 346 (William E. Kapp)

Albert Kahn Associates: introductory photos p. 45 (Detroit Opera House interior), p. 329 (Rotunda interior), p. 339 (Kahn at Mason and Rice); architect's photo p. 343 (Albert Kahn); site photos for entries 10a, 36, 48, 49, 52, 93, 95, 102, 109, 112, 119, 120, 124, 134b, 144, 194a-b, 196, 197, 198, 199, 203b, 204, 211, 224a-b, 234, 294, 340, 361a, 363a-f

Balthazar Korab: introductory photos p. xvi (Introduction), p. 4 (Indian Villiage), p. 5 (Brush Park), p. 6 (Civic Center), p. 7 (Downtown skyline), p. 35 (Greektown after dark), p. 83 (Financial District), p. 153 (Cultural Center), p. 189 (Hamtramck), p. 209 (Palmer Woods), p. 247 (Lafayette/Gratiot), p. 261 (Belle Isle Bridge), p. 287 (Cranbrook), p. 291 (Grosse Pointe), pp. 305 (Cranbrook), p. 307 (Art Museum and Library, Eliel Saarinen House), p. 321 (GM Technical Center), p. 323 (Water tower, Interior stair); architect's photo p. 347 (Eero Saarinen); site photos for entries 1, 2, 4, 5, 6, 7, 8b, 10b, 11, 12, 13, 14, 15, 16a-b, 17, 19a-b, 20, 21a-c, 22, 24, 25, 26, 27, 28, 30, 31b, 32, 33, 34, 35, 37, 38, 39, 40, 41, 42, 47, 51a-b, 53, 57a-b, 58b, 59, 60, 61, 62, 63, 64, 65, 67, 68, 69, 70, 71, 72, 73, 74, 75, 76, 77, 78, 79, 80, 81, 82, 84, 85a, 86, 87, 88, 89, 90, 91, 92, 96, 97, 98, 99, 101, 103, 106, 108, 111, 113, 114, 115, 117, 121, 122, 123,126, 127, 129, 130, 134a, 135, 136, 137, 138a, 139a-b, 140a-b, 142a-b, 143, 147, 158, 159, 160, 161, 163, 164, 165, 166, 169a-b, 171, 172, 173, 176, 177a-b, 179, 180, 181, 182, 183, 184a-b,185,186, 187, 188, 189, 190, 191a, 192a, 193, 200, 201, 202, 203a, 206, 207, 209, 210, 212, 213, 214, 221, 222, 223, 227, 228, 229, 230, 231, 232, 235, 236, 237, 239, 243, 246, 248, 249, 250, 251, 254a, 257, 258, 259a-b, 260, 267, 268, 269, 271a-b, 272, 274, 276, 277, 280b, 281, 282, 283, 284, 285, 287, 289, 290, 291, 292, 293, 295, 296, 299, 305, 306, 308, 310, 312a-b, 313, 314, 315, 317, 319, 320, 323, 325, 326, 327, 328, 329, 330, 332, 336, 337, 338, 339, 341, 342, 343a-b, 344, 345a-b, 346, 347, 348a-b, 349, 350, 351, 352, 353, 354, 355, 356, 357, 358, 359, 360, 361b, 362, 364, 365, 367

Barton Malow: site photo for entry 104

Beth Singer: site photo for entry 324

Burton Historical Collection, Detroit Public Library: introductory photo p. 3 (Frontier Detroit); site photo for entry 85b

Chris Lark: site photos for entries 10a, 52

City of Detroit-Historic Designation Advisory Board: introductory photo p. 229 (Dry Dock Engine Works interior); site photo for entries110, 116, 131, 133a

Cranbrook Archives: introductory photo p. 13 (Civic Center); architect's photo p. 344 (Saarinen)

Eric Hill: introductory photos p. 71 (Washington Boulevard), p. 169 (Milwaukee Junction), p. 217 (Most Holy Trinity in context), p. 255 (Elmwood Cemetery); site photos for entries 18, 31a, 44, 45, 50, 54, 55, 66, 83, 118, 132, 133b, 141, 145, 148, 149, 153, 154, 156a-b, 157, 167, 178, 191b, 195a-b, 205, 208, 215, 216, 217, 218, 219, 233, 238, 244, 245, 253, 254b, 261, 266, 270, 275, 280a, 288, 298, 300, 301, 302, 303, 304, 307, 311, 316, 322, 331, 333a, 366

Fred Golden: site photo for entry 242

Frederick Crowther: site photo for entry 46

Gensler Associates: site photo for entry 278

Glen Clavin Moon: site photos for entries 43, 263, 264, 265, 368

HarleyEllis: site photo for entries 3, 9, 100

Hedrich-Blessing: site photos for entries 23, 29, 56, 58a, 125 , 226

Henry Ford Museum: site photo for entry 369

John Gallagher: site photo for entry 252

Justin Maconochie/Hedrich-Blessing: introductory photo p. 45 (Detroit Opera House interior); site photo for entry 49

Kessler Francis Cardoza: architect's photo p. 347 (William Kessler)

Manning Brothers: site photo for entry 309

New Center Council: introductory photo p. 175 (New Center)

Pewabic Pottery: architect's photo p. 343 (Mary Chase Perry Stratton)

Raimund Koch: site photo for entry 262

Rich Castillo: site photo for entry 150

Rossetti Architects: introductory photo p. 291 (Bon Secours Hospital)

Rundell Ernstberger: introductory photo p. 96 (Campus Martius)

SHPO: introductory photo p. 191 (Boston-Edison); site photos for entries 94, 146, 151, 152, 155, 162, 168, 174, 175, 220, 225, 240, 241, 247, 255, 256, 279, 286, 297, 321, 333b, 334, 335

Sims-Varner: site photo for entry 8a

SmithGroup: architect's photo p. 342 (Fred L. Smith); site photos for entries 105, 107, 138b, 192b, 273, 318

Wayne State University: introductory photo p. 141 (Main Campus)

Yamasaki & Associates: architect's photo p. 346 (Minoru Yamasaki); site photo for entry 170

Zachary Associates: site photo for entry 128

Colophon

Managing Editor: Kathryn Wildfong
Production and Design Manager: Alice Nigoghosian
Design: Savitski Design, Ann Arbor, Michigan
Printer: University Lithoprinters, Ann Arbor, Michigan
Bindery: John H. Dekker & Sons Bookbinding, Grand Rapids, Michigan
Paper: 70 lb. Sterling Litho Matte
Font: Bauer Bodoni and Univers Condensed

Front cover photograph: Skyline view of Detroit from Windsor.
Back cover photographs (top to bottom): Guardian Building, no. 108; Detroit Receiving Hospital, no. 136; Cranbrook Art Museum and Library, p. 307; Detroit Opera House, no. 49; Pewabic Pottery Company, no. 319. All cover photographs by Balthazar Korab except the Detroit Opera House which was taken by Justin Maconochie/Hedrich-Blessing.